Computer Models of
Process Dynamics

Computer Models of Process Dynamics

From Newton to Energy Fields

Olis Rubin
Brooklyn, Pretoria, South Africa

IEEE PRESS

WILEY

Published by John Wiley & Sons, Inc., Hoboken, New Jersey.
Published simultaneously in Canada.

For general information on our other products and services or for technical support, please contact our Customer Care Department within the United States at (800) 762-2974, outside the United States at (317) 572-3993 or fax (317) 572-4002.
Wiley also publishes its books in a variety of electronic formats. Some content that appears in print may not be available in electronic formats. For more information about Wiley products, visit our web site at www.wiley.com.

Library of Congress Cataloging-in-Publication Data Applied for

ISBN: 9781119885658 [Hardback]

Cover Design: Wiley
Cover Images: © zhengshun tang/Getty Images; Courtesy of Olis Rubin

Set in 9.5/12.5pt STIXTwoText by Straive, Pondicherry, India

To Judy
She brought beauty, goodness and love in my life.
We give thanks for all the blessings that we have received, together with our children

Contents

Preface

"It is unworthy for excellent men to lose hours like slaves in the labor of calculation which could safely be relegated to anyone else if machines were used"

Gottfried Wilhelm Leibniz (1685)

My first job was with a large electrical engineering enterprise where I had been moved to a division that designed and installed heavy duty motor drives. Our division had just acquired an analog computer that was barely large enough to simulate these machines. I was lucky to be chosen to work with my friend Gopal to see what we could achieve with this "new-fangled contraption." Our first project was to investigate the performance of a Ward-Leonard (generator–motor) set that drove a huge mining machine. The computer gave us a new "window to the world," through which we could see what was happening inside the motor. All that we had learned as undergraduates now fell into place. Our basic training had considered the steady state operation of electric motors, while the lectures on dynamic behavior were entirely mathematical. We could now construct a computer model that allowed us to see the hardware, the differential equations, and the transient behavior of shafts and other variables. This is what a computer model can do for us!

Leibniz would have been elated if he could have foreseen how far machines could take us, beyond just saving us laborious calculations. Digital computers now provide us with platforms that make the physical modeling process almost effortless, leaving us free to think about more important questions. This book is written to show how a computer can be programmed to simulate motion in general. We will not include the growing market for new user interfaces, such as virtual reality or networking. These fields should be left to the expert attention of specialists.

In addition to setting the wheels in motion along a path that led to the computers of today, Leibniz was also the co-founder of differential calculus. The creation of a dynamic model is deeply rooted in mathematical analysis. We will sacrifice theoretical rigor in order to simplify the mathematics in a way that is intelligible to the working engineer and computer professional. Wherever possible we will explain mathematical operations by means of computer programs that approximate their behavior.

Thanks go to the many reviewers whose suggestions helped to bring this book into its present form. I hope that it will give readers the benefit of experience that was gained by working with many colleagues on diverse projects. Thanks to Philip de Vaal, whose enthusiastic support strengthened me to persevere in the face of setbacks, and to Becker van Niekerk, whose industry constantly invigorated me to complete this project. This is the second time that Aileen Storry has helped me bring a book to see the light of day. Thanks to the professionalism of the Wiley team, led by Kimberly, Mustaq and Patricia, that managed the publication process.

I must thank my dearest wife for her constant, unstinting support. Not only is her spelling better than mine, but she has a way of provoking me to write more lucidly for you, the reader. May it thus give you food for thought, and better equip you for the future!

1

Introduction

1.1 Engineering uses of computer models

Computer models are used throughout every phase of industrial research, design, and development. Simulation studies can play a large part in the concept phase of an engineering project since computer models can usually be created in less time and cost less than hardware prototypes. The very creation of such models forces everyone to delve deeper into the underlying physics of the plant. This can give valuable insight into plant operation that can aid the plant designers. If such simulators are developed before the plant is built, they can be used to evaluate the design before expensive decisions are made, and thereby help to avoid costly mistakes. In the later stages of a development program, we can greatly reduce the time and cost of commissioning and qualification by using simulator studies to reduce the scale of hardware testing. The model can also be used to determine safety limits and emergency procedures by simulating tests that would be hazardous in the real plant. There is also a growing market for training simulators to ensure the competence of the operators who will run the plant. We can foresee that this will tie up with the creation of virtual reality and the computer game industry.

Computer modeling of dynamic processes has a long association with control engineering, where there is often an interest in the speed with which the system settles to a required operating condition. The designers generally make use of feedback control loops, where they have to allow for the time response of the plant to control inputs. Computer models were used to study simple servomechanisms, and this led to their extensive use in very large and complex feedback control problems. They have been widely employed in the aerospace industry for the design of flight control systems. The process control industry has applied computer modeling to such large-scale studies as optimizing a complete

Computer Models of Process Dynamics: From Newton to Energy Fields, First Edition.
Olis Rubin.
© 2023 The Institute of Electrical and Electronics Engineers, Inc.
Published 2023 by John Wiley & Sons, Inc.

chemical process. The growing field of robotics will also make use of dynamic models.

"The purpose of computing is insight, not numbers."

R.W. Hamming (1962)

Computer models also find application in many diverse scientific fields, including areas that are known as the softer sciences. As we use machinery to perform manual labor, we can use computers to mechanize difficult repetitive mathematical processes and thereby free our minds to consider questions of a more intellectual nature.

1.1.1 Mission statement

This book is written for you, the professional worker in the field of computer modeling, who wishes to widen your horizon and needs to consider new approaches, applications, and advanced techniques. When we use the word "model" we are thinking of a program that simulates the dynamic behavior of a physical phenomenon. Perhaps you have not already entered the field, but wish to apply your training in applied mathematics and experience with computers to explore the behavior of an object that evolves in this way. This book proceeds from basic methods of programming and sets up mathematical models of fairly common objects that can be described by reasonably simple equations.

A series of case studies covers a myriad of different topics in order to provide a vista of the challenges that fall within this discipline. These topics have been fitted into a framework that progresses from introductory material to subjects of increasing complexity. You will meet scores of examples that have been carefully chosen to take you step by step along a logical learning curve that leads to greater enlightenment.

It is shown how the computer has progressed from being a mere tool to convert mathematical equations into numbers. We can interact with it as with virtual reality where its graphical output makes the equations become alive.

There is another mission to be accomplished. If there is to be synergy between yourself and the computer, the simulation process has to stand firmly on the following legs:

Techniques of computer modeling,
Mathematical analysis, and
Imagination, Inspiration, and Creative Thinking

1.2   The subject matter

The book provides a long series of case studies that are based on personal experience. The emphasis is on the simulation of moving objects or the propagation of energy in a physical medium. Computer models are presented to the reader either as program listings or as block diagrams. Most of them are programmed on the MATLAB® or Scilab® platforms:

MATLAB is a registered trademark of The MathWorks, Inc.
Scilab is registered under the GPLv2 license (previously CeCILL) as circulated by
   CEA, CNRS, and Inria.
The computer code fragments use statements that are easily understood by Python
   and C users.

Chapter 2 gives an introduction to computer programming, using the instruction sets from MATLAB and Scilab. This firstly shows how to perform various repetitive operations, and then goes on to consider the use of a digital computer to simulate differential equations. These techniques will serve as a springboard for the creation of even the most advanced computer models.

Chapter 3 serves as an object lesson to show how creative thinking is a tool in the model building process. It explains how scientific theories are actually conceptual models that describe physical phenomena and shows how the evolution of science depended on a series of inspired guesses. It describes the development of three different mathematical frameworks that are used in later chapters to illustrate the creation of various computer models.

Chapter 4 shows how differential equations can be implemented as computer models, which can then be exploited to produce graphs and numbers. It also shows how mathematical tools based on calculus can be used to find analytical solutions that satisfy the equations. It thereby illustrates how problems can be studied by two independent methods to increase our confidence in the results.

Chapter 5 considers the creation of differential equations that describe the motion of point masses and their implementation as computer models. It also shows how analytical solutions can be used to perform cross-checks, to verify the computed results.

Chapter 6 then considers the motion of a rigid body and the creation of a flight simulator in the aircraft industry.

Chapter 7 analyses the flow of heat through a solid body by exploiting mathematical methods that are based on the concept of scalar and vector fields. These are used to show how the evolution of a temperature field can be described by a partial differential equation. It is demonstrated how a computer model can be created by approximating the body as a series of finite elements, where each individual element can be described by an ordinary differential equation.

Chapter 8 analyses wave propagation of an energy field through a continuous medium. It again demonstrates how a computer model can be created by approximating the medium as a series of finite elements. Methods are used that are similar to those described in Chapter 7. The analysis of the physical phenomena discussed in these two chapters is much more complex than the study of mechanical motion. The case studies use a combination of computer modeling, mathematical analysis, and physical analogies as a way to gain a better understanding of the physical processes that are considered.

Chapter 9 widens our horizon by exploring the realm of uncertainty and statistical analysis. The examples that appear in this chapter consider various topics, which range from imperfect theoretical knowledge to measurement noise, as well as business models and digital images.

Chapter 10 shows how simulation engineers can work as members of a design team within an engineering project. At the beginning of the project the computer model can be used as an electronic prototype that is created more quickly and cheaply than hardware. It also provides the facility for checking the sensitivity of the product to variations in parameters within the design tolerances. There must be a configuration management process to keep track of changes to the model during the course of the project. The need for formal procedures is emphasized in order to create trustworthy models. This includes cross-checks on simulation results by means of mathematical analysis to see that the computer model has been implemented correctly.

When engineers use computer models to assist them with making critical design decisions they must remember that the solutions obtained with the computer are greatly dependent on the equations that were created to represent the physical hardware. Approximations in these equations result in approximate solutions. The equations used in this book may be sufficient for an introduction to the topic, and indeed many have been used for preliminary investigations of the problems that will be discussed. However, before readers attempt serious investigations of this type, it is recommended that they satisfy themselves about the form of the equations that they choose to use.

The moment of truth arrives when the hardware is tested. After this, the computer model can still serve as the means whereby we can quickly and efficiently predict the behavior of the hardware under different operating conditions.

1.3 Mathematical material

The advance of science led to the creation of new mathematical methods that describe the new theoretical concepts. Thus, Newton's laws of motion led to the creation of vector analysis, while Maxwell's equations required the concept of a vector field. Such mathematical analysis forms an integral part of the modeling process, both in the definition of the models and in checking the results. It was thus preferable to include selected mathematical material in separate appendices that can be studied separately or consulted when referred to in the chapters.

Appendix A describes frequency response techniques that are used in engineering, such as the design of feedback controllers. It shows how MATLAB and Scilab can determine linear state equations and transfer functions that approximate a given computer model.

Appendix B describes the use of vectors to create kinetic models of point masses and rigid bodies.

Appendix C describes the application of vector fields to solve diffusion and wave equations.

Appendix D discusses the mathematical modeling and analysis of random events.

1.4   Some remarks

Mathematical modeling began when Galileo and Newton married the sciences of astronomy and mathematics. Many professions have since used calculus to analyze systems of every description. As the calculations became more complex, scientists began to create computer models. This began with the creation of analog computers and the development of sophisticated simulation techniques. Some of the books that were written on the subject are listed below and are still a valuable source of information to anyone who wishes to create computer models. Once the model has been mathematically defined, it is now possible to use a digital simulation platform that greatly simplifies its programming on the computer. We can then experiment with the model and obtain answers with astonishing rapidity. This creates a risk that we sometimes forget to take some time off to consider where we are going. The IBM Corporation used to hand out posters that continue to give good advice "THINK." The scientists of yesteryear can still serve as a role model in this regard.

This book aims to show how creative thinking, mathematical analysis, and computer models can be used together to achieve a synergy that may not otherwise be apparent to the reader. It also takes true wisdom to decide how realistic a model must be and what is enough to satisfy our needs.

Bibliography

Abbasov, I.B. (2019). *Computer Modeling in the Aerospace Industry*. New York: Wiley.
Hamming, R.W. (1962). *Numerical Methods for Scientists and Engineers*. New York: McGraw-Hill.

Karplus, W.J. (1958). *Analog Simulation*. New York: McGraw Hill.

Korn, G.A. and Korn, T.M. (1956). *Electronic Analog Computers*. New York: McGraw Hill.

Paynter, H.M. (1960). *A Palimpsest on the Electronic Analog Art, Dedham*. MA: Philbrick Researches.

Raczynski, S. (2014). *Modeling and Simulation*. New York: Wiley.

Rogers, A.E. and Connoly, T.W. (1960). *Analog Computation in Engineering Design*. New York: McGraw Hill.

Rubin, O. (2016). *Control Engineering in Development Projects, Dedham*. MA: Artech House.

Shearer J.L., Murphy, A.T. and Richardson, H.H., *Introduction to System Dynamics*, Reading, MA: Addison-Wesley, 1967

Soroka, W.W. (1954). *Analog Methods in Computation and Simulation*. New York: McGraw Hill.

Tomovic, R. and Karplus, W.J. (1962). *High Speed Analog Computers*. New York: Wiley.

2

From Computer Hardware to Software

This chapter spends less than 5% of its time on the computer and over 95% of its time on the software.

> "For the machine is not a thinking being, but simply an automaton which acts according to the laws imposed upon it."
>
> Ada, Countess of Lovelace, 1843
> (*Source:* In the Public Domain, Rights Holder Augusta Ada King)

We will code computer models in a programming language that bears no resemblance to the code that controls the computing circuits.

2.1 Introduction

The mission statement in Chapter 1 described a learning curve that progresses from basic programming to the most challenging techniques of computer modeling. This chapter begins by giving a short introduction to the digital computer. It will then go on to describe a programming language that will typically be used in later chapters. It will also show some fundamental techniques whereby this language can be used to perform relatively complex tasks. Later chapters will consider models of continuous motion by means of differential equations; thus we require methods whereby a digital computer, which is a discrete device, can emulate continuous behavior. Section 2.7 presents techniques whereby this can be achieved.

2.2 Computing machines

Our word "calculate" comes from the Roman *calculus* (a pebble). A primitive abacus used pebbles that were laid in furrows of sand. Over many centuries machines were developed to speed up such calculations. Leonardo da Vinci (1452–1519) left

Computer Models of Process Dynamics: From Newton to Energy Fields, First Edition.
Olis Rubin.
© 2023 The Institute of Electrical and Electronics Engineers, Inc.
Published 2023 by John Wiley & Sons, Inc.

sketches of the mechanisms that are used in a mechanical adding machine. Pascal (1623–1662) invented a calculator that was used by his tax-collector father. Then Babage (1791–1871) attempted to create a machine that had the capability of the modern computer (Swade, 1991).

> One evening I was sitting in the rooms of the Analytical Society at Cambridge…, with a table of logarithms lying open before me. Another member…called out. 'Well, Babage, what are you dreaming about?' to which I replied, 'I am thinking that all these tables might be calculated by machinery."
>
> Charles Babage

Babage's first machine, the "Difference Engine," had an ability to repeat calculations that had never been achieved before. He abandoned this to embark on a much more ambitious project, the "Analytical Engine." This machine embodied many of the features of modern electronic computers. It was programmable using punched cards, so complex actions could be achieved by means of a group of more elementary instructions. It had a "store" where numbers and intermediate results were held and a separate "mill" where the arithmetic processing was performed. The machine could implement computing loops and was capable of performing conditional branching:

A form of : IF … THEN … ELSE

The machine would have been the size of a small locomotive – 15 feet high, 6 feet across, and, in one version, 20 feet long. Had it been built, "calculating by steam" would have been a prophetic wish come true.

In 1944 Aiken built an electromechanical version of Babage's Analytical Engine (Trask, 1971). Bernstein (1963) describes the operation of this machine: "One could go in and listen to the gentle clicking of its relays, which sounded like a room full of ladies knitting." This was followed in 1945 by the ENIAC, an electronic digital computer that contained 18 000 thermionic valves that consumed 150 kW of electricity (Trask, 1971). The invention of transistors and integrated circuits then allowed the creation of low-cost, high-performance microprocessors.

2.2.1 The software interface

Digital computers are able to perform complex operations by executing many simple actions in discrete steps. The first computers were programmed by writing each step separately in binary code. Such a set of instructions, known as a program, can then be loaded into the computer memory bank. The computer then performs the particular operation by reading the instructions from memory and executing them step-by-step. Special programs were then developed and installed in the computer that allow us to write our instructions in a simpler language. Such an installed program then translates our statements into binary instructions that are executed by the computer. Today there can be several layers of software that act as an interface between the user and the actual computer hardware.

With the advent of personal computers (PCs) in the 1980s the stage was set for the development of the digital simulation platforms of today. The first PCs were slow and had little memory, but John Little anticipated that they would eventually be capable of effective technical computing and initiated the development of the product that is known as MATLAB® (Moler, 2006). This can execute program files to perform many scientific and engineering tasks. Numerical results can then be displayed or plotted in high-resolution graphics.

2.3 Computer programming

Scientific computations can be done through underlying software that allows us to write our instructions in a language that resembles the equations that are familiar to mathematicians. A typical instruction to perform an arithmetic calculation takes the form of a statement that has the following format:

variable = expression;

Mathematicians write equations in this way to define variables as algebraic functions of other variables. The above instruction will cause the computer to perform a calculation that is defined by the *expression* on the right-hand side of the equal (=) sign, and save the result as the *variable* that is defined on the left-hand side. This is saved as a binary number in its memory. It is necessary to identify the location (address) of this *variable* in the memory bank, so that it can be retrieved for later use. The underlying software platform that supports the scientific language provides a user interface where numbers are displayed as decimals, while the address of the *variable* is displayed as a name that is written in alphanumeric characters.

Several scientific languages have been developed, each of which has a slightly different algebraic syntax.

The program listings given in this book are extracted from programs that were created and run on either the Scilab or the MATLAB software platform. Programs that are saved in a file with the extension *.sce* can be run by Scilab, while files with the extension *.m* can be run by MATLAB. The individual instructions in these programs can also be typed and run in the command windows of the respective platforms. The next sections (2.3.1–2.3.6) give a short introduction to the basic syntax that is used. Readers who write programs using these platforms can consult their built-in Help facilities for further information. User Guides are also available, which give more basic training.

2.3.1 Algebraic expressions

MATLAB and Scilab perform arithmetical calculations on numerical objects. The instruction to perform a particular calculation is created by typing a statement of the form that was shown in the previous section. For example, we could define the radius of a circle by the following statement:

```
r = 1.2;
```

This would instruct the computer to save the numerical value of the radius in its memory bank. If we now type the letter r in the command window we would see the following:

```
r =
   1.2
```

This quantity is now available for further use. If we are using Scilab we could calculate the area within this circle by the following statement:

```
A = %pi * (r^2);
```

Scilab has a predefined variable %pi that is equal to the ratio of a circle's circumference to its diameter, while MATLAB uses the symbol pi to identify this number. The brackets define the order of execution. The above statement will thus cause the square of the radius to be calculated before it is multiplied by %pi.

Now suppose that we have defined the length of a cylinder by the symbol L. We could then calculate its volume by the following statement:

```
V = (%pi*(r^2)) * L;
```

Other arithmetic operations are similarly coded. Their default order of execution is as follows:

^	exponentiation
+	addition
-	subtraction
*	multiplication
/	division

Scilab and MATLAB allow us to create variables "on the fly" as they are defined by statements within a program. Their numerical values can then be changed by subsequent statements. If a statement refers to a calculation that involves a variable y that has not been previously created, the program will end and display an error message:

```
Undefined variable: y
```

MATLAB and Scilab are designed to perform arithmetical calculations on numerical vectors and matrices, where scalars are regarded to be 1-by-1 matrices. Suppose that we have created the following scalars:

```
a11 = 1;
a12 = 2;
a21 = 3;
a22 = 4;
```

We could then create the following row vectors:

```
R1 = [a11, a12];
R2 = [a21, a22];
```

If we now type the name R1 in the command window we would see the following:

```
R1 =
    1.          2.
```

These row vectors can then be combined to form a matrix:

```
M = [R1; R2];
```

If we now type the name M in the command window, we would see the following:

```
M =
    1.          2.
    3.          4.
```

We can also address the individual elements in a matrix, in order to use their values in further calculations. For example, if we type the M(1,2) in the command window we would see the following:

```
ans =
    2.
```

Similarly, if we type the M(2,1) in the command window we would see the following:

```
ans =
    3.
```

Alternatively, we could have created the following column vectors:

```
C1 = [a11; a21];
C2 = [a12; a22];
```

If we now type the name C1 in the command window we would see the following:

```
C1 =
    1.
    3.
```

These column vectors can then be combined to form the same matrix:

```
M = [C1, C2];
```

We can also address the row and column vectors in a matrix. For example, if we type M(2, :) in the command window we would see the following:

```
ans =
    3.              4.
```

while if we type M(:,2) in the command window we would see the following:

```
ans =
    2.
    4.
```

A matrix N can be added to or subtracted from a second matrix (M) provided that they have the same dimensions. Consider the following statement:

```
A = M + N;
```

The individual elements of the matrices are added together, so that A(i,j) = M(i,j) + N(i,j).

Two matrices M and N can be multiplied using the following statement, provided that the number of columns of M equals the number of rows of N:

```
A = M * N;
```

For example, if M is a row vector [m1, m2] and N is a column vector [n1; n2], the above statement produces the scalar product:

$$A = (m1 \ n1) + (m2 \ n2)$$

If M is a square matrix the expression M^2 is equivalent to M*M while M^3 is equivalent to M*M*M.

Similarly, M^0.5*M^0.5 is equal to M and M^1.5 is equal to M*M^0.5.

Two matrices can be multiplied element-by-element provided that they have the same dimensions. The following statement gives such a matrix that has the same dimensions as M and N:

```
A = M .* N;
```

The expression M./N gives element-by-element division, while the expression M.^2 is equivalent to M.*M.

The Help facilities and User Guides give better information on such operations; for example, how to divide one matrix by another.

2.3.2 Math functions

MATLAB and Scilab have built-in functions, such as:

sqrt	square root
sin	sine
cos	cosine
tan	tangent
asin	arcsine
atan	arctangent
atan2	four quadrant arctangent
exp	exponential to base e
log	natural logarithm
log10	log to base 10
factorial(4) = 1*2*3*4	
M'	matrix transpose (row vector to column vector and vice versa)

If M is a matrix, the expression sqrt(M) will apply the square root operation element-by-element. Other functions operate in the same way. We can also nest functions, as shown by the following example:

    s = sqrt(exp(A))

This brings us to complex numbers. If we type the expression sqrt(-1) in the Scilab command window we would see the following symbol for the unitary imaginary number:

    ans =
      i

Scilab has predefined this quantity, so the statement c = 3 + (4.5*%i) creates a complex variable.

If we then type the symbol c in the command window, we would see the following:

    c =
      3. + 4.5i

We can similarly create a complex matrix such as `M + (N*%i)`.

Unlike `sqrt(M)`, the expression `M^0.5` can operate on a real matrix to give a complex matrix.

The Help facilities and User Guides give better information on available functions.

2.3.3 Computation loops

We are now coming to those features that distinguish a computer from a calculator.

Consider the calculation of the following polynomial to produce a variable y as a function of a given variable (x):

```
y = a0 + a(1)*x + a(2)*x^2 + ... + a(99)*x^99
```

where the coefficients are defined as the elements of a vector:

```
[a(1), a(2), ... ,a(99)]
```

We can use a calculator as follows, to calculate the individual terms and add them successively to a running total:

```
y = a0
y = y + a(1)*x
y = y + a(2)*x^2
//////////
y = y + a(99)*x^99
```

On a computer, we can avoid the laborious process of separately programming each individual step by creating a computing loop. MATLAB and Scilab have statements that allow us to do this as follows:

```
y = a0;
K = 99;
for k = 1:K
        y = y + a(k)*x^k;
end;
```

All the operations that appear between the `for` statement and the `end` keyword will be executed 99 times. In this example there is a single operation, which calculates a term `a(k)*x^k` and adds it to the running total (y). The computing loop goes around from `for` to `end` and back to `for`. The `for` loop uses a counter, the variable k, to keep track of the number of times that the operation has been iterated. This is a true variable that can be used within the calculations. In this example it has been used to address the elements `a(k)` of the vector, and also to determine the power to which the variable x must be raised. The

expression 1:K refers to an actual vector. The statement V = 1:K; would produce a row vector of the form:

```
V =
    1.   2.  3.  ...  K
```

Rather than calculating a polynomial with a given number of terms, we may
wish to compute the variable y to an accuracy of 1%. MATLAB and Scilab allow
us to do this as follows:

```
y = a0;
k = 1;
z = a0;
while z<y
        y = y + a(k)*x^k;
        k = k + 1;
        z = 100*a(k)*x^k;
end;
```

In this case there are three operations between the while statement and the
end keyword. Before it begins the first iteration, the computing loop tests to
see whether the expression z<y is true. The symbol < is a relational operator. With
MATLAB the statement u = z<y would produce a variable u that is set to one if x is
less than y, and to zero if x is not less than y. The last statement in the loop computes the next term of the polynomial and then goes back to the test (z<y). If the
next term is less than 1% of the running total, the program exits from the loop.
With Scilab the statement u = z<y produces a Boolean variable that is %T (for true)
or %F (for false).

Computing loops can also be nested. Thus we could use the following program to
calculate y for M values of x that are stored in a vector (X):

```
Y = [];
for m = 1:M
        x = X(m);
        y = a0;
        for k = 1:K
                y = y + a(k)*x^k;
        end;
        Y = [Y, y];
end
```

The M values of y have been stored in a row vector (Y).

2.3.4 Decision making

The while loop considered in the last section used the result of an expression (z<y) to decide whether to continue iterating or exiting from the loop. This expression uses the relational operator < to test whether x is less than y. MATLAB and Scilab have relational operators that include the following:

<	less than
>	greater than
==	equal to
~=	not equal to

The boolean variables %T (for true) and %F (for false) used by Scilab can be combined to test whether several conditions are satisfied. MATLAB can similarly combine binary variables. This is achieved by means of the logical operators:

&	logical AND
|	logical OR
~	logical NOT

Many programs must decide between several courses of action that could be taken to achieve a given objective. For example, consider the description of a motor that moves through a distance (x) to drive a machine through mechanical links. There could be play P in the links before x causes any motion (y) of the machine. Suppose that the equivalent gear ratio of the links can then be expressed by the following relationship:

```
y = N*(x - P)
```

We may then have an endstop that prevents y from moving beyond a position E. Suppose that the links can bend elastically, allowing the motor to move beyond the point (E/N) +P. We may decide to use a gross approximation in order to model this behavior by a mathematical function $y = f(x)$ that has the following properties:

```
Y = 0: when x is less than P
Y = N*(x - P): when x lies between P and (E/N)+ P
Y = E: when x exceeds (E/N)+ P
```

We can realize this function by means of the following program:

```
if x < P
       y = 0;
elseif x < (E/N)+ P
       y = N*(x - P);
else   y = E;
end
```

We see that the region where y moves from zero to E satisfies two conditions that could be combined into the expression (x> = P) & (x< (E/N) + P).

More complex programs can use various combinations of loops and if statements.

2.3.5 Graphics

MATLAB and Scilab can create various plots of numerical results. The bulk of the examples in this book use the statement plot(X,Y) to plot a graph of a vector Y versus the vector X. The elements X(i) can represent the values of an independent variable, while the elements Y(i) can represent a function of X(i). Frequency responses can be plotted against a logarithmic frequency axis. Section 6.3.4 shows how this is done in Scilab, while Section 10.4.1 shows similar MATLAB instructions. A three-dimensional plot is shown in Figure 7.14. This was created by the Scilab statement plot3d(X,Y,Z). The MATLAB and Scilab Help facilities and User Guides give better information on available graphics features.

2.3.6 User defined functions

We have seen the power that an iterative loop has given a computer. The concept of a function extends this power by allowing us to call up a computing procedure *at will, at different points in the program*. Appendix A.3 gives an example of the coding of a function in Scilab. The MATLAB Help facility and User Guide give information on the coding of an equivalent function.

2.4   State transition machines

A digital computer is a state transition machine. At every clock pulse there is a change in the pattern of bits (0 or 1) that is stored in its memory bank and its electronic registers. The execution of a line of code typically involves one or more of the following actions, each of which changes the state of the machine:

load a program statement into the control unit
load a variable into the processor
execute the statement to compute the value of a variable
save the variable in memory

We will now describe a digital machine whose state is determined by the pattern of bits that is stored in a single shift register. Every clock pulse will cause a change in its state, which is determined by hard-wired interconnections. The machine resembles an elementary computer, where the program consists of these interconnections. We thus have a single statement that is endlessly repeated. The device can also be implemented on a microcontroller as an algorithm that is repeated whenever it receives an interrupt signal from the clock. The algorithm can be tested by a program that uses a `for` loop to simulate the repetitions that occur in the actual hardware. We will use Scilab for running such a test.

2.4.1 A binary signal generator

Consider a device that uses various digital elements to produce a sequence of binary pulses. Binary data is stored in bistable flip-flops, each of which stores a single bit in a transistor that is switched ON or OFF. The flip-flops are interconnected in a string to form a shift register. When the machine receives a clock pulse, the pattern of bits in the register is moved by one position down the line. Logic operations are performed by AND, OR, and NOT gates.

We can also implement the device as an algorithm on a microcontroller. The state of the shift register is given by a vector (x) whose elements are either ones or zeros and an input signal $z = 1$ or 0. We will begin with a state vector (x) that has three elements. Whenever the microcontroller receives an interrupt signal from the clock the pattern of bits will be shifted:

```
from x(2) to x(3)
from x(1) to x(2)
from z to x(1)
```

We can implement the algorithm by the following Scilab program:

```
for k=1:4
      x(3)  = x(2);
      x(2)  = x(1);
      x(1)  = z(k);
      X  = [X ; x];
end
```

Suppose that the initial state is $x = [0\ 1\ 0]$ and $z = [1\ 1\ 1\ 1]$.

The last statement in the loop gathers the row vectors (x) that show the evolution of the state into a matrix (X) that can then be displayed as:

X(:,1)	X(:,2)	X(:,3)
0.	1.	0.
1.	0.	1.
1.	1.	0.
1.	1.	1.
1.	1.	1.

Having verified the operation of the shift register, we wish to implement a binary feedback loop by using an exclusive-or gate to combine x(3) and x(2) and feeding its output (z) back to x(1). This implies that z will be 1 provided that one input is 1 and the other is 0. The expression x(3) ~= x(2) can be used to realize an exclusive-or function, so the Scilab program can be modified as follows to test the feedback algorithm:

```
x = [1, 0, 0];
X = x;
for k=1:7
        z = x(3)~ = x(2);
        x(3) = x(2);
        x(2) = x(1);
        x(1) = z;
        X = [X; x];
end
```

The last statement in the loop gathers the row vectors (x) that show the evolution of the state into a matrix (X) that can then be displayed as:

X(:,1)	X(:,2)	X(:,3)
1.	0.	0.
0.	1.	0.
1.	0.	1.
1.	1.	0.
1.	1.	1.
0.	1.	1.
0.	0.	1.
1.	0.	0.

By going down the rows we see that the system cycles through seven different states before returning to the initial condition. This implies that the state vector (x) cycles through every binary number except the number 000. The three elements x (1), x(2), and x(3) cycle through the same sequence with a delay of one step between them. We will truncate the matrix (X) to its first seven rows and then use the following command to convert these binary sequences into signals that switch between +1 and -1:

```
S = 2*X - 1;
```

The resulting matrix is made up of the following column vectors:

S(:,1)	S(:,2)	S(:,3)
1.	-1.	-1.
-1.	1.	-1.
1.	-1.	1.
1.	1.	-1.
1.	1.	1.
-1.	1.	1.
-1.	-1.	1.

Element-wise multiplication of these three column vectors by S(:,1) gives the following:

```
S(:,1).*S(:,1)        S(:,1).*S(:,2)        S(:,1).*S(:,3)
1.                    -1.                   -1.
1.                    -1.                    1.
1.                    -1.                    1.
1.                     1.                   -1.
1.                     1.                    1.
1.                    -1.                   -1.
1.                     1.                   -1.
```

If we pass the variables S(:,1), S(:,2), and S(:,3) through digital to analog converters (DACs), they will produce signals that will switch between +1 and -1 at the sample instants k*T, where k = 1, 2, 3, ... We will define the variables s(k,1), s(k,2), s(k,3) to denote the values of these signals over the intervals between the instants k*T and (k + 1)*T. We see that the signal s(k,2) lags behind s(k,1) by one time step, while s(k,3) lags behind by one further time step. The three column vectors:

```
S(:,1).*S(:,1)        S(:,1).*S(:,2)        S(:,1).*S(:,3)
```

could also be generated as time varying signals by forming the products:

```
p(k,1)  =  s(k,1)*s(k,1);
p(k,2)  =  s(k,1)*s(k,2);
p(k,3)  =  s(k,1)*s(k,3).
```

We can define the correlation function between the signals s(k,1), s(k,2), and s(k,3) to be the following functions:

```
A(1)  =   the mean value of p(k,1)
A(2)  =   the mean value of p(k,2)
A(3)  =   the mean value of p(k,3)
```

We see that the signal p(k,1) is equal to a constant (1) at all times, and thus A(1) = 1.

On the other hand, the signals p(k,2) and p(k,3) switch between +1 and -1, to give A(2) = -1/7 and A(3) = -1/7.

   Mathematicians define these values to be the autocorrelation function of the signal s(k,1), and would say that there is relatively little correlation between the signal s(k,1) and its delayed forms, s(k,2) and s(k,3). We will return to this subject in a short while.

   Binary sequences were originally studied as a branch of coding theory, and have been extensively tabulated (Peterson, 1961). They can be generated by binary state transition machines that have the same structure as the above device. An important class of machines will cycle through all possible states except the condition where all elements are zero. If the state vector has n elements, the cycle will go through $2^n - 1$ states.

   We will create such a maximal length sequential network with eight elements, so the cycle will go through 255 states. In the previous network with three elements, we arbitrarily chose the signal flow to go from element 1 to 2 to 3. We will show that this choice was arbitrary by now reversing the flow to go from element 8 to 7, and from there down to element 1. The signal (z) that is fed back to the element x(8) is generated by the modulo 2 sum of x(1) + x(3) + x(4) + x(5). The signal generator can be implemented by the following Scilab program:

```
x = [1, 0, 0, 0, 0, 0, 0, 0];
X = x;
for k = 1:299
    z = x(1) + x(3);
    if z>1, z = 0; end
    z = z + x(4);
    if z>1, z = 0; end
    z = z + x(5);
    if z > 1, z = 0; end
    for m = 1:7
        x(m) = x(m + 1);
    end
    x(8) = z;
    X = [X ; x];
end
S = 2*X - 1;
```

   We have used a `for` loop to perform the seven data shifts from x(m + 1) to x(m), and have programmed the modulo 2 additions by using `if` statements. We then use the column vector S(:,1) to produce a time varying signal s (k,1) that is shown in the top plot of Figure 2.1. This shows how the signal

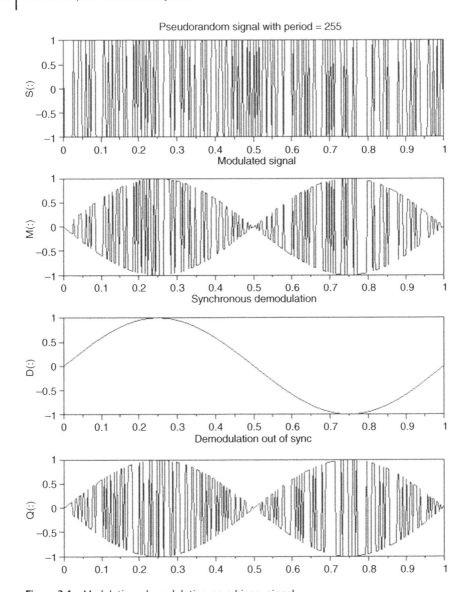

Figure 2.1 Modulation–demodulation on a binary signal.

appears to switch randomly between +1 and -1, doing so many times per cycle. Such waveforms are called pseudorandom binary signals (PRBS).

By analogy to the previous network with three elements, we can show that there is now even less correlation between the signal s(k,1) and its delayed forms, s(k,2), s(k,3), ...

The product:

```
p(k,1) = s(k,1)*s(k,1);
```

is equal to a constant (1) at all times.

Other products:

```
p(k,d) = s(k,1)*s(k,d);
```

switch between +1 and -1 to give A(d) = -1/255.

Some communication systems use such binary signals as their carrier. The signal s(k,1) can be amplitude modulated by a sinusoidal signal that is generated as a function of time (T) by the following instructions:

```
T = [0:299]'/299;
M = S.*sin(T*2*%pi);
```

The second plot in Figure 2.1 shows the resulting signal M(:), which can be used to produce a time-varying signal m(k) that goes to the transmitter. The receiver can then demodulate m(k) by the following instruction:

```
D = S.*M;
```

This operation is equivalent to the following:

```
D = S.*S.*sin(T*2*%pi)
```

which corresponds to a time-varying signal:

```
s(k,1*s(k,1*sin(k*2*%pi/299) = sin(k*2*%pi/299)
```

The sinusoidal signal can then be extracted by this process, as shown by the third plot in Figure 2.1, where the carrier has disappeared.

The bottom plot in Figure 2.1 shows what happens if the demodulator is out of synchronism by one step. This operation corresponds to a time-varying signal:

```
s(k,1)*s(k,2)*sin(k*2*%pi/299)
```

The product:

```
p(k,2) = s(k,1)*s(k,2)
```

switches between +1 and -1, to give A(2) = -1/255.

The transmitted signal can be cleanly extracted, provided that we know what carrier is being used, and the demodulator can be synchronized with the original modulator. Any phase shift in the demodulating signal will produce an output similar to the bottom plot in Figure 2.1.

2.4.2 Operational control of an industrial plant

The operation of a large industrial plant will probably involve several phases between startup and shutdown. We may need a higher-level supervisory controller that schedules lower-level controllers in order to drive the plant through the various phases of operation. This could be programmed in a process automation system or perhaps in a programmable logic controller (PLC). Figure 2.2 is a simplified generic flowchart that includes procedures for starting such a plant, operating it, and shutting it down. The rectangular blocks represent the different states of the controller, while the connecting lines represent transitions from one state to another. The labels on these lines represent the conditions that cause the controller to initiate the transitions. The signal *mode* could appear on the operator's console in order to indicate the operating state of the plant. The system is initialized by going into the STANDBY state (*mode 0*).

The operator starts up the plant by sending a command *c1*. The supervisory controller then enters the STARTUP state (*mode 1*) and issues commands to lower-level plant controllers that cause the plant to follow a startup sequence. When the condition *c2* is satisfied, the supervisory controller enters the OPERATIONAL state (*mode 2*) and the plant can begin production. There are various conditions *c3*, *c4*, *c5*, and *c6* that cause the system to go back to STANDBY.

The flowchart could serve as a functional specification for programmers to create embedded code, using a language such as C-star to operate the automation system. They could perhaps explore concepts by using a scientific language such as Scilab to simulate a startup from the STANDBY state. For example, this could define a function, such as the following, to simulate the actions that are executed during the startup procedure:

```
function c = STARTUP()
    mode = 1;
    // < startup actions >
    c=%T;
endfunction
```

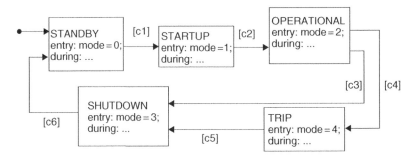

Figure 2.2 Flowchart to illustrate operation of a supervisory controller.

The symbol $//$ is used by Scilab to indicate that the following text is not to be executed. We have used it here to indicate that the programmer will insert the relevant *statements*.

The following code fragment shows how a while loop could be used to simulate a startup from STANDBY up to OPERATIONAL, and a shutdown back to STANDBY:

```
mode = 0;
c1 = STANDBY()
while ~c6
    if c1 then
        c1 = %F;
        c2 = STARTUP()
    elseif c2
        c2 = %F;
        c3 = OPERATIONAL()
    elseif c3
        c3 = %F;
        c6 = SHUTDOWN()
    end
end
STANDBY()
```

This example illustrates how a flowchart can be used to describe program flow. It also gives an example of a user-defined function. We leave it to readers to add the code that causes the plant to trip when condition *c4* is met, and to think why we should differentiate between this and condition c3.

Rubin (2016, pages 187–196) gives an example of how to simulate the supervisory control of a generating unit in an electrical power station, with figures that show the system behavior.

2.5 Difference engines

Charles Babage's concept studies for the design of a mechanical computer were described in Section 2.2. His ideas arose from a project to construct a machine that he called a "Difference Engine." This could calculate and print mathematical tables such as logarithms and trigonometric functions. Its operation can be explained by describing how it would calculate a table of integers and their squares. This would involve an input shaft (x), an intermediate shaft (z), and an output shaft (y). If x is advanced by 1 unit, z will be advanced by 2 units, while

y will then be advanced by z units. The motion of these shafts can then be modeled by the following computer program:

```
disp("x      y")
x = 1:9;
z(1)  = 1;
y(1)  = 1;
for k = 1:8
     z(k+1)  = z(k)  + 2;
     y(k+1)  = y(k)  + z(k+1);
     disp(string(x(k+1))+"      "+string(y(k+1)))
end
```

This displays the following result:

x	y
2	4
3	9
4	16
5	25
6	36
7	49
8	64
9	81

We can explain its operation by considering the following relationships:

$$z(x) = 2(x - 1) + 1$$
$$z(x + 1) = z(x) + 2 = 2x + 1$$
$$y(x) = x^2$$
$$y(x + 1) = y(x) + z(x + 1) = x^2 + 2x + 1 = (x + 1)^2$$

2.5.1 Difference equation to calculate compound interest

Consider a bank account that earns compound interest where the interest is paid monthly.

Suppose that the account was opened by depositing an amount $x(1) = 1000$ at the beginning of a month, which we will refer to by an index $k = 1$. The bank could then use software that increases the balance of the account by a discrete step at the beginning of the next month. It could then generate a statement by saving the corresponding balance in a vector (x) whose elements $x(2), x(3), \ldots$ keep track of the balance at the beginning of month 2, 3, ... This procedure can be simulated by the following computer program:

```
x(1)=1000;
for k=1:12
    x(k+1) = A * x(k);
end
```

If A equals 1.0066667, the program will generate the following vector:

```
x =
    1000.  1006.6667    1013.3778 ...      ...      1082.9999
```

which corresponds to an annual interest rate of slightly above 8%.

The statement x(k+1) = A*x(k) is known as a difference equation. It is being repeated for successive values of the index: k = 1, 2, 3, ...

The balance at time (k) can be calculated by the following simple compound interest formula:

$$x(k) = A^k x(1)$$

2.6 Iterative programming

A common situation in digital simulation involves the solution of nonlinear implicit equations. For example, chemical engineers may need to determine the boiling point of a mixture that contains two or more volatile liquids within a vessel that operates at a given pressure (P). If the most volatile liquid begins to boil at a temperature (T), the resulting pressure (P) is a complex function f(T) that cannot readily be inverted. We would then need to devise an iterative trial and error procedure to determine T as a function of P. If we have guessed that T has a value U, we can use this to calculate f(U). If f(U) deviates from the given pressure (P) we can revise U and repeat the process. The key is to find a method for revising U so that the iteration converges to the correct answer. There are a host of possible techniques that may converge rapidly in some situations but diverge in others. This typically takes the form of a numerical instability where the series of new guesses oscillate around the correct solution with ever-increasing deviations.

The following very simple example illustrates the use of an iterative program to search for the value of the mathematical constant "e" that causes the function e^t to be equal to its derivative $d(e^t)/dt$. The program approximates the derivative by the difference:

$$D(t) = [\exp(t + dt) - \exp(t)]/dt$$

where dt is reasonably small.

For example, if dt = 0.001 then at t = 1 the difference between $D(t)$ and e^t is equal to

$$D(1) - \exp(1) = 0.0013596$$

We store our initial guess for the number "e" in a variable a(1) and use it to calculate the following deviation:

```
d = a(1)^t - ((a(1)^(t+dt) - a(1)^t) / dt)
```

This can then be used to revise the estimate as a variable a(2), which is combined with a(1) to form a vector (a).

We could then use a for loop to iterate the process:

```
t = 1;
dt = .001;
a(1) = 2;
y = a(1)^t;
d = (a(1)^(t+dt) - a(1)^t)/dt;
K = 0.9;
disp("a                 y                 d")
for k = 1:9
    a(k+1) = a(k) + K*(y-d);
    y = a(k+1)^t;
    d = (a(k+1)^(t+dt) - a(k+1)^t) / dt;
    disp(string(a(k+1))+" "+string(y)+" "+string(d))
end
```

This displays the following result:

a	y	d
2.5519026	2.5519026	2.3918425
2.6959566	2.6959566	2.6750496
2.7147729	2.7147729	2.7126206
2.71671	2.71671	2.7164959
2.7169027	2.7169027	2.7168815
2.7169218	2.7169218	2.7169197
2.7169237	2.7169237	2.7169235
2.7169239	2.7169239	2.7169239
2.7169239	2.7169239	2.7169239

The last iterations show that if a is equal to 2.716 923 9 and t = 1, then the variables y and d are equal to a. This corresponds to the number "e" up to the third decimal place. If we reduce the magnitude of dt, a will approximate "e" more closely.

Iterative programs can also be used to solve algebraic equations. For example, the quadratic equation:

$$x^2 - x - 1 = 0$$

can be written as

$$x = \sqrt{(x+1)}$$

We could use a `while` loop to search for the value (x) that equals $\sqrt{(x+1)}$:

```
K = 1;
while abs(x(k)-sqrt(x(k)+1)) > 1e-6
        x(k+1) = sqrt(x(k)+1);
        k = k+1;
end
```

If we run this with an initial value `x(1)` = 3, we obtain the following series of numbers:

```
x =
    3
    2
    1.7320508
    . . . . .
    1.6180369
    1.6180349
```

If $x = 1.618\ 034\ 9$ is a root of the above equation we can solve for a second root (x_2) where

$$(x - 1.6180349)(x - x_2) = 0.$$

2.6.1 Inverse functions

Section 2.3.2, Math Functions, gave a list that included inverse functions. For example, if x lies between `-%pi/2` and `%pi/2` radians, the following statement gives $X = x$:

```
X = a sin( sin(x) )
```

The following function does not have a convenient inverse:

```
y = sin(x) + 0.3*sin(3*x)
```

We thus need to devise an iterative procedure to calculate x for a given y. Suppose that we run this from an initial value x (1) = 0, that gives y (1) = 0. We can then use the following `while` loop to search for a value of x that gives a value of y equal to a required quantity (Y):

```
x(1)  =  0;
y(1)  =  sin(x(1))  +  0.3*sin(3*x(1));
k=1;
while  abs(Y-y(k))  >  0.001
      x(k+1)  =  x(k)  +  (Y-y(k))
      y(k+1)  =  sin(x(k+1))  +  0.3*sin(3*x(k+1));
      k  =  k+1;
end
```

If we run this for Y = 0.8, the program ends with the following result:

```
x  =  0.5238954
y  =  0.8002568
```

showing that `sin(0.5238954)+0.3*sin(3*0.5238954)` is approximately equal to 0.8. There is a restriction in that Y lies within the range between −0.9 and +0.9.

2.7 Digital simulation of differential equations

In the fifth century BCE Pythagoras of ancient Greece thought of space as a matrix of equispaced points. Motion through space would then consist of a series of finite jumps from point to point. Pythagorean motion can be simulated on a digital computer by means of difference equations that resemble the simple example shown in Section 2.5.1. However, the famous paradox of Zeno (495–435 BCE) showed that this view of the world was inadequate (Jeans, 1950). Zeno considered a race between Achilles and a tortoise, where the tortoise receives H yards head start. If Achilles runs 10 times faster than the tortoise, the distance that he must run in order to catch up with the tortoise is given by a series whose terms eventually become infinitesimally small:

H + H/10 + H/100 + H/1000...

This analysis is an ancient precursor to modern-day calculus, where we view space as a continuum and the continuous flow of time as being infinitely divisible.

Later chapters will consider models of continuous motion by means of differential equations. We thus need to devise methods whereby a digital computer, which is a discrete device, can emulate continuous behavior. Such methods will necessarily be approximate.

Newton and Leibnitz derived differential calculus by taking the limit of a finite difference as the time step was reduced to zero. In actual fact we solve the differential equations by an integration process. However, the process of integration is the opposite of differentiation, where we add up all the infinitesimal variables $v(t)$ to generate the function $x(t)$. Suppose that we create a computer model that approximates the integration process as the sum of finite differences. We will show how this approach can create an adequate approximation to the behavior of differential equations, provided that we make the time step small enough.

Take the simple example:

$$dX/dt = a\, X(t)$$

We happen to know that the analytic solution of this equation describes the evolution of $X(t)$ as a continuous function of time (t), where the evolution from an initial state $X(0) = X0$ is given by

$$X(t) = X0\exp(a\ t)$$

If the parameter (a) is positive X will grow, while if it is negative X settles towards zero.

We can then define a sampled signal $x(k)$ to be the value of $X(t)$ at $t = kT$, where T is the period between samples, while $x(k)$ is an element of a discrete array $x(0), x(1)$, $x(2)$, ... The transition from $x(k)$ to $x(k + 1)$ is given by integrating $X(t)$ over the time interval T. We can also make use of the analytic solution to show that the transition is given by

$$x(k + 1) = \exp(akT + aT) = \exp(aT)\exp(akT) = \exp(aT)x(k)$$

This equation can be written as follows:

$$x(k + 1) = x(k) + E(T)\, x(k)$$

where $E(T)$ is a *constant* that can be expanded as a Taylor series:

$$E(T) = \exp(aT) - 1 = (aT) + (aT)^2/2! + (aT)^3/3!\ ...$$

This is a difference equation, analogous to the compound interest formula used in Section 2.5.1, 2.1.9.

2.7.1 Rectangular integration

Nonlinear differential equations do not produce exponential evolution, so we cannot use the above analysis to derive a difference equation that gives the same answers as the continuous system at the sample instants. However, we can make use of the above polynomial expression for $E(T)$ to create a difference equation that possibly approximates the behavior of a nonlinear differential equation.

Consider the above differential equation and its corresponding difference equation:

$$dX/dt = aX(t)$$
$$x(k + 1) = x(k) + E(T)x(k)$$

We will use a truncated polynomial (aT) in place of $E(T)$ so that the difference equation becomes

$$R(k + 1) = R(k) + aT\,R(k)$$

where the evolution of the resulting $R(k)$ will hopefully follow that of $x(k)$.

We would then simulate the continuous process by means of the following computer program:

```
R(1)  = Xo;
for k=1:K
    R(k+1)  = R(k)  + T*a*R(k);
end
```

If we run this from $Xo = 1$, the resulting sequence $R(k)$ for $T*a = -0.02$ will be as shown below:

k	$\exp(kT - T)$	$R(k)$
1	1.	1.
2	0.980198	0.98
3	0.960789	0.9604
4	0.941764	0.941192
5	0.923116	0.922368
6	0.904837	0.90392

We have also shown the computed function $\exp(kT - T)$ that corresponds to the evolution of the continuous process. The difference between them is known as the *truncation error*, and can be reduced by choosing a smaller time step (T).

The increment $T*a*R(k)$ approximates the integral of $aX(t)$ by the last sampled value $aX(kT)$ times T. This equals the area of a rectangle with a height $= aX(kT)$, which stands on a base $= T$. For this reason, the approximation is known as *rectangular integration*. An example of such a rectangular signal, which is produced by sampling a continuous sinusoid, is shown in Figure A.3, Appendix A.7.1, while Appendix A.7.3 shows analytically that simulating a differential equation by rectangular integration introduces a delay. This is proportional to the time step (T) and causes the truncation error. We see that the formula for the future value R $(k+1)$ is based on the present value $R(k)$. For this reason, it is known as a *predictor*.

We can use rectangular integration to simulate nonlinear differential equations. An example of this is shown in the next section, where we will use a higher-order integration algorithm.

We can also perform rectangular integration in the following way, over a *double interval*:

```
D(1)  = Xo;
D(2)  = Xo*exp(a*T);
for k=2:K
    D(k+1)  = D(k-1)+ 2*a*T*D(k);
end
```

This avoids bias by calculating the slope halfway between $k - 1$ and $k + 1$. In the current situation it gives an improvement in the third decimal place. In order to start this process from D(1) we need to find some way to estimate D(2). We have "cheated" in the above program by calculating its true value. The formula for the future value D(k+1) is based on the present value D(k) and the past value D(k-1) and so it is again a *predictor*.

2.7.2 Trapezoidal integration

Rectangular integration is based on the assumption that a variable $X(kT + t)$ remains at the value $X(kT)$ over the period from kT to $kT + T$. Once we have computed its future value $X(kT + T)$ we can use the new data to revise this assumption. For example, we could use the following linear interpolation:

$$X(kT + t) = X(kT) + (t/T)\,[X(kT + T) - x(kT)]$$

The integral of this expression from kT to $kT + T$ is

$$J = T\,X(kT) + (T/2)\,[X(kT + T) - X(kT)] = (T/2)\,[X(kT + T) + X(kT)]$$

This is equivalent to finding the area of a trapezium. For this reason, it is known as trapezoidal integration.

We can then simulate the differential equation $dX/dt = aX(t)$ as follows:

```
P(1)  = Xo;
P(2)  = Xo*exp(a*T);
C(1)  = Xo;
C(2)  = Xo*exp(a*T);
for k=2:K
    P(k+1)  = C(k-1)+ 2*a*T*C(k);
    C(k+1)  = C(k)  + a*(T/2)*(P(k+1)+C(k));
end
```

This has first used a *predictor* to find P(k+1) and then implemented a *corrector* that uses trapezoidal integration. If we run this from Xo = 1 with T*a = −0.02, the sequence C(k) is the same as exp($kT - T$) up to the fifth decimal place.

We will now use the above method to simulate the following nonlinear differential equation:

$$dX/dt = -X^2$$

With the initial condition $X(0) = 1$, its analytic solution is known to be

$$X(t) = 1/(1 + t)$$

We can simulate the continuous process by means of the following computer program:

```
P(1)  = 1;
P(2)  = 1/(1+T);
C(1)  = 1;
C(2)  = 1/(1+T);
for k = 2:K
    P(k+1) = C(k) - T*C(k)^2;
    C(k+1) = C(k) - T*((P(k+1)+C(k))/2)^2;
end
```

If we run this with T = 0.2, the resulting sequence C(k) will be as shown below:

k	$1/(1 + kT - T)$	C(k)
1	1.	1.
2	0.8333333	0.8333333
3	0.7142857	0.7166281
4	0.625	0.6281106
5	0.5555556	0.5588069
6	0.5	0.5031387

The truncation error continues to diminish when the program runs beyond $k = 6$.

One approach to improving the accuracy of such simulations is to compute the incremental motion in infinitesimally small steps, but this introduces several practical problems, such as those due to finite word length, memory capacity to store huge quantities of data, and the time taken to compute motion over a meaningful distance. Digital simulation platforms such as MATLAB and Scilab use combinations of various integration methods to ameliorate these difficulties. Some of these are summarized by Hamming (1962). Chapter 4 gives some comparative examples where systems are simulated on such platforms or by means of programs that use simple difference equations. Section 5.3.2 gives an artificial illustration to show how there may then be a tradeoff between truncation errors and roundoff errors.

2.7.3 Second-order integration

Consider the differential equation:

$dX/dt = F(X[t])$

We will approximate the evolution of $F(X[t])$ over one sample period by a polynomial:

$F(X[kT + t]) = Y(t) = a0 + a1\,t + a2\,t^2 + a3\,t^3$

The integral of $Y(t)$ over the period from $t = 0$ to $t = T$ is equal to

$J = a0\,T + a1\,T^2/2 + a2\,T^3/3 + a3\,T^4/4$

Simpson's formula for numerical integration approximates this as

$\underline{J} = (T/6)\,(\,Y[0] + 4Y[T/2] + Y[T]\,)$

We then see that

$Y(0) = a0$

$4\,Y(T/2) = 4a0 + 2a1\,T + a2\,T^2 + a3\,T^3/2$

$Y(T) = a0 + a1\,T + a2\,T^2 + a3\,T^3$

Substituting these into Simpson's formula then gives

$\underline{J} = a0T + a1\,T^2/2 + a2\,T^3/3 + a3\,T^4/6$

which differs from J by an amount a3 $T^4/12$.

Consider the differential equation:

$dX/dt = -X^2$

Suppose that we have calculated $X(kT)$ and now need to find $X(kT + T)$. We must first find an estimate $\underline{X}(kT + T)$ and the midpoint value $\underline{X}(kT + \frac{1}{2}T)$. We can use Simpson's formula to compute a better estimate for $X(kT + T)$:

$$X(kT + T) = X(kT) + (T/6)\left(X[kT] + 4\underline{X}[kT + 1/2T] + \underline{X}[kT + T]\right)$$

The following computer program implements the Runge-Kutta iterative method to achieve this:

```
x(1)  = 1;
for  k=1:K
      x1 = -T * x(k)^2;
      x2 = -T * (x(k)+x1/2)^2;
      x3 = -T * (x(k)+x2/2)^2;
      x4 = -T * (x(k)+x3)^2;
      x(k+1)  = x(k)  +T*(x1 +2*x2 +2*x3 + x4)/6;
end
```

If we run this with $T = 0.5$, the resulting sequence x(k) will be as shown below. This demonstrates the improvement that can be achieved by using second-order integration. The accuracy of the Runge-Kutta method is good, even with the relatively large step length:

```
k          1 / (1 + kT - T)        x(k)
1          1.                      1.
2          0.6666667               0.6666766
3          0.5                     0.5000288
4          0.4                     0.4000252
5          0.3333333               0.3333531
6          0.2857143               0.2857297
7          0.25                    0.2500122
8          0.2222222               0.2222321
```

2.7.4 An Example

Consider the following differential equation where $X(0) = 0$:

$$dX/dt = X^2 + 1$$

This equation was chosen because we know that the solution is $X(t) = \tan(t)$. We wish to create a computer program that generates a discrete signal x(k) that corresponds to the values of $X(t)$ at instants kT, starting from x(1) $= 0$. To get started we need to estimate the next value by a Taylor polynomial:

$$x(2) = x(1) + T(dX/dt) + T^2(d^2X/dt^2)/2 + T^3(d^3X/dt^3)/6 + T^4(d^4X/dt^4)/24$$

where the derivatives of X are computed at $t = 0$ and thus $dX/dt = 1$ and $d^2X/dt^2 = 2X(dX/dt) = 0$.
We then see that

$$d^3X/dt^3 = 2X(d^2X/dt^2) + 2(dX/dt)^2 = 2$$

It turns out that d^4X/dt^4 is zero at $t = 0$, so that the following polynomial gives a reasonable approximation:

$$x(2) = x(1) + T + T^3/3$$

With $T = 0.2$, this gives $x(2) = 0.2026667$.

We can use x(1) and x(2) as starting values to *predict* xp(3) by doing rectangular integration over a double interval, and then *correcting* this result by doing trapezoidal integration. This corresponds to the following computer program:

```
T = 0.2;
    x(1) = 0;
    x(2) = x(1) + T + T^3/3;
    D = [0;0];
    for k=2:K
        dx = x(k)^2 + 1;
        xp(k+1) = x(k-1) + 2*T*dx;
        dxp = xp(k+1)^2 + 1;
        x(k+1) = x(k) + T*(dx+dxp)/2;
        e = [e; xp(k+1)-x(k+1)];
    end
```

The numbers dx and dxp are the values of dX/dt computed at states x(k) and xp(k).

The resulting sequence x(k) for $T = 0.2$ is compared below with the analytic solution to the differential equation:

```
tan(kT - T)    x(k)           e(k)
0.             0.             0.
0.2027100      0.2026667      0.
0.4227932      0.4241154      -0.0076859
0.6841368      0.6876135      -0.0129973
1.0296386      1.0375603      -0.0243200
1.5574077      1.5757145      -0.0574884
2.5721516      2.6148376      -0.1841268
```

The difference e(k) between the predicted xp(k) and the corrected x(k) is an indication of the accuracy of the results. It may be used in a routine that takes corrective action, e.g. to reduce the time step (*T*).

2.8 Discussion

After an introduction to the digital computer this chapter presented many of the important facilities that are available in a scientific language. The syntax used corresponds to either MATLAB or Scilab, which are the languages that will be widely used in the rest of the book. It was then shown how these facilities could be used to implement various programming techniques. This represents the first step on the road to becoming proficient in the programming of computer models. Since this book is mainly concerned with the simulation of continuous systems, considerable attention was spent on programming techniques that approximate continuous behavior by discrete operations. More general engineering applications are covered in the literature, such as Kuo and Kaiser (1966).

This chapter presents examples that were chosen to illustrate the flexibility that the digital computer offers its programmers. It is reasonable to state that the limitation no longer lies with the computer, but with the know-how of the user. We have illustrated the general principles that underlie the creation of a computer program. Readers will still have to put in the hours before they can expect to obtain meaningful results in their particular area of endeavor.

As stated in Chapter 1, the successful creation of a computer model generally depends on three skills. As well as becoming proficient in programming techniques, it is usually necessary to perform mathematical analysis. We will address this topic when we consider specific case studies. Chapter 1 also underlines the importance of creativity. Chapter 3 gives inspiring examples of this from the world of science.

Exercises

1 Consider the assembly of a physical object, such as building a house, preparing a meal, or assembling a device of your own choice.

   Draw up a list of constituent components, and of work to be done.

   Draw up a procurement plan that includes the order of operations.

   Draw up a sequential procedure (in words) that can be used as a plan to create the object.

2 If you are involved with a plant that goes between distinct operating states, can you describe this process by means of a flow diagram, such as that shown in Figure 2.2. If the material within the plant moves between different units, can you draw a material flow diagram?

3 Readers can create their programs on the platform and operating system of their choice.

   We assume that the platform has a window where commands can be typed and executed.

   We will refer to this as a command line window and to the execution as [enter].
   The command syntax given here is based on MATLAB or Scilab.

   Type in the following:

```
A = 2; B = 3; C = 4 [enter]
D = A^B [enter]
E = D + C [enter]
```

Confirm that D equals A^B and E equals D + C. Otherwise consult the user documentation to find the syntax used by the platform of your choice.

We assume that the platform has a code editor window where lines of code can be typed and stored in an executable file. MATLAB executable files have the extension .m while Scilab uses the extension .sce.

Type the above lines of code in the code editor window and save in an executable file called `myfile`.

In the MATLAB command line window, type in the following:

```
myfile [enter]
```

If `myfile.m` is in the MATLAB path, the above commands will be executed. In the Scilab command line window, type in the following:

```
exec('C:\..PATH..\Simulation\myfile.sce', -1) [enter]
```

If the path is correctly typed, the above commands will be executed.
Experiment with the various programming features that are listed.
This will help you to perform the exercises that follow.

4   Readers should consult the Help facilities and User Guides of the platform for information on their graphics features.

Create the compound interest program shown in Section 2.5.1, and use it to plot x vs. k.

If it is to be used by a bank, what questions do they need to answer before you start coding?

If you round off downwards or upwards after the second decimal place, how will the plot change?

Calculate the exponential function of (k/n) and plot it on the same graph for different values of n.

Experiment with different values of A and n in order to match the plots better.

5   Modify the program shown in Section 2.6.1 in order to find the root of the quadratic equation to an accuracy of four decimal places. After this can you find its second root (x_2)?

Modify the iterative program to search for this second root and run it with various initial values of x.

6   Create a binary signal generator that uses a shift register with three states, $x(1)$, $x(2)$, and $x(3)$. A program that does so is shown in Section 2.4.1, where the vector x has three elements.

Run the program for 21 steps. How many cycles does it generate?
Calculate the period as $N = 2^n - 1$, where $n = 3$.

Convert the binary signal into a signal that switches between $+1$ and -1 (see Section 2.4.1).

Calculate the correlation between this signal and its delayed forms.

Plot the correlation function vs. the delay between the signals.

If a customer requires a binary signal that does not repeat itself before 1000 clock pulses, what value of n will you use? Design a generator that will produce this binary signal. You may need to consult the book by Peterson (1961) or its equivalent.

7   Create a program that simulates a three-bit binary adder; where $1 + 1 = 0$, carry 1.

Run it for 21 steps and see how many cycles are generated.

8   Modify the Babage engine program shown in Section 2.5 to also print $z(k + 1)$ at each step.

How does this tie up with the difference between squares?

9   Create the program described in Section 2.7.1 that simulates rectangular integration, and plot the evolution of the output (R) from various initial conditions. Do the same with the program described in Section 2.7.2, with outputs P and C.

10   Suppose that you have generated a sine wave with a frequency of 10 Hz and you now wish to create a quadrature signal that lags it by 90 degrees (see Appendix A.2).

If you decide to use rectangular integration to generate the quadrature signal to an accuracy of 1 degree, can you make a rough estimate of the maximum step length that you may use?

11   Turing wrote an essay *Intelligent Machinery* (1948) that describes a machine that can load data from memory and interpret it as an instruction to perform one of the following operations:

Change the memory address from which the next data will be taken.
Change the data in the current memory address.
Stop.

Readers may be interested to search the literature for further details on such a machine and try to create a computer program that models its operation.

References

Bernstein, J. (1963). *The Analytical Engine*. New York: Random House.

Hamming, R.W. (1962). *Numerical Methods for Scientists and Engineers*. New York: McGraw-Hill.

Jeans, J. (1950). *The Growth of Physical Science*. London: Readers Union.

Kuo, F.F. and Kaiser, J.F. (1966). *System Analysis by Digital Computer*. New York: Wiley.

Moler, C. (2006). *The Growth of MATLAB and the MathWorks over Two Decades, Natick*. MA: The MathWorks Inc.

Peterson, W.W. (1961). *Error Correcting Codes*. New York: Wiley.

Rubin, O. (2016). *Control Engineering in Development Projects*. Boston: Artech House.

Swade, D. (1991). *Charles Babbage and His Calculating Engines*. London: Science Museum.

Trask, M. (1971). *The Story of Cybernetics*. London: Studio Vista.

3

Creative thinking and scientific theories

We will see that what are commonly regarded as scientific facts are often the creation of scientists.

> "As far as the laws of mathematics refer to reality, they are not certain, and as far as they are certain, they do not refer to reality"
>
> Albert Einstein
> (*Source:* Rights Managed)

When we create models that are based on such "scientific facts" we should ensure that the problem at hand falls within the circumstances that were considered by the scientist.

3.1 Introduction

As pointed out in Chapter 1, the creation of computer models stands on the following legs:

Techniques of computer modeling,
Mathematical analysis, and
Imagination, Inspiration, and Creative Thinking

Rather than trying to teach how to improve creativity, we will show how great scientists of the past created theoretical models to describe the behavior of natural phenomena. This will serve as a role model for readers when they need to exercise their imagination to create computer models for given applications.

The study of science is ultimately the search for law and order in physical phenomena. In order to achieve this we first need to take measurements, after which we need to do calculations. We will be looking at scientific achievements that were

Computer Models of Process Dynamics: From Newton to Energy Fields, First Edition.
Olis Rubin.
© 2023 The Institute of Electrical and Electronics Engineers, Inc.
Published 2023 by John Wiley & Sons, Inc.

made in a world without modern scientific instruments or machines to perform laborious calculations. Mathematical analysis was in its infancy and had to be developed by the same scientists who were investigating the physical processes. These deficiencies implied that researchers had to rely heavily on creative thinking, so the early history of science provides ample examples of this faculty.

This chapter presents three independent narratives. Sections 3.2 and 3.3 describe how the science of dynamics was created. Section 3.4 considers the study of electromagnetism, while Section 3.5 looks at fluid dynamics. The related material will be used in examples that appear in later chapters. The narratives presented here are restricted to a few key events that reveal how scientific progress depended on a few inspired guesses, which form the keystones in a logical structure that is typically taught in an engineering course. There is extensive literature that relates the history of science in greater detail (see Jeans, 1950).

3.2 The dawn of astronomy

Astronomy has been one of the most persistent activities in science. The ancient Egyptians used the rising of the star Sothis (Sirius) as an astronomical clock which ticked a year every 365¼ days, allowing them to predict the coming of the Nile floods. The true scientific spirit first began to flourish several centuries later when the ancient Greeks tried to understand rather than merely to know. Their work serves as a prime example of how creative thinking, supported by mathematics, forms part of the modeling process. Without proper laboratories they were able to create theoretical mental models to explain the motion of the solar system. Computer models of planetary orbits continue to be used in this age where we create satellites of our own.

Anaxagoras (c500–428 BCE) made an inspired guess by modeling the Moon, the Earth and the Sun as spherical objects, where the Moon and the Earth are illuminated by the Sun. He then explained that the Moon is eclipsed when the Earth comes between it and the Sun, while the phases of the Moon depended on the relative angles between the Sun the Moon and the Earth. Two centuries later Aristarchus of Samos (c310–230 BCE) treated these observations in a truly scientific spirit. His calculations appear in a work, *On the Sizes and Distances of the Sun and the Moon*, that has fortunately survived the destruction of the ages.

His reasoning is an object lesson on how to create a mathematical model. Aristarchus reasoned that at half Moon the Sun, Moon, and Earth must form a right-angled triangle. He measured the angular difference between the Sun and the Moon and then took the unprecedented step of doing triangulation to determine the relative distances of the Sun and the Moon. This technique was used by land surveyors, but Aristarchus dared to use it on the heavens. The exact moment of half Moon is difficult to determine, but his calculation nevertheless showed that the distance to the Sun is orders of magnitude greater than the distance to the Moon. At a solar eclipse the Moon almost covers the face of the Sun, so the more distant Sun must be correspondingly larger than the Moon. Aristarchus had observed the shadow of the Earth during a lunar eclipse and concluded that it is twice the size of the Moon, so obviously the Earth is much smaller than the Sun. Archimedes wrote in his *Psammites* that Aristarchus put forward the hypothesis that the Earth moves around the Sun along a circular orbit. Unfortunately, this act of genius was not accepted for 17 centuries, and the official model of the solar system continued to state that the Sun moved around the Earth. Nevertheless, the ancient Greeks showed us how creative thinking can perform an essential role when we are looking for a solution in an unexplored situation.

3.3   The renaissance

"Whoever in discussion adduces authority uses not intellect but rather memory"

Leonardo da Vinci
(*Source:* In the Public Domain)

The era of the Renaissance represents an age where some began to question the official authority of the church. In his magnum opus, *De Revolutionibus Orbium Coelestum*, Copernicus (1473–1543) challenged the official model of the solar system. He suggested that the Earth rotates relative to the fixed stars, and showed how this can explain their apparent daily revolution in the sky. Copernicus then suggested that the Earth moves around the Sun, and showed how this can explain the motion of the planets through the night sky. The resulting model of the solar system would then consist of the Earth and the other planets all moving in circular orbits around the Sun.

Tycho Brahe (1546–1601) had measured how Mars sometimes moves rapidly across the sky and sometimes more slowly. Kepler (1571–1630) found that he could match this data to within eight minutes of arc by assuming that the Earth and Mars followed circular orbits around the Sun. He then found empirically that he could obtain a better fit to the observations by modeling the orbit of a planet as an ellipse, where it gains speed as it falls towards the Sun and loses speed as it moves away from the Sun. This empirical model opened up a new question: Why did the planets move in ellipses, rather than any other curve? This question would only be answered after the discovery of an entirely new science.

3.3.1   Galileo

Galileo Galilei (1564–1642) can properly be regarded as the father of modern physical science. His greatest contribution was to combine experimental methods with creative thinking and mathematical analysis. In a series of brilliant experiments, he would almost single-handedly create the science of mechanics and dynamics. He fortunately left his findings to posterity in a strikingly lucid volume: *Discorsi e Dimonstrazione Mathematiche, intorno á due nuoue scienze* (*Dialogs Concerning Two New Sciences,* translated by Crewe and de Salvio, 1954). He began by dropping a cannon-ball and a musket-ball from the top of the leaning tower of Pisa and showed that they simultaneously reached the ground. Having disproved the age-old theory that different bodies fell at different rates he performed a series of experiments, based on meticulous analysis, to formulate the science of dynamics.

We can gain some idea of the prevailing ignorance of his day from the fact that he took four axioms and six theorems to define speed to be distance divided by time. The Pythagoreans regarded space to be a series of discrete points, allowing distance to be expressed exactly by an integer number and time to consist of a similar series of discrete events. Zeno (495–435 BCE) had devised several well-known paradoxes that questioned this view. The writings of Galileo imply that he regarded space as a continuum and the continuous flow of time as being infinitely divisible.

Galileo created a mathematical model to explain the result of the Pisa experiment. This postulated that the motion of falling bodies obeyed a law of uniform acceleration. We typically use the acceleration due to gravity at sea level. From this, he proved theoretically that if a body starts from rest and is uniformly accelerated, then the distance that it travels in a given time (t) is proportional to t^2. He verified this by means of a simple mechanical model that consisted of a ball rolling down an inclined plane. This simulated free-fall in a slowed down time scale that was measured with a water-clock (*clepsydra*). By creating a simple mechanical model, he could verify a basic law of kinematics. Today we may use different technology, but we can still learn a great deal from Galileo.

Galileo also performed experiments with a pendulum that consisted of a ball hanging on a fine thread. He found that the ball reached the same height at the end of its swing as it had at the point of release and ascribed this to an exchange between height and momentum (*impeto*). Galileo had to avoid writing about the motion of planets around the Sun since he had been before the Inquisition, in a trial that was rightly described as the disgrace of the century. There was an express order prohibiting the printing of any of his work, *nulla excepto*. Fortunately, Elzevir risked the wrath of Rome and printed it in Leyden in 1638 (Jeans, 1950).

3.3.2 Newton

Isaac Newton (1642–1703) extended the work of Galileo to replace Kepler's empirical model of the solar system by mathematical equations. This is described in his book: *Philosophiæ Naturalis Principia Mathematica*, which many regard as the greatest scientific work ever produced by the human intellect.

Newton invented differential and integral calculus, as well as introducing many new ideas into physical science. He generalized Galileo's law of uniform acceleration by postulating a force of gravity that caused an apple to fall to the ground, and concluded that the same force kept the Moon and the planets in their orbits. He then introduced the following three axioms, known as his laws of motion, which he used in a mathematical model that described the orbit of the Moon around the Earth:

1) Every body perseveres in its state of rest or of uniform motion in a straight line, unless it is compelled to change that state by impressed forces.
2) Change of motion (i.e. the rate of change of momentum) is proportional to the motive force applied and takes place in the direction in which such force is applied.
3) To every action there is always opposed an equal reaction.

Newton saw clearly that he had created a mathematical framework from what was only a working hypothesis. He was aware that he could not define an inertial reference for measuring speed, while his concepts of force, mass, and momentum were questionable. Brushing these reservations aside, he proceeded to apply a numerical test on the motion of the Moon. We will broadly describe his reasoning, using mathematics that is familiar to us.

It is a reasonable approximation to assume that the Moon orbits around the Earth on a circle of radius (R) with a constant tangential velocity (v). Its angular rate will then be

$$w = v/R$$

It is shown in Appendix B.2 that its centripetal acceleration will be

$$a = v^2/R = w^2 R$$

Newton now proposed that the Earth exerted a gravitational force on the Moon. The second law of motion implies that this force will cause a centripetal acceleration of the Moon. He then assumed that this force is given by the following equation:

$$f = G M/R^2$$

where f is the force per unit mass of Moon body, M is the total mass of the earth, and G is a constant. Newton had reasoned that it is the same force of gravity that causes objects on the surface of the Earth to fall with an acceleration (g) and that its value is given by the same equation:

$$g = G M/r^2$$

where r is the radius of the Earth.

Astronomers had estimated the size of the earth and the distance to the Moon, so Newton knew that the ratio (R/r) was equal to 60. Since the measured acceleration due to g was equal to 32 ft s^{-2} he could calculate the gravitational force on the Moon:

$$f = g\,(r/R)^2$$

Newton could calculate the angular rate (w) from the period (T) of the Moon's orbit:

$$w = 2\pi/T$$

where T is 27.32 days, not to be confused with the phases of the moon (29.53 days) that results from its combined motion around the Earth and the Sun. Since he knew the distance (R) to the moon he could thus calculate the centripetal acceleration:

$$a = 4\pi^2 R/T^2$$

and found that the result was pretty close to the other value (f).

We will now look at why Newton chose the above law for gravitational force. Most of the planets revolve around the Sun in orbits that are nearly circular. Keppler's empirical model further states that the period of a planetary orbit is given by

$$T^2 = K\,r^3$$

where K is a constant while r is its distance from the Sun. Its motion around the orbit corresponds to an angular rate (w), where

$$w^2 = (2\pi/T)^2 = 4\pi^2/K\,r^3$$

whence the centripetal acceleration can be written as

$$a = w^2\,r = 4\pi^2/K\,r^2$$

For a planet to move around the Sun in a stable orbit regardless of its distance from the Sun, the force of gravitation must vary proportionally with $1/r^2$. Newton's law of universal gravitation is expressed more generally as

$$F = G\,m_1\,m_2/r^2$$

where two bodies having masses m_1 and m_2, which are separated by a distance (r), attract one another with a gravitational force (F).

We have seen how a series of inspired guesses were used by Newton to create a logical framework that is now taught in engineering courses. It is a further example of how creative thinking, combined with mathematics, helps us to model physical objects. Even though advances in science led to Einstein's model of gravity as a distortion of space–time, Newton's equations are still accurate enough to serve in the creation of programs that navigate our space probes. In Chapter 4 we will show

how the mathematical model of planetary motion can be solved analytically, while it is also implemented as a computer model.

3.4 Electromagnetism

Ancient Greek navigators used the magnetic properties in lodestone from Magnesia (μαγνησ) while the word "electricity" is derived from the Greek word (ηλεκτρον) for amber. However, it was not until the nineteenth century that scientists created the science of electromagnetism. This is an interesting case study that illustrates how mathematicians and experimental physicists co-operated to arrive at a mathematical model that explains the experimental results. Readers are referred to Maxwell (1888) for a detailed description of the experiments that were performed, and the laboratory instruments that were designed. Many were striking examples of nineteenth century craftmanship that well deserved their places in museums.

One of these was the balance that Coulomb used in 1785 to measure the force between two electrostatic charges. The instrument was designed so that the electrostatic force produced a measurable torsion of a fine wire or glass fiber. By measuring the charges Q and Q_1 and varying the distance (r) between them, he created a mathematical model, known as *Coulomb's law*. This states that the electrostatic force between two point charges is proportional to $Q\,Q_1/r^2$, where like charges repel and unlike charges attract one another.

Faraday then found experimentally that a charge Q inside a conducting sphere attracts unlike charges, which thus flow to the inside surface of the sphere, while like charges are repelled, causing the outside surface of the sphere to carry a total charge Q. Faraday had the inspiration to imagine that the charge Q (coulomb) drives a radial *electric flux* through the surrounding medium, where the *flux density* (coulomb/m^2) is defined as:

$$\mathbf{D} = \mathbf{r}\, Q/\left(4\pi r^2\right)$$

where r is the distance from the charge, while $\mathbf{r}$ is a unit vector that points outward from the charge. Since this flux is normal to the surface of the sphere, its integral over the whole surface is equal to Q, as confirmed by experiment.

Gauss (1777–1855) modeled this by a vector field (Jordan, 1953) that satisfies the equation:

$$\text{div}(\mathbf{D}) = q \tag{3.1}$$

where q is the charge density (coulomb/m^3) at any point, while the divergence function div($\mathbf{D}$) is discussed in Appendix C.4. The analysis of vector fields is presented in Davis (1967).

3.4.1 Magnetic fields

When Öersted reported his discovery (Jeans, 1950) that a compass needle was deflected by an electric current, Ampère immediately investigated the properties of the magnetic field. It was shown experimentally (Jordan, 1953) that if a current ($\mathbf{I}$) flows through a long straight wire it produces a field that follows concentric circles that lie in a plane normal to the wire. Jordan (1953) defines a vector quantity $\mathbf{B}$, called *magnetic flux density*, to represent the strength of the field, and describes how its magnitude (B) can be measured. Stoke's theorem (Jordan, 1953) can be used to show that $\mathbf{B}$ can be modeled by a vector field that satisfies the equation:

$$\text{curl}(\mathbf{B}) = \mu\, \mathbf{J}$$

where $\mathbf{J}$ is the current density (amps m^{-2}) flowing at a given point, μ is the permeability (henry m^{-1}) of the medium that surrounds the wire, while the function curl ($\mathbf{B}$) is discussed in Appendix C.4.2. The *magnetic intensity* ($\mathbf{H}$) of a field that produces a flux density ($\mathbf{B}$) was defined to be

$$\mathbf{H} = \mathbf{B}/\mu$$

whence

$$\text{curl}(\mathbf{H}) = \mathbf{J} \tag{3.2}$$

Now consider a capacitor where a current flowing into one plate deposits charge upon it while the current flowing from the other plate removes charge. If the plates are separated by a perfect insulator there cannot be any physical charge flowing between them, but the difference in their charges creates a voltage difference. There is thus an electric flux density ($\mathbf{D}$) between the plates. Maxwell modified Equation (3.2) by observing that a change in electric flux also produces a magnetic field (Jordan, 1953). When operating in a perfect insulator, Equation (3.2) is replaced by

$$\text{curl}(\mathbf{H}) = \partial\mathbf{D}/\partial t \tag{3.3}$$

3.4.2 Electromagnetic induction

Faraday made an inspired guess that an electric current should induce a current to flow in another circuit. In 1831, after 10 years of research, he wound two closely coupled copper coils with one connected to an electric battery and the other to a galvanometer. He finally noticed that the galvanometer moved when the battery was disconnected. In a further experiment he found that he could induce a current to flow through a coil by moving a magnet in its proximity. *Faraday's induction law* states (Jordan, 1953) that the induced voltage around a loop is equal to $-d\Phi/dt$, where Φ is the total magnetic flux going through the loop. This relationship is best expressed in terms of an *electric field* $\mathbf{E} = \mathbf{D}/\varepsilon$, which is measured in volts m^{-1}. Stoke's theorem (Jordan, 1953) can then be used to show that $\mathbf{E}$ can be modeled by a vector field that satisfies the equation

$$\text{curl}(\mathbf{E}) = -\partial\mathbf{B}/\partial t = -\mu\,\partial\mathbf{H}/\partial t \tag{3.4}$$

3.4.3 Electromagnetic radiation

In 1864 Clerk Maxwell used the above equations to show that an electromagnetic wave would be propagated through space at the speed of light. By taking the curl of Equation (3.4) and reversing the order of differentiation he obtained the following:

$$\text{curl}[\text{curl}(\mathbf{E})] = -\mu\,\text{curl}(\partial\mathbf{H}/\partial t) = -\mu\,\partial\,\text{curl}(\mathbf{H})/\partial t$$

Substituting Equation (3.3) in this equation then gave

$$\text{curl}[\text{curl}(\mathbf{E})] = -\mu\,\partial^2\mathbf{D}/\partial t^2 = -\mu\,\varepsilon\,\partial^2\mathbf{E}/\partial t^2 \tag{3.5}$$

Since there is no electric charge in space, Equation (3.1) can be written as

$$\text{div}(\mathbf{D}) = 0$$

This means that $\text{div}(\mathbf{E}) = 0$, which then implies that $\text{curl}(\mathbf{E})$ is at right angles to $\mathbf{E}$, and therefore $\text{curl}(\text{curl}(\mathbf{E}))$ is in the direction of $\mathbf{E}$.

After some algebraic manipulation Maxwell found that

$$\text{curl}(\text{curl}(\mathbf{E})) = -\text{div}[\text{grad}(\mathbf{E})] \tag{3.6}$$

Combining Equations (3.5) and (3.6) then gives a three-dimensional wave equation (see Section 8.2.1):

$$\text{div}[\text{grad}(\mathbf{E})] = \left(1/c^2\right)\partial^2\mathbf{E}/\partial t^2$$

where $1/c^2 = \mu\varepsilon$, while the meaning of div[grad( )] is discussed in Appendix C.4.

In 1887 Hertz succeeded in making electrical equipment emit waves which were of the kind that Maxwell had predicted. The vast field of radio transmission resulted from this experiment. Rather than characterizing it by its frequency ω, we generally refer to its wavelength as $\lambda = c/\omega$. Radio astronomers are interested in electromagnetic radiation whose wavelength is a million times longer than that of visible light, while some γ rays are a million times shorter. Maxwell's model of electromagnetic phenomena spurred the development of modern science, which had a profound influence on the technology of today.

We have viewed the intense effort that went into the creation of the mathematical apparatus mentioned above. This work would have been in vain had it not been for the creative thinking of a few inspired scientists.

3.5 Aerodynamics

Artist, scientist, inventor, and genius – one wonders what Leonardo da Vinci would have achieved if he had more suitable measuring instruments to advance his studies on the flow of water and air. His capacity for taking pains went with the imagination to design his famous "flying machines."

See his notebooks, translated by MacCurdy (1938).

Much later, in the mid seventeenth century, von Guerike invented the air-pump and demonstrated the power of atmospheric pressure (see Jeans, 1950). Boyle and Hooke used an air-pump to compress a given quantity of gas, where they found that the product of pressure (P) and volume (V) remained constant (see Jeans, 1950).

Gassendi had earlier advanced the idea that a gas is composed of hard, rapidly moving particles that randomly bounce off one another (see Jeans, 1950). This model explains how atmospheric pressure acts on a solid surface, by the impulses caused when molecules of air impact on the surface. Clausius used the molecular model of gaseous behavior to show mathematically that the pressure exerted by the gas is proportional to the kinetic energy of its molecules. Joule had shown that when the gas is heated, the product (PV) increases, whence it was concluded that its temperature varies proportionately with its kinetic energy (see Jeans, 1950). This led to the definition of an absolute temperature scale (T) where $T = 0$ corresponds to zero energy. The above relationships could then be combined into a single equation:

$$PV = RT$$

where R is proportional to the number of molecules in the given quantity of gas.

Bernoulli used this kinetic model of gaseous behavior to predict what should happen if a stream is flowing at a velocity (v). He assumed that some of the random molecular motion would be converted into directed motion (v). The directed kinetic energy per unit volume of the stream is given by

$$q = 1/2\,\rho\,v^2$$

where ρ is the density of the gas.

Bernoulli's theorem states that the pressure exerted on a surface that is parallel to the stream would then be diminished by the amount q. This is because the mean kinetic energy of molecules that strike the surface is reduced by the amount q (see von Karman, 1954).

This change in pressure was exploited in the perfume sprays of yesteryear, which performed the same function as the aerosol cans of today. They consisted of a pipe that had a nozzle on one end and a rubber bulb at the other end. By squeezing the bulb the lady caused air to flow through the pipe. This reduced its pressure, causing perfume to be sucked through a narrow tube that was connected to the pipe. Bernoulli thereby contributed to the cosmetic industry.

Bernoulli's theorem is of great importance to aeronautical engineers, since it allows them to calculate the lift force that is developed by a wing. We will return to this subject in Section 8.6.

As a rough guide, the number of molecules in the atmosphere at sea level is well in excess of 10^{25} molecules per cubic meter. An average molecule undergoes more than ten billion collisions per second. Under these conditions the error introduced by assuming that the aerodynamic flow field is continuous is far less than the other approximations that are typically made.

This model of how a gas behaves was once again created by the inspiration of a few scientists.

3.5.1   Vector flow fields

Leonardo da Vinci made detailed drawings of the lines that water follows when it flows around obstacles in its path. Such streamlines can be seen in a wind tunnel by injecting visible matter into the gas that flows around a model that is held in a fixed position. The three-dimensional flow of a gas follows analogous streamlines around solid objects in its path. We can use the concepts given in Appendix C to describe this by a vector flow field, where $\mathbf{V}(x, y, z)$ is a three-dimensional velocity vector that defines the flow at any point. The direction of flow is aligned with $\mathbf{V}$, while the speed (v) of flow is equal to its magnitude.

For incompressible flow the density of the fluid (ρ) is the same at any point in the field. The mass flow into any volume element must equal the outflow, whence

$$\rho \operatorname{div}(\mathbf{V}) = 0$$

Thus the divergence of the velocity vector $\operatorname{div}(\mathbf{V})$ is zero.

We define an irrotational flow field to have $\operatorname{curl}(\mathbf{V})$ equal to zero. Appendix C.4.2 shows that the velocity vector $\mathbf{V}(x, y)$ for a two-dimensional irrotational flow is given by the gradient of a scalar field. This field can be defined mathematically as a potential function $P(x, y)$ that satisfies Laplace's equation:

$$\operatorname{div}[\operatorname{grad}(P)] = 0$$

Section 8.6 shows how we can define potential functions that produce streamlines that go around a solid cylinder. The resulting velocity of the flow will vary along the surface of the cylinder, allowing us to apply Bernoulli's theorem in order to calculate the force on the cylinder. The resulting forces agree with the findings of d'Alembert and Rayleigh. In the mid eighteenth century d'Alembert towed ship models in still water and measured the drag force. He then developed a mathematical model that allowed him to calculate this force. In his book *Essai d'une nouvelle théory de la résistance des fluides* he considered a circular cylinder in a uniform flow field. His analysis gave the paradoxical result that the drag on the cylinder was absolutely zero. Then in 1878 Lord Rayleigh published a paper *On the Irregular Flight of a Tennis-Ball* that shed some light on the mechanism whereby aerodynamic forces are produced by airflow. With a circular cylinder in the same flow field, he found that by adding circulatory flow around the cylinder he could produce a lateral force, known as the Magnus effect. In the 1920s Flettner used a rotating vertical cylinder to "sail" a boat. The design was technically sound, but was too costly to be a commercial success!

Was it the inspiration of some unknown tennis player who first "cut the ball" that prompted Rayleigh to create a model that explains the existence of an aerodynamic lift force on the wing of an aircraft? This model forms the basis of computational fluid dynamics which can be combined with wind tunnel tests to assist with the design of aircraft.

3.6 Discussion

This chapter has introduced us to many creative thinkers who formulated scientific models that described the behavior of the real world. Consider the scientists who modeled the motion of the planets in the solar system. When we look up at the sky, it seems to be obvious that the Sun, Moon and stars are moving around the Earth. Aristarchus took a great leap of imagination when he turned this around by thinking that the Earth may just be another planet that moves around the sun. What is even more surprising is the fact that he arrived at this conclusion by making simple observations that needed virtually no measuring instruments. Copernicus performed complex calculations without the help of computers to deduce the laws of planetary motion from astronomical measurements. It then took the genius of Galileo and Newton to construct the physical laws that allow us to create a model that will be used in Section 5.2 to simulate the motion of a planet.

Two contemporaries of Newton (Pascal and Leibniz) constructed primitive calculators, but it took considerably more than two centuries before scientists and mathematicians had computers to assist them in their problem solving. One can only marvel at the insight of our predecessors, who achieved so much in the intervening centuries. How did Euler visualize motion in three dimensions and Lagrange describe even more complex motion without the assistance of the computing facilities and displays that we have today? How did Fourier and Laplace see a spectrum of a complex signal without a computer to build it out of basic elements?

The ease with which we can now interact with a computer makes it very tempting to play with the keyboard and mouse instead of taking time off to consider where this is taking us. However, we still need to use independent reasoning and creative thinking to define the tasks that are implemented on the machine. That computer giant, the IBM corporation, used to hand out posters that showed a single word "THINK."

Section 3.4 described the formulation of a scientific model that described electromagnetism. It required a series of brilliant achievements to establish the interactions between seemingly unrelated physical phenomena. Someone had the imagination to realize that the voltage across a voltaic pile was related to the electrostatic potential produced by a charge. Someone had the inspiration to use a voltaic pile as a source that drives an electric current through a conductor. There was then a fortuitous discovery that an electric current produces a magnetic field. After showing that an electrostatic charge induced a similar charge on a neighboring object, Faraday imagined that an electric current could similarly induce a current through a nearby conductor. It took him over ten years of fruitless experiments before he discovered how to prove this and thereby founded electrical engineering as we know it today. It was Maxwell who created a mathematical model that linked up all these physical phenomena and used it to predict the propagation of electromagnetic radiation through space. This opened the way for the many varied uses of electromagnetic waves that we know today. It also provided a stepping stone that led to the creation of modern physics.

Optical devices such as spectacles, telescopes, and microscopes use lenses and mirrors that can be designed by using Euclidean geometry to calculate the path followed by rays of light (Bragg, 1933). Light can also be separated into the colors of the rainbow by a diffraction grating. This is a metal plate with many closely spaced parallel lines scratched on its surface. We can explain the operation of a diffraction grating by assuming that light consists of electromagnetic waves, where the spacing between the lines on the grating can match the wavelength of the various colors. Such a grating can be used in a spectroscope to detect the presence of various elements by the wavelengths of their emission or absorption spectra. These instruments are routinely used by chemists and astrophysicists. Section 8.5 presents a computer model that calculates the interference between waves that is produced by an equispaced array of point sources. This can be compared with the operation of a diffraction grating and can also be applied to the analysis of a phased array radar or radio telescope. Bragg (1933) describes many other phenomena that can be explained by modeling light as a form of wave propagation.

Section 3.5 then went on to consider the efforts to create a mathematical model of aerodynamics. A model was first created to describe the properties of a "perfect gas." This corresponded fairly closely to the atmosphere at sea level. The next problem was to create a model of fluid flow around the wing of an aircraft.

A mathematical model was created to describe the flow of a hypothetical fluid that had certain simplified properties. Section 3.5.1 describes how this model made use of an algebraic potential function, while Section 8.6 shows how it is used to calculate the flow around a simple geometric figure. Unfortunately, this approach is very limited when we wish to apply it to a practical situation, so the aviation industry had to rely on wind tunnels to verify their designs. After more than a century of research it became possible to create computer programs that combine the elements of potential flow with the complex flow patterns of air. Computational fluid dynamics now has a place together with the wind tunnel in the aviation industry.

There are situations where we need new ideas before we can create a model of a given object. This is where we need creative thinking. It is hoped that readers will use the above examples from the past as a role model to assist them with meeting the challenges of the present.

References

Bragg, S.W. (1933). *The Universe of Light*. London: G. Bell & Sons.

Davis, H.F. (1967). *Introduction to Vector Analysis*. Boston: Allyn and Bacon.

Galilei, G. (1954). *Dialogs Concerning Two New Sciences* (trans. H. Crewe and A. de Salvio). New York: Dover.

Jeans, J. (1950). *The Growth of Physical Science*. London: Readers Union.

Jordan, E.C. (1953). *Electromagnetic Waves and Radiating Systems*. London: Constable.

MacCurdy, E. (1938). *The Notebooks of Leonardo da Vinci*. London: Jonathan Cape.

Maxwell, J.C. (1888). *An Elementary Treatise on Electricity*, 2e. Oxford: Clarendon Press.

von Karman, T. (1954). *Aerodynamics*. New York: McGraw Hill.

4

Calculus and the computer

The study of mathematics is primarily concerned with the manipulation of equations. We will create models on a computer that manipulates arrays of numbers.

> "The Analytical Engine weaves algebraic patterns just as the Jacquard loom weaves flowers and leaves."
>
> Ada, Countess of Lovelace, 1834
> (*Source:* In the Public Domain, Rights Holder Augustus Ada King)

It is better to use more than one approach when studying a problem. A mathematical solution and a computed result will show us two faces of the same coin. We thereby gain more insight than we would by finding a single result.

4.1   Introduction

While scientists were investigating the nature of the world around us mathematicians were developing methods for analyzing its behavior. While Newton imagined that the orbit of the Moon around the Earth was governed by his laws of motion, he also developed the calculus to verify his hypothesis. This started a "gold rush" where mathematicians sought to tabulate the derivatives and integrals of countless functions. The next phase was to find ways of solving differential equations. This intellectual exercise also had applications in science and engineering, which prompted engineers to design mechanical "models" that mechanized the solution. These were then implemented on electronic analog computers, which initiated the search for practical digital simulation. Chapter 2 discusses numerical techniques that can be used to approximate the integral of a variable. Advances in this area went hand-in-hand with improvements in computer graphics, to produce

Computer Models of Process Dynamics: From Newton to Energy Fields, First Edition.
Olis Rubin.
© 2023 The Institute of Electrical and Electronics Engineers, Inc.
Published 2023 by John Wiley & Sons, Inc.

simulation platforms such as MATLAB and Scilab. This chapter gives examples that show how it may be easier to find a numerical solution to a mathematical problem than to use classical analysis. The computer simulation models are implemented in a block diagram form, which assists us to visualize the signal flow that is inherent within such differential equations. The studies are done on the Scilab platform, but could just as easily be done on MATLAB. It is also shown how a model can be implemented by computer code. The code fragment uses statements that are common to MATLAB and Scilab, and should be easily understood by Python and C users.

The case studies in this chapter show that the numerical results given by computer models are comparable with the analytical solutions to the differential equations. Even though the creation of a model may be easier than the determination of an analytic solution, this does not mean that the mathematical approach is obsolete. In Section 4.8 we will expand the reasons for using analytical methods as well as computer simulation when studying a problem.

4.2 Mathematical solution of differential equations

Leibnitz (1646–1716) was the co-founder of *Acta Eruditorum*, the only privately owned scientific journal in Europe at the time, where he published a series of papers that familiarized mathematicians with differential and integral calculus in a notation that was simpler and more convenient than that of Newton. Descartes (1596–1650) had explained the principles of analytic geometry in his *Discours de la Méthode*. Calculus could then be combined with cartesian geometry to create differential equations that model the physical motion of material objects. This started an era of more than two centuries that provided an abundance of brilliant thinkers who formulated the tools of applied mathematics that are available to us today. Newton had applied his laws of motion to bodies that were small enough to be treated as point masses. Euler (1707–1783) showed how to apply Newton's laws to a rigid body that moved in a three-dimensional space while it rotated about its center of gravity. Hamilton (1805–1865) and Clerk Maxwell (1831–1879) described the laws of dynamics in the vector notation shown in Appendix B. Lagrange (1736–1813) transformed these laws so that they could be applied to even more general mechanical systems.

Now that scientists could create differential equations that model the physical motion of natural objects, the next problem was to find mathematical methods to solve them. Tables of derivatives were created, which included formulae such as:

$$d \sin(wt)/dt = w \cos(wt)$$

$$d \cos(wt)/dt = -w \sin(wt)$$

This implies that $x(t) = -X \sin(wt)$ is a ready-made solution to the following differential equation:

$$\mathrm{d}^2x/\mathrm{d}t^2 = -w^2x$$

Now suppose that a given system is described by a differential equation of the form:

$$A_n\, \mathrm{d}^n x/\mathrm{d}t^n + \cdots + A_2\, \mathrm{d}^2 x/\mathrm{d}t^2 + A_1\, \mathrm{d}x/\mathrm{d}t + x(t) = u(t)$$

A similar technique can be used to find the response of this system to a sinusoidal input $u(t) = -U \sin(\omega t)$. If the system is stable, it will eventually settle to an oscillation where $x(t)$, $\mathrm{d}x/\mathrm{d}t$, $-\mathrm{d}^2 x/\mathrm{d}t^2$, etc. are all sinusoidal functions of time at the same frequency (ω) and where their amplitudes and phases are such that they satisfy the above equation. The frequency response of the system can be calculated by varying ω and determining the resulting amplitudes and phases. Fourier (1768–1830) had introduced the use of a harmonic series to represent functions. This was found to be particularly useful for the analysis of linear constant systems that obey the principle of superposition. If the input to such a system is expressed as the sum of individual signals, the response of the system can be expressed as the sum of the individual responses to the respective signals. If the input signal can be expressed by means of a Fourier series, its output can be determined from its frequency response.

Now consider the derivative formula:

$$\mathrm{d}e^u/\mathrm{d}t = e^u\, \mathrm{d}u/\mathrm{d}t$$

This implies that the exponential function: $x(t) = \exp(at) = e^{at}$ is a ready-made solution to the following differential equation:

$$\mathrm{d}x/\mathrm{d}t = ax$$

Laplace (1749–1827) generalized frequency response analysis by considering signals that are formed by combining sinusoidal and exponential functions. This allowed him to transform variations in time to functions of a complex frequency, where we can analyze differential equations by classical algebraic methods. Appendix A gives further details. Engineers now had powerful methods for determining the response of linear constant systems as a matter of routine.

Picard (1856–1941) developed an iterative method for finding analytic functions that are solutions of a nonlinear, time-varying differential equation. This method will be demonstrated in Section 4.4, Picard's Method for Solving a Nonlinear Differential Equation, while Section 4.4.1, Mechanization of Picard's Method, shows how it can be mechanized as a computer model. Taylor (1685–1731) published an account on the use of power series to represent given functions. Section 4.4.3, Approximate Solution by Taylor Series, shows how a Taylor series can be used instead of Picard's method to solve the differential equation. The rest of the chapter goes on to show how exponential, sinusoidal, and Bessel functions can all be expanded as Taylor series.

4.3 From physical analogs to analog computers

In addition to his illustrious scientific career, in 1879 Lord Kelvin devised a mechanical computer that consisted of rotating drums, cables, and dials. Its purpose was to plot the predicted times of high tides around Britain, as well as the high-water marks. Time-varying differential equations of the following form were used to model the motion of the sea:

$$dy/dt = v(t)f(t)$$
$$dv/dt = -y(t)$$

The solutions to these equations are functions $V(t)$ and $Y(t)$ over the interval $0 < t < T$. Kelvin initially considered finding these functions by mechanizing Picard's iterative method (see Section 4.4). This used the following idea. If an estimate of $V(t)$ was available, it could be used to form dy/dt. Kelvin could then construct a mechanical integrator that computed $Y(t)$. This could be used to form dv/dt, which could then be sent to a second mechanical integrator that computed $V(t)$. This procedure could be iterated until $V(t)$ and $Y(t)$ converged to a consistent solution.

While building the machine Kelvin found that it was far simpler to run the two differential equations simultaneously and connect them in a feedback loop. This meant that dx/dt was continuously updated as $v(t)$ was changed and dv/dt was continuously changed as $y(t)$ was updated. Feedback loops were well known by this time. In 1788 Watt used a flyball governor to regulate the speed of steam engines, and in 1868 Maxwell published a paper in the *Proceedings of the Royal Society* that analyzed the stability of such governors.

Kelvin's work was continued in 1925, when Dr Vannevar Bush of MIT constructed a general-purpose analog computer that used mechanical units to solve differential equations. Electrical analogs were introduced in the 1920s when network analyzers were used to simulate electrical power grids. A major advance in analog computing came when vacuum tubes and transistors were used to build operational amplifiers. Several enterprises competed to produce reliable user-friendly, economically competitive analog computers, which held the field for many decades. Digital computers have now supplanted the analog computer but some of us may still remember them with nostalgia; they somehow brought us closer to the physical world than the digital simulation of today.

A great deal of research went into the digital simulation of differential equations, and in the 1970s several enterprises developed in-house platforms that ran on the mid-sized computers of the day. As the word length and speed of commercial machines increased, digital simulation started taking over from the analog installations. The phenomenal progress in computer hardware went hand in hand with advances in operating systems and software. The simulation platforms MATLAB with Simulink and Scilab with Xcos allow users to create dynamic models in a window that displays them as block diagrams. This chapter shows examples that use the Scilab platform to create such block diagrams, while they also show how the dynamic models can be implemented as computer code.

4.4 Picard's method for solving a nonlinear differential equation

Picard (1856–1941) developed a general iterative method for solving differential equations. The procedure can be illustrated by considering the following nonlinear differential equation:

$$dx/dt = -x^2$$

We wish to find $x(t)$ that satisfies this equation over the interval: $0 < t < 1$, where its initial condition is given by

$$x(0) = 1, \text{ where } dX/dt = -x(0)^2 = -1$$

We start the iteration by making an educated "guess" that a function of time $_0X(t)$ approximates a solution to the equation. We can satisfy the above initial conditions by assuming that

$$_0X(t) = 1 - t$$

We can then compute the integral of $[_0X(t)]^2$ over the period from $t = 0$ to $t = 1$:

$$_1X(t) = 1 - \int [_0X(\tau)]^2 \, d\tau = 1 - \int (1 - \tau)^2 \, d\tau = 1 - t + t^2 - \tfrac{1}{3} t^3$$

Since $_1X(t)$ satisfies the differential equation. we can use it as a revised estimate of $x(t)$. We can iterate this process by computing the integral of $[_1X(t)]^2$ over the same period:

$$_2X(t) = 1 - \int \left(1 - \tau + \tau^2 - \tfrac{1}{3}\tau^3\right)^2 \, d\tau = 1 - t + t^2 - t^3 + \cdots$$

Since the integrand is a third-order polynomial, $_1X(t)$ will be fourth order. If we iterate this process the order of the polynomial $_nX(t)$ will keep growing, and the mathematics becomes more and more tedious. In this particular case, we can deduce that the polynomial is tending towards the binomial series $\Sigma (-t)^n$ that corresponds to the following function:

$$x(t) = 1/(1 + t)$$

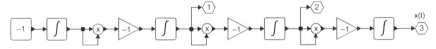

Figure 4.1 Mechanization of Picard's method for solving $dx/dt = -x^2$.

We can use a table from a textbook to show that its derivative satisfies the differential equation:

$$dx/dt = -1/(t+1)^2 = -x^2$$

4.4.1 Mechanization of Picard's method

Section 4.3 described how Lord Kelvin planned to mechanize Picard's method in order to solve a differential equation by using mechanical integrators. We can do the same by implementing the integrators on a digital simulation platform. The block diagram shown in Figure 4.1 shows the mechanization of the procedure used in the previous section, where there are three iterations of the time integral. This was created by using Scilab software, where the triangular blocks act as gains, while the square blocks, $[\int]$, are integrators, and the round blocks are multipliers. This again solves the differential equation:

$$dx/dt = -x^2$$

The integrators are all initialized to $x(0) = 1$, and the system is run to a final time $t = 1$, which is the limit of convergence of the binomial series $\Sigma\,(-t)^n$.

The three outputs of the model should thus correspond to the polynomials $_nX(t)$ for $n = 1$, 2, 3 that would be produced by the analytic application of Picard's method. The upper plot of Figure 4.2 shows how they converge towards the actual solution, $1/(1 + t)$, which is indicated by symbols $(\mathbf{x})$. The integration step length was set to one millisecond.

4.4.2 Feedback model of the differential equation

Section 4.3 goes on to describe how Lord Kelvin finally built a machine that implemented a feedback loop to solve the differential equations. The block diagram shown in Figure 4.3 can be used to solve the differential equation:

$$dx/dt = -x^2$$

The Scilab elements within the feedback loop again consist of a multiplier, a gain block, and an integrator. These are identical to those that were repeated three times in Figure 4.1. In Figure 4.3 the output (x) of the integrator is continuously fed back in order to calculate its input $(-x^2)$. The iterations that were done by

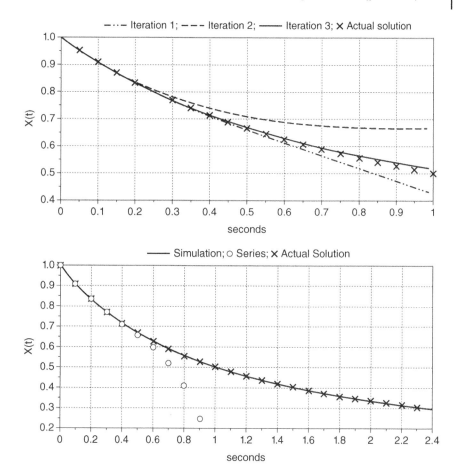

Figure 4.2 Results of using various methods to solve the differential equation.

Figure 4.3 Simulation of $dx/dt = -x^2$.

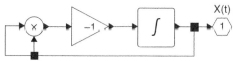

Picard are now implicitly done by the feedback loop. Since the input to the integrator (dx/dt) equals $-x^2$, this computer model implicitly solves the above differential equation. The lower plot in Figure 4.2 shows the settling of this model from an initial condition $x(0) = 1$ as a solid curve, while the actual solution is again indicated by symbols (**x**). The simulation steplength was set to one millisecond.

We could have simulated the differential equation by means of a program such as that shown below:

```
for k=1:n
        t(k+1)  =  t(k)  + dt;
        x(k+1)  =  x(k)  -  dt*x(k)^2;
end
```

4.4.3 Approximate solution by Taylor series

There is yet another way to solve the differential equation:

$$dx/dt = -x^2$$

where $x(t) = X0$ at $t = 0$.

We can simplify matters by defining the following vector of derivatives:

$$\mathbf{d}(t) = \left[dx/dt, d^2x/dt^2, ...\right] = \left[-x^2, -2x(dx/dt), ...\right]$$

The Taylor expansion of $x(t)$ about $t = 0$ is based on the derivatives at this point. These can be calculated by the following Scilab function, where the variable D(k) represents the value of the kth derivative at $t = 0$:

```
function D  =  myDE_at0(X0)
        D(1)  =  -X0^2;
        D(2)  =  -2*X0*D(1);
        D(3)  =  -2*X0*D(2)  -  2*D(1)*D(1);
        D(4)  =  -2*X0*D(3)  -  6*D(1)*D(2);
        D(5)  =  -2*X0*D(4)  -  8*D(1)*D(3)  -  6*D(2)*D(2);
endfunction
```

We can then use Taylor's method to calculate the coefficients $a(k)$ of the following power series:

$$P(t) = a0 + a(1)\,t + a(2)\,t^2 + a(3)\,t^3 + \cdots$$
$$dP/dt = a(1) + 2\,a(2)\,t + 3\,a(3)\,t^2 + \cdots$$
$$d^2P/dt^2 = 2\,a(2) + 3!a(3)\,t + \cdots$$

At $t = 0$ we have $P(t) = -a0$; $dP/dt = -a(1)$; and $d^kP/dt^k = -k!\,a(k)$.

The coefficients $a(k)$ must satisfy the condition that the terms (d^kP/dt^k) are equal to D(k). The following Scilab function computes the Taylor polynomial up to the fifth-order derivative:

```
function X  =  seriesExpansion(X0,T)
        X  =  X0*ones(T);
        D  =  myDE_at0(X0);
```

```
for k=1:5,
    a(k)  =  D(k)/factorial(k);
    X = X + a(k)*T.^k;
end
endfunction
```

If `X0 = 1` this function produces a truncated binomial series:

```
X  =  X0*ones(T)  -  T  +  T.^2  -  T.^3  +  T.^4  -  T.^5
```

If T is positive, this will be an alternating series. Textbooks on calculus show that we can test for the convergence of this series by verifying that the successive terms keep reducing, to eventually approach zero. Readers can use this test with examples that occur in later chapters.

The symbols (**o**) in the lower plot of Figure 4.2 represent the variation of X vs T. We see that after t = 0.4 seconds the series starts diverging from $1/(1 + t)$, which is indicated by symbols (**x**). We can extend the domain by adding more terms to the series.

4.5 Exponential functions and linear differential equations

Section 2.7 considered the use of difference equations to approximate the differential equation

$$dx/dt = a\,x(t)$$

Scilab programs were used to verify the performance of these difference equations by recording their evolution from the initial condition $x(0) = 1$. A program is given in Section 2.7.1 that uses rectangular integration. When this program is run with $a = -1$ and a step length equal to 0.2 seconds, $x(t)$ settles from the initial condition, as shown by the dashed curve in Figure 4.4. A program that uses trapezoidal integration is given in Section 2.7.2, which gives the solid curve shown in Figure 4.4.

It is known that the evolution of the above differential equation with $a = -1$ is given by an exponential function $x(t) = e^{-t}$, where the constant (e) can be approximated by 2.7182818. We can calculate the value of e^{-t} at $t = 2, 3, 4, \ldots$ as

$$e^{-t} = 1/e^2, 1/e^3, 1/e^4$$

It is more difficult to calculate e^{-t} when t is a fraction. However, we see that

$$e^{-0.5} = 1/\text{sqrt(e)}$$
$$e^{-1.5} = e^{-0.5}/e$$

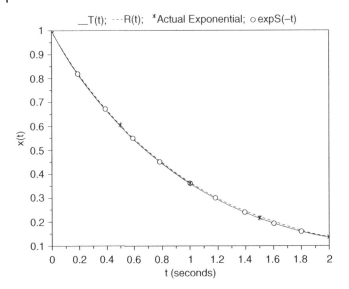

Figure 4.4 Simulation result compared with series expansion and exponential expression.

The symbols (*) in Figure 4.4 represent e^{-t} at $t = 0.5, 1, 1.5$, and 2. This confirms that rectangular and trapezoidal integration give a good approximation to exponential settling.

4.5.1 Taylor series to approximate exponential functions

We will use a Taylor expansion about $t = 0$ to find the solution of the linear differential equation:

$$dx/dt = a\,x(t)$$

The differential equation implies that: $d^k x/dt^k = a^k x(t)$ so the kth derivative is equal to a^k at $t = 0$. Using the reasoning that was described in Section 4.4.3, we find that $x(t)$ is given by a Taylor series:

$$T(t) = 1 + (a\,t)/1! + (a\,t)^2/2! + \cdots + (a\,t)^n/n!$$

Suppose that we define our time scale so that $a = 1$. The following Scilab function will then compute the Taylor polynomial of order (n) to achieve a precision S:

```
function x = expS(at, S)
        n = 2;
        Rn=%inf;
        while abs(Rn)>S
                x=1;
```

```
        for k=1:n
          x=x+at^k/factorial(k);
        end
        n=n+1;
        Rn=at^(n+1)/factorial(n+1)/x;
    end
endfunction
```

For example, we can use this function with `S = 1e-5`.

The symbols (**o**) in Figure 4.4 represent the output of the function `expS(at,S)`, for the following values of `at`:

```
    at = 0., -0.2, -0.4, -0.6, -0.8, -1
```

This confirms that the Taylor expansion gives a good approximation to exponential settling.

The above Scilab function also gives the following results:

```
    expS(0.1,S) = 0.905
    expS(0.2,S) = 0.81867
    expS(0.3,S) = 0.740837
```

We see that the following are true, to an accuracy of 0.1%:

```
    expS(0.2,S) = expS(0.1,S)*expS(0.1,S)
    expS(0.3,S) = expS(0.1,S)*expS(0.2,S)
```

This gives further confirmation that the exponential settling is equivalent to e^{-t}.

4.6 Sinusoidal functions and phasors

Consider the following linear differential equations:

$$dx/dt = -w\,y(t)$$
$$dy/dt = w\,x(t)$$

These can be simulated by difference equations that use trapezoidal integration:

```
dt = 0.1;                    // steplength [s]
T = 0:dt:359.9;              // time [s]
w = %pi/180;                 // frequency [rad/s]
X(1:2) = [1;cos(w*dt)];   // initial condition + first
                             // step
```

```
jY(1) = 0;
for k=1:3598
    jY(k+1) = jY(k) + (w*dt/2)*(X(k)+X(k+1));
    X(k+2) = X(k+1) - (w*dt/2)*(jY(k)+jY(k+1));
end
jY(k+2) = jY(k+1) + (w*dt/2)*(X(k+1)+X(k+2));
```

The motion of `jY(k)` vs that of `X(k)` is plotted on the left-hand side of Figure 4.5. This gives a circle that has its center at the origin of the XjY plane. The plot of `jY` vs time on the right-hand side is a good approximation to the function $y(t) = \sin(wt)$. A plot X vs time would correspond to $x(t) = \cos(wt)$.

We can combine the variables $x(t)$ and $y(t)$ into a complex number $z(t) = x(t) + jy(t)$, where "j" is defined as the imaginary number $(\sqrt{-1})$. We can then think of the left-hand plot in Figure 4.5 as showing $x(t)$ and $jy(t)$ as the Cartesian coordinates of a point that is moving in a complex plane, where x is the component on the real X axis while y is the imaginary component on the jY axis. The left-hand plot in Figure 4.5 also shows radial lines that indicate the position of the moving point at times $t = 0$, 45, 90, 135, 180, 225, 270, 315 seconds. Since the frequency (w) is `%pi/180` rad s^{-1}, the angles between these lines are all equal to 45 degrees. We can regard these radial lines to be vectors $\mathbf{z}(t) = x(t)\,\mathbf{i} + y(t)\,\mathbf{j}$, where $\mathbf{i}$ is a unit vector along the real axis while $\mathbf{j}$ is along the imaginary axis.

Such rotating vectors are known as phasors. The **o** symbols on the tips of the phasors correspond to the **o**s on the sine wave. We can thus see that the phasor $\mathbf{z}(t)$ rotates anticlockwise at an angular rate of w rad s^{-1} while its length remains constant, since

$$\cos^2(wt) + \sin^2(wt) = 1$$

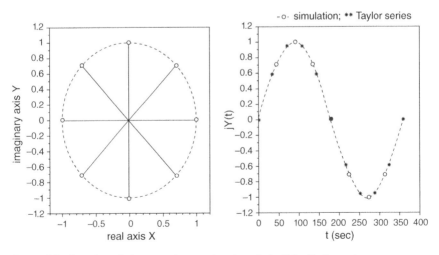

Figure 4.5 Rotation of phasor and approximation of sin (*t*) by Taylor series.

The phasor representation of sinusoidal signals is used by communication engineers to describe the modulation of carrier systems and by electrical engineers to describe the behavior of alternating current power lines. It is common practice to represent a rotating phasor by a single vector that points in its direction at $t = 0$. In this case the phasor points along the real axis, since

$$\mathbf{z}(0) = \cos(0) + j \sin(0) = 1$$

4.6.1 Taylor series to approximate sinusoids

We can compute a Taylor expansion of $x(t) = \sin(t)$ about $t = 0$. Let us define a vector of derivatives:

$$\mathbf{d}(t) = \left[dx/dt, d^2x/dt^2, d^3x/dt^3, ...\right] = [\cos(t), -\sin(t), -\cos(t), ...]$$

and use the notation that $D(n)$ represents the value of the nth derivative at $t = 0$. Since $\sin(0) = 0$ and $\cos(0) = 1$, these are given by

```
D(1)  = 1
D(2)  = 0
D(3)  = -1
```

etc.

The Taylor expansion for $\sin(t)$ is thus an alternating series that contains only odd powers of t.

It can be computed up to the 19th derivative by means of the following Scilab program:

```
function x = sinN(t)
    x = t;
    j = -1;
    for k=3:2:19
        x = x + j*t.^k/factorial(k);
        j=-j;
    end
endfunction
```

We can then compute a single cycle of this function as follows:

```
T = 0:.2*%pi:2*%pi;
X = sinN(T);
```

The resulting values of X are shown by the symbols (*) on the right-hand side of Figure 4.5. It corresponds to the series:

$$\sin(t) = t/1! - t^3/3! + t^5/5! - t^7/7!...$$

We similarly approximate the cosine function by a Taylor series:

$$\cos(t) = 1 - t^2/2! + t^4/4! - \ldots$$

4.7 Bessel's equation

Bessel functions are often used to describe spatial distributions in cylindrical objects, such as heat conduction and modes of vibration. Previous generations took great pains to compute these functions and document them in voluminous handbooks of mathematical tables. Today we can compute them with little difficulty.

Consider the following form of Bessel's equation:

$$t^2 \left(d^2x/dt^2 \right) + t(dx/dt) + t^2 x = 0$$

This differential equation can again be solved with Scilab. The block diagram is shown in Figure 4.6.

The settling of this model from $x(0) = 1$ is shown in Figure 4.7, where the simulation step length was 1 ms.

The function $x(t)$ can be approximated by a convergent power series of the form:

$$x(t) = x_0 + x_1 + x_2 + x_3 + \cdots$$

$$x_k(t) = a_k \, t^k$$

where we can satisfy the initial condition by making $a_0 = 1$.

This series can be differentiated term by term, to give

$$dx/dt = dx_1/dt + dx_2/dt + \cdots$$

$$dx_i/dt = i \, a_i \, t^{i-1}$$

Differentiating a second time then gives

$$d^2x/dt^2 = d^2x_2/dt^2 + d^2x_3/dt^2 \ldots$$

$$d^2x_i/dt^2 = i(i-1) \, a_i \, t^{i-2}$$

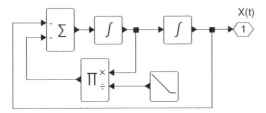

X(t)

Figure 4.6 Simulation of Bessel's equation.

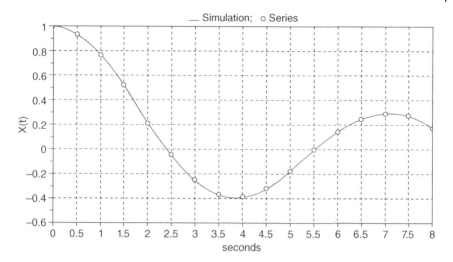

Figure 4.7 Resulting Bessel function.

If we substitute these expressions into the Bessel equation, we then get

$$t^2(a_0 + a_1 t + a_2 t^2 ...) + t(a_1 + 2a_2 t + 3a_3 t^2 + 4a_4 t^3 ...)$$
$$+ t^2(2a_2 + 3 \times 2a_3 t + 4 \times 3a_4 t^2 ...) = 0$$

Since this equation must be satisfied for all values of t, the coefficients of each power of t must be zero. We see that the coefficients a_1, a_3, ... of odd powers of t must all be zero. We then have for t^2:

$$t^2(a_0 + 2a_2 + 2a_2) = 0$$

Thus:

$$a_2 = -a_0/2^2$$

For t^4 we have:

$$t^4(a_2 + 4a_4 + 4 \times 3a_4) = 0$$

giving

$$a_4 = -a_2/4^2$$

This recurrence relation allows us to compute the coefficients, where, for t^k:

$$a_k = -a_{k-2}/k^2$$

The following program uses this to create a vector (A) with components: $A(1) = a_0$, $A(2) = a_2$, $A(3) = a_4$, etc.:

```
A = 1;
for k = 1:11
    j = 2*k;
    A(k+1) = -A(k)/j^2;
end
```

The function $x(t)$ is given by the following series:

$$x(t) = 1 + a_2 t^2 + a_4 t^4 + a_6 t^6 \ldots$$

For a given vector (T), where $T(k)$ represents the instant t_k, we can use the following program to compute a vector (X), where $X(k) = x(t_k)$:

```
n = max(size(T));
X = ones(1,n);
for k = 1:11
    j=2*k;
    X = X + A(k+1)*T.^j;
end
```

The resulting values of $X(k)$ are shown by the symbols (**O**) in Figure 4.7.

4.8 Discussion

We are now in the happy position of enjoying the fruits of our mathematical heritage and also having powerful computer tools that give numerical answers. When continuous time processes are modeled on digital platforms the primary challenge is to find algorithms that operate on a discrete variable so as to obtain results that approximate the integration of a continuous variable. Advances in this area went hand-in-hand with improvements in computer graphics, to produce the powerful simulation platforms that we have today.

The examples given in this chapter show that computer models can be created quickly and easily to simulate the behavior of differential equations. In the particular cases that were considered the computer could find numerical answers with less effort than solutions could be found by mathematical analysis.

Even though the creation of a model may be easier than the determination of an analytic solution, this does not mean that the mathematical approach is obsolete. Firstly, it is recommended practice to follow more than one path when studying a problem, since this allows us to improve our confidence in the answers by doing cross-checks on the results. Secondly, once the mathematicians have arrived at an analytic function, it may be a simple matter to mechanize it in a computer program. Scientific languages will generally include several such functions in their statement sets. These typically include exponential and trigonometric functions and their inverses. There is a third reason for using analytic functions. Consider the function `exp(a*t)`. Its shape is characterized by the parameter a. Its time constant is given by `1/a` (see Section 10.2.4). This makes it very easy for us to sketch the response to a step input that is approximated by an exponential function (or the settling from an initial condition).

Scientists began to use computer tools to create models that simulated the evolution of physical processes. Chapter 5 shows how the motion of a planet can be modeled by differential equations that are formulated in polar coordinates. These equations are implemented as a computer model that produces an elliptical plot of planetary motion. It is then shown how an analytical solution of these highly nonlinear differential equations requires considerably more work to produce comparable elliptical orbits.

Exercises

Readers can create their models on the platform of their choice, where the chosen platform will include its own operating and plotting tools.

1   Create the simulation model described by Figure 4.3 and plot the free settling from the initial conditions

$$x(0) = 1, x(0) = 0.5, \text{ and } x(0) = 2.$$

Can you find the analytic solutions for these situations, and compare them with the simulation results?

Now plot the free settling from $x(0) = 1$ when the simulation model is modified to the following:
a) $dx/dt = -2x^2$
b) $dx/dt = x^2$

2   Create a simulation model that satisfies the equation:

$$dx/dt + x = u.$$

Plot the free settling from $x(0) = 1$.

Plot the transient response from $x(0) = 0$, to step inputs $u = 1$ and $u = 2$.

Create the function `[x,n]=expS(t,S)` given in Section 4.5.1 and run with different accuracies (`S`).

Compare these answers with those given by `exp(t)` and with the free settling of the model.

3   Create the simulation program that is given in Section 4.6 and plot the motion of X and jY vs. T.

Run it with the initial conditions: X(1:2) = [1;1] and jY(1) = 0.

Rewrite the program with rectangular integration and compare the results with varying step length.

4   Create the Bessel model shown in Figure 4.6 and plot the free settling from $x(0) = 1$.

Modify the model to simulate the following second-order differential equation:

$$dx^2/dt^2 + a(dx/dt) + x = 0$$

where a equals 1.

Plot the free settling from the different initial conditions:

$$x(0) = 1; dx/dt|_0 = 0$$
$$x(0) = 0; dx/dt|_0 = 1$$
$$x(0) = 0; dx/dt|_0 = -1$$
$$x(0) = 1; dx/dt|_0 = -1$$

Now change the parameter (a) to 0 and plot the free settling from $x(0) = 1$. Can you find the analytic solution for this situation, and compare it with the simulation result?

Repeat with the parameter values: $a = 0.5$, $a = 2$, and $a = 4$.

Bibliography

Karplus, W.J. (1958). *Analog Simulation*. New York: McGraw Hill.

Korn, G.A. and Korn, T.M. (1956). *Electronic Analog Computers*. New York: McGraw Hill.

Rogers, A.E.a. and Connoly, T.W. (1960). *Analog Computation in Engineering Design*. New York: McGraw Hill.

Rubin, O. (2016). *Control Engineering in Development Projects*. Boston: Artech House.

Soroka, W.W. (1954). *Analog Methods in Computation and Simulation*. New York: McGraw Hill.

Tomovic, R. and Karplus, W.J. (1962). *High Speed Analog Computers*. New York: Wiley.

5

Science and computer models

We have now acquired the skills that are needed to create a computer model that describes the behavior of a simple physical object.

> "Mechanics is the paradise of the mathematical sciences because by means of it one comes to the fruits of mathematics."
>
> Leonardo da Vinci
> (*Source:* In the Public Domain)

By taking this first step we will start our journey along a path that leads us to create models of ever greater and greater complexity.

5.1 Introduction

Chapter 4 has shown us how to implement computer models that help us to study the behavior of differential equations. It is now time to put this skill to practical use. This chapter will show us how the motion of physical objects can be modeled by differential equations. The studies make use of simple objects that should be familiar to most of us, so that we can concentrate on basic principles of mathematical modeling without being burdened with the study of complicated physics. For instance, there is an example in Section 5.3.2, that shows how a digital simulation program could produce truncation or roundoff errors.

In Section 5.2 we will show how we can simulate the orbit of a planet around a Sun. The history of this subject is described in Chapter 3, where it is related to how Newton made an inspired guess that the Earth exerts a gravitational pull on the Moon that causes it to move in an orbit around us. He then set about explaining the form of this orbit by postulating that it obeyed his laws of motion. It will be

Computer Models of Process Dynamics: From Newton to Energy Fields, First Edition.
Olis Rubin.
© 2023 The Institute of Electrical and Electronics Engineers, Inc.
Published 2023 by John Wiley & Sons, Inc.

shown how Newton's mathematical framework can be used to derive a set of differential equations that describe the motion of the planet. These equations will then be implemented as a computer model, which is used to show how the shape of the orbit depends on the velocity of the planet when it is at a given position. The case study avoids going into details that would detract from the primary objective, to illustrate the basic modeling process. Similar techniques could be employed to create a computer program that can serve as a test-bed for finding a control strategy to inject a spacecraft into an orbit that meets given mission requirements. The rest of the chapter then goes on to describe the creation of a computer model to simulate the motion of a pendulum. Galileo studied this motion in the laboratory to demonstrate the interchange between the potential energy and kinetic energy as the pendulum swings to and fro. The model creates plots that illustrate the effect of nonlinearity on oscillatory motion. The modeling of oscillatory motion is of special interest to scientists and engineers. For example, aeronautical engineers are concerned with the pitch oscillation of an aircraft, which has a marked resemblance to the swinging of a pendulum. Economic cycles of supply and demand also appear to be oscillatory. Many industries, including process control, flight control, and robotics, involve feedback control loops that may begin to oscillate.

The case studies considered in this chapter serve as stepping stones that lead to the creation of more complex models that are needed by industry. Several of these will be presented in later chapters.

5.2 A planetary orbit around a stationary Sun

Chapter 3 gave a brief history of how the motion of the Earth, Sun, Moon, and planets have been studied over the millennia. This included Kepler's elliptical orbits and Newton's laws of gravity and motion. The gravitational force exerted by the Sun on a planet is equal and opposite to that exerted by the planet on the Sun, so the Sun will also move in a small orbit. If the Sun is much more massive than the planet, we can ignore its motion, and define its position to be at the origin of the coordinate system.

The planet will move in a plane, where we can describe its position in cartesian coordinates by a vector:

$$\mathbf{X} = [x, y]$$

Its position can also be described in polar coordinates (r, Q) that are related as follows to the cartesian coordinates:

$$x = r \cos (Q)$$
$$y = r \sin (Q)$$
$$r^2 = x^2 + y^2$$

$$\tan(Q) = y/x$$

Newton's law of gravity can be expressed by the following form:

$F_g = M/r^2$ = the gravitational force per unit mass on the planet

M = the mass of the Sun *times* the universal gravitational constant

This force acts radially towards the Sun, so the equations of motion for the planet can be written as

$$d^2x/dt^2 = -(M/r^2)\cos(Q) = -(M/r^3)x$$
$$d^2y/dt^2 = -(M/r^2)\sin(Q) = -(M/r^3)y$$

The combination of the centrifugal and the gravitational forces cannot produce tangential acceleration of the planet, so its angular momentum cannot change. We can include this constraint in the above differential equations, but it is easier to rewrite the equations of motion in polar coordinates.

The angular momentum per unit mass of the planet is equal to

$$H = r^2 w$$

where

$$w = dQ/dt$$

The centrifugal force per unit mass on the planet is thus given by

$$F_c = rw^2 = r(H/r^2)^2 = H^2/r^3$$

The evolution of $r(t)$ is thus described by the following differential equation:

$$d^2r/dt^2 = (H^2/r^3) - (M/r^2) \tag{5.1}$$

This nonlinear differential equation can be simulated by means of Scilab. The block diagram is shown in Figure 5.1. Equation (5.1) defines the variation with time of the radial distance (r) between the Sun and the planet. The orbit of the planet is described by two polar coordinates, r and Q. The variation of Q with time is given by the following differential equation, which is also implemented in Figure 5.1:

$$dQ/dt = H/r^2$$

The shape of the orbit depends on the initial conditions of the integrators. If dr/dt is set to zero, the planet is either at its apogee or its perigee. When the gravitational and centrifugal forces are equal ($F_g = F_c$), the planet follows a circular orbit, shown in Figure 5.2, where the radius is given by

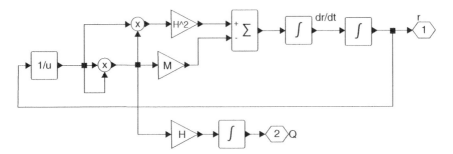

Figure 5.1 Simulation of planetary orbit.

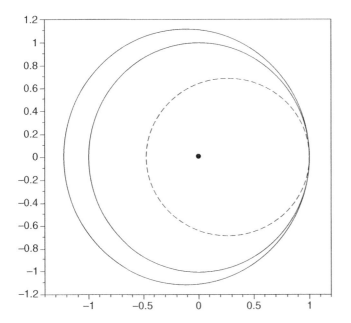

Figure 5.2 Shape of planetary orbits.

$$r = H^2/M$$

A circular orbit has a constant tangential speed (rw), where

$$dQ/dt = w = M^2/H^3$$

The orbit starts at perigee when F_g is less than F_c. This is shown by the outer orbit in Figure 5.2, while the dashed line shows an orbit that starts at apogee where F_g is greater than F_c. These plots have been normalized to give $r = 1$ at $t = 0$, and correspond to $Q(0) = 0$, so one axis of the ellipse is horizontal. If $Q(0)$ is positive, the ellipse will be rotated anticlockwise.

The time to complete a circular orbit is given by Kepler's third law, where

$$T^2 = 4\pi^2/w^2 = 4\pi^2 r^2/H^2 = 4\pi^2 M/H^3$$

5.2.1 An analytic solution for planetary orbits

We can linearize the differential Equation (5.1) by the following transformation of coordinates:

$$r = 1/s$$

whence we have

$$dr/ds = -1/s^2$$

Substituting s for r in the formula for angular momentum then gives

$$H = w/s^2 = -(dQ/dt)(dr/ds)$$

Now, by the chain rule for differentiation:

$$dr/dt = (dr/ds)(ds/dQ)(dQ/dt) = -H(ds/dQ)$$

whence

$$d^2r/dt^2 = -H\,d(ds/dQ)/dt = -H\left(d^2s/dQ^2\right)(dQ/dt) = -H^2 s^2 \left(d^2s/dQ^2\right)$$

Substituting the expression for d^2r/dt^2 given by Equation (5.1) then gives

$$H^2 s^2 \left(d^2s/dQ^2\right) = \left(H^2/r^3\right) - \left(M/r^2\right)$$

and again substituting s for r in this expression:

$$H^2 s^2 \left(d^2s/dQ^2\right) = \left(s^3 H^2\right) - \left(s^2 M\right)$$

The evolution of $s(Q)$ is thus described by a linear differential equation:

$$d^2s/dQ^2 = -s + \left(M/H^2\right) \tag{5.2}$$

The analytic solution to this equation is a sinusoidal oscillation of the form:

$$s(Q) = \left(M/H^2\right) + B\,\cos(Q - q)$$

The position vector of the planet is thus given by an explicit function of the polar angle (Q):

$$\mathbf{X} = r\,[\cos(Q), \sin(Q)] = [\cos(Q), \sin(Q)]/s(Q)$$

This describes an elliptical orbit, such as those shown in Figure 5.2. The parameters B and q determine the size and shape of the orbit. When s is constant the orbit is a circle. This implies that d^2s/dQ^2 must be zero, and therefore, from Equation (5.2):

$$s = M/H^2$$

In the case of an elliptical orbit the tangential speed (v) of the planet varies sinusoidally with angle, as shown by the following equation:

$$v = rw = H/r = H\,s(Q)$$

5.2.2 A difference equation to model planetary orbits

Chapter 2 showed how continuous integration over an interval (dt) can be approximated by a difference equation. For example, the system shown in Figure 5.1 can be approximated by the following program:

```
for k=1:n
    t(k+1) = t(k) + dt;
    dUdt = (H^2)/(r(k)^3) - M/(r(k)^2);
    U(k+1) = U(k) + dt*dUdt;              // rectangular
                                          // integration

    drdt = (U(k+1)+U(k)) / 2;
    r(k+1) = r(k) + dt*drdt;              // trapezoidal
                                          // integration

    Q(k+1) = Q(k) + dt*M^2/H^3;
end
x = cos(Q).*r;
y = sin(Q).*r;
```

This program approximates the continuous evolution of $r(t)$ by taking samples `r(k)`. Rectangular integration is equivalent to holding the last sample until the next sample is taken. This operation is described graphically in Appendix A, Section A.7.1. It effectively adds a time delay in the feedback loop shown in Figure 5.1 and therefore alters its behavior. The planetary orbit will therefore slowly diverge from the actual ellipse. Trapezoidal integration is a better approximation to the continuous evolution of $r(t)$ but still introduces some error. In the above program it is not possible to use trapezoidal integration of `dUdt` since the next value `r(k+1)` is not yet known. With 545 samples over an orbital period, the divergence after the first orbit was typically found to be 0.01% of the initial radius. Since the Scilab simulation platform also implements a sampled system, there can be a small divergence from the true orbit. This will be reduced since Scilab uses an advanced integration scheme.

5.3   Simulation of a swinging pendulum

Consider a pendulum that has a weight that is attached to one end of a weightless rod. The rod can swing freely about a pivot that is attached to the other end, causing the weight to move along the arc of a circle. We will define the rotation of the rod by an angle Q, where $Q = 0$ when the weight hangs vertically below the pivot. When $Q = 180$ degrees the weight is vertically above the pivot. There is a downwards vertical force (mg) that acts on the weight, where

   m = mass of the weight (kg)

   g = acceleration due to gravity at the surface of the Earth (ms^{-2})

When the pendulum swings away from $Q = 0$, the gravitational force on the weight will have a component that is normal to the rod. This produces a moment proportional to $-mg \sin(Q)$. The resulting motion of the weight is described by the following second-order differential equation:

$$mL^2 \left(d^2Q/dt^2 \right) = -mgL \sin(Q) - ZmL^2 (dQ/dt)$$

where L is the distance in meters between the pivot and the weight while Z is a coefficient of damping due to friction and air resistance (s^{-1}).

We will define Q to increase as the pendulum swings anticlockwise. When Q lies between 0 and 180 degrees, $\sin(Q)$ is positive, so the weight produces a clockwise moment that pulls the pendulum back towards $Q = 0$. As the weight passes the vertical line above the pivot, Q moves to the region between 180 and 360 degrees, and the weight produces an anticlockwise moment that pulls the pendulum further forward towards $Q = 360$ degrees, where the weight is again hanging vertically below the pivot. We thus have a symmetrical situation where a rotation of the pendulum from its lowest position produces a moment that pulls the pendulum back towards the lowest position.

Galileo demonstrated that the state of the pendulum at any instant depended on both the angle (Q) and the angular rate at which the pendulum is swinging:

   $dQ/dt = W$

The above second-order differential equation can then be written as

   $dW/dt = -(g/L) \sin(Q) - ZW$

The second-order equation of motion has been split into two first-order differential equations that are known as the state equations of the system. The block diagram in Figure 5.3 shows how they can be simulated on the Scilab platform where the two integrators give the evolution of $Q(t)$ and $W(t)$.

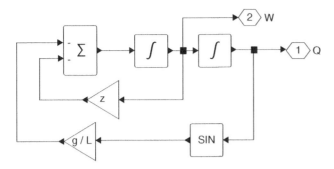

Figure 5.3 Simulation of a pendulum.

The initial angle (Q) of the pendulum was set to -1.5 rad while its angular rate (W) was -1.5 rad s^{-1}, so the rod was just below the horizontal and the pendulum was swinging outwards. The component of the force (mg) normal to the rod reaches a maximum when Q equals 90 degrees and reduces as the pendulum swings beyond this value. This is simulated in the model by the nonlinear function block sin(Q). The resulting motion of the pendulum is shown in Figure 5.4, where the solid curve represents the angle (Q) while the dashed curve is the angular rate.

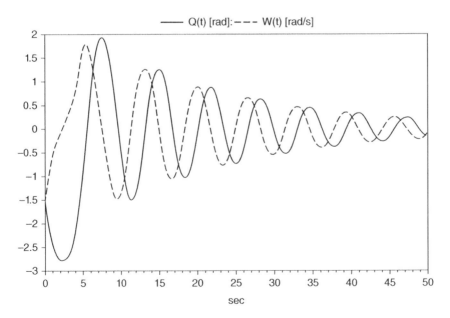

Figure 5.4 Swinging motion of pendulum.

The oscillatory motion is initially highly distorted but becomes close to a damped sine wave as the amplitude of the swings decreases and $\sin(Q)$ is nearly linear.

5.3.1 A graphical construction to show the motion of a pendulum

In the *Journal de Mathématiques pures et appliquées* (1881–1882), Poincaré introduced the idea of plotting the position of a body versus its velocity in what is known as a "phase plane." The motion of the pendulum is plotted in this way in Figure 5.5. The damped oscillatory motion is now an inward spiral, shown in the figure as a dashed curve. We refer to this curve as a state trajectory, since it describes the motion of the vector [Q W].

The slope of the state trajectory at any point in the phase plane is given by

$$dW/dQ = (dW/dt)/(dQ/dt) = [-(g/L)\sin(Q) - ZW]/W$$
$$= -[(g/L)/W]\sin(Q) - Z$$

If we equate dW/dQ to a particular slope (M), we can derive the following equation:

$$[(g/L)/W]\sin(Q) = M + Z$$

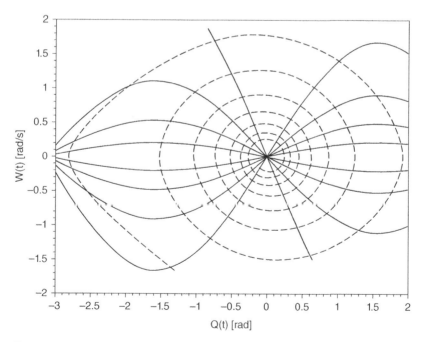

Figure 5.5 Phase plane plot with isoclines.

giving:

$$W = - (g/L) \sin (Q)/(M + Z)$$

We can use this equation to plot a curve in the phase plane that defines the points where the slope of the state trajectory has the value M. This curve is known as an "isocline." The solid curves in Figure 5.5 correspond to the isoclines for

$$M = 5, 2, 1, 0.5, -0.5, -1, -2, -5 \left[\text{rad s}^{-1} \text{ per rad} \right]$$

Since we know the slope of the state trajectory where it crosses each of these isoclines, we can construct a piecewise linear curve that approximates the state trajectory. If we plot more isoclines, the straight-line segments between them will be shorter, allowing us to draw a better approximation to the state trajectory. This graphical method allows us to draw the phase plane plot of a system without actually solving the differential equations. We could also use it as a cross-check to verify the model.

5.3.2 Truncation and roundoff errors

The simulation model shown in Figure 5.3 can also be implemented by the following program:

```
for k=1:n
    t(k+1)  = t(k)  + dt;
    dWdt  =  (-g/L)*sin(Q(k))  -  Z*W(k);
    W(k+1)  =  W(k)  + dt*dWdt;
    Q(k+1)  =  Q(k)  + dt*W(k+1);
end
```

The solid curve in Figure 5.6 was generated by the above program with dt = 0.01 s. The dashed curve shows how $\mathbf{Q}(t)$ deviates from the nominal solution when dt is increased by a factor 30.

Early computers used a much smaller wordlength than the double precision arithmetic that produced these curves. This could produce roundoff problems when the steplength (dt) was reduced to avoid such truncation errors. The dash–dotted curve in Figure 5.6 shows the result of artificially rounding off the integrands by the following operations:

```
    W(k+1)  =  W(k)  + round(140*dt*dWdt)/140;
    Q(k+1)  =  Q(k)  + round(140*dt*W(k+1))/140;
```

Most digital simulation platforms operate with double word lengths, which usually obviates this problem.

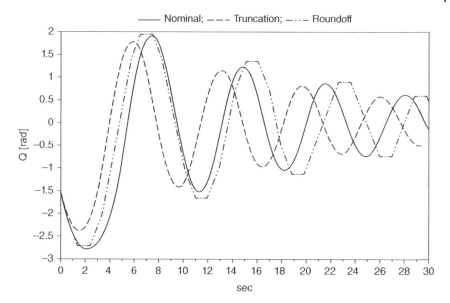

Figure 5.6 Simulated truncation and roundoff.

5.4 Lagrange's equations of motion

Lagrange's equations can be derived from Newton's laws of motion. They were published in his book *Méchanique Analytique*, where he wrote the following preface:

> We have already several treatises on mechanics, but the plan of this one is entirely new. I intend to reduce this science, and the art of solving its problems, to general formulae, the simple development of which provides all the equations needed for the solution of the problem. The methods that I explain require neither geometrical nor mechanical construction or reasoning, but only algebraic operations.

If we neglect any effects, such as friction, that dissipate energy, Lagrange's equations can be written as follows:

$$\mathrm{d}(\partial T/\partial w_k)/\mathrm{d}t - (\partial T/\partial q_k) + (\partial U/\partial q_k) = F_k$$

where $k = 1, 2, 3, \ldots, n$.

q_k	$=$	a generalized coordinate of the kth station
w_k	$=$	dq_k/dt
T	$=$	kinetic energy of the system
U	$=$	potential energy of the system
F_k	$=$	a generalized external force acting on the kth station

We will illustrate the formal procedure by again deriving the equations of motion for a pendulum. We will define the state of the system to be given by the following generalized coordinates, which comply with the above format:

q_1 = angular displacement of the pendulum from the vertical [rad]

$w_1 = dq_1/dt$ = angular rate of the pendulum $\left[\text{rad s}^{-1}\right]$

We then define the pendulum by means of the following parameters:

m_1 = mass of the weight [kg]

L_1 = length of the pendulum [m]

Z_1 = damping coefficient (which will be neglected)

The position and velocity of the weight can then be expressed in cartesian coordinates:

$x_1 = L_1 \sin (q_1)$

$y_1 = L_1 \cos (q_1)$

$dx_1/dt = L_1 \cos (q_1) \, dq_1/dt = L_1 \cos (q_1) \, w_1$

$dy_1/dt = - L_1 \sin (q_1) \, dq_1/dt = - L_1 \sin (q_1) \, w_1$

When the weight rises above its lowest position it acquires the following potential energy:

$U_1 = m_1 \, g \, [L_1 - y_1] = m_1 \, g \, L_1 \, [1 - \cos (q_1)]$

Its derivative corresponds to the restoring moment about the pivot of the pendulum produced by the gravitational force acting on the weight:

$\partial U_1/\partial q_1 = m_1 \, g \, L_1 \, \sin (q_1)$

The kinetic energy due to the motion of the weight is given by

$T_1 = 1/2 \, m_1 \, \left[(dx_1/dt)^2 + (dy_1/dt)^2\right] = 1/2 \, m_1 \, L_1{}^2 \, w_1{}^2$

Its derivative corresponds to the angular momentum of the pendulum:

$\partial T_1/\partial w_1 = m_1 \, L_1{}^2 \, w_1$

The rate of change of momentum is then given by

$d(\partial T_1/\partial w_1)/dt = m_1 \, L_1{}^2 \, dw_1/dt$

The kinetic energy is independent of the position of the weight, so

$$\partial T_1/\partial q_1 = 0$$

Substituting these quantities into Lagrange's equation provides the equation of motion for the pendulum.

$$m_1 L_1{}^2 (dw_1/dt) + m_1 g L_1 \sin(q_1) = m_1 L_1{}^2 (d^2 q_1/dt^2) + m_1 g L_1 \sin(q_1) = 0$$

Note that we have not included any damping of the motion. There are no forces, apart from gravity, acting on the pendulum, so F_k is zero.

5.4.1 A double pendulum

Now consider the addition of a second pendulum, that swings about a pivot point fixed to the bottom of the first pendulum. Suppose that it is defined by the following parameters:

m_2 = mass of the lower weight [kg]

L_2 = length of the lower pendulum [m]

The augmented state of the system defined by adding the following generalized coordinates:

q_2 = angular displacement of the lower pendulum from the vertical [rad]

$w_2 = dq_2/dt$ = angular rate of the lower pendulum $\left[\text{rad s}^{-1}\right]$

The position of the lower weight is given by $(x_1 + x_2, y_1 + y_2)$, where

$$x_2 = L_2 \sin(q_2)$$

$$y_2 = L_2 \cos(q_2)$$

The potential energy of the second pendulum is then

$$U_2 = m_2 g L_1 \left[1 - \cos(q_1)\right] + m_2 g L_2 \left[1 - \cos(q_2)\right]$$

Its derivative corresponds to the restoring moment on the lower pendulum due to gravity:

$$\partial U_2/\partial q_2 = m_2 g L_2 \sin(q_2) \approx (m_2 g L_2)\, q_2$$

The total restoring moment about the pivot of the upper pendulum is then given by

$$\partial(U_1 + U_2)/\partial q_1 = m_1 g L_1 \sin(q_1) + m_2 g L_1 \sin(q_1) \approx (m_1 + m_2) g L_1\, q_1$$

The velocity of the lower weight can be expressed as follows in cartesian coordinates:

$$V_X = dx_1/dt + dx_2/dt$$
$$V_Y = dy_1/dt + dy_2/dt$$
$$dx_2/dt = L_2 \cos(q_2) w_2$$
$$dy_2/dt = -L_2 \sin(q_2) w_2$$

so that its kinetic energy is given by

$$T_2 = 1/2 m_2 [V_X^2 + V_Y^2] = 1/2 m_2 [L_1^2 w_1^2 + L_2^2 w_2^2 + 2L_1 L_2 w_1 w_2 \cos(q_2 - q_1)]$$

The angular momentum of the lower pendulum will then be given by

$$\partial T_2/\partial w_2 = m_2 L_2^2 w_2 + m_2 L_1 L_2 w_1 \cos(q_2 - q_1)$$

so that the rate of change of momentum is given by

$$d(\partial T_2/\partial w_2)/dt = (m_2 L_2^2) dw_2/dt + m_2 L_1 L_2 \cos(q_2 - q_1) dw_1/dt$$
$$- m_2 L_1 L_2 w_1 (w_2 - w_1) \sin(q_2 - q_1)$$

We can also calculate the following partial derivative:

$$\partial T_2/\partial q_2 = -m_2 L_1 L_2 w_1 w_2 \sin(q_2 - q_1)$$

For small motion about the vertical we can simplify these expressions before substituting them into Lagrange's equation, which gives the following equation of motion for the lower pendulum:

$$(m_2 L_2^2) dw_2/dt + (m_2 L_1 L_2) dw_1/dt + (m_1 + m_2) g L_1 q_1 = 0$$

We similarly have for the motion of the upper pendulum:

$$[(m_1 + m_2) L_1^2] dw_1/dt + (m_2 L_1 L_2) dw_2/dt + m_2 g L_2 q_2 = 0$$

These two equations of motion can be expressed in the following matrix form:

$$\underline{M} \, d^2 Q/dt^2 + \underline{K} \, Q = 0$$

where Q is a vector with components $\{q_1; q_2\}$ and the variables Q and dQ/dt define the state of the system at any instant.

These matrices can be entered into the Scilab workspace by the following statements:

```
K = [ (m1+m2)*g*L1    0                // generalized
      0               m2*g*L2 ];       // stiffness matrix
M = [ (m1+m2)*L1^2    m2*L1*L2         // generalized
      m2*L1*L2        m2*L2^2 ];       // mass matrix
H = inv(M) * K;
```

We then have a modified form of state equation:

$$d^2Q/dt^2 = -\underline{H}\,Q$$

Suppose that the lengths L_1 and L_2 are now made equal to 1 m, while the masses m_1 and m_2 are equal to 0.2 kg.

The system can then be simulated as shown in Figure 5.7. This model superficially resembles that of a single pendulum, shown in Figure 5.3. The obvious differences are the absence of the sin(Q) block and the inner feedback loop. These are simply because we have neglected the damping term and have linearized the equations by assuming small motions about the vertical. However, Figure 5.7 differs significantly from the model of a single pendulum. The gain (-H) of the triangular block is now a matrix, while its input is a vector $Q(t)$ that models the angular positions (q_1 and q_2) of the upper and lower pendulum. The matrix product ($-\underline{H}\,Q$) is then a vector that models the angular accelerations ($d\mathbf{W}/dt$).

If we release the upper pendulum from an initial angle while the lower pendulum is hanging below it, the resulting motion will be as shown in Figure 5.8. The solid curve represents the angular motion $q_1(t)$ of the upper pendulum while the

Figure 5.7 Simulation model of double pendulum.

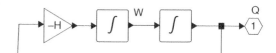

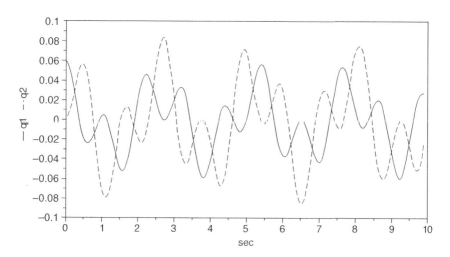

Figure 5.8 Oscillation of double pendulum.

dashed curve is that of the lower pendulum. These follow a complex pattern that is generated by two sine waves.

5.4.2 A few comments

The above matrix methods can handle higher-order systems where the states (**Q** and **W**) are n-dimensional vectors. The simulation model shown in Figure 5.7 can also be implemented by the following program, where Q and W are vectors and H is a matrix:

```
for k=1:n
    t(k+1)   =  t(k) + dt;
    W(:,k+1) =  W(:,k) - dt*H*Q(:,k);
    Q(:,k+1) =  Q(:,k) + dt*W(:,k+1);
end
```

We can introduce a generalized damping matrix into the state equations, as follows:

$$\underline{\mathbf{M}}\, d^2Q/dt^2 + \underline{\mathbf{Z}}\, dQ/dt + \underline{\mathbf{K}}\, \mathbf{Q} = \mathbf{0}$$

For large oscillations we can no longer linearize the equations of motion.

5.4.3 Modes of motion of a double pendulum

The following Scilab function computes a diagonal matrix (D) that contains the eigenvalues of H and a matrix (T) whose column vectors are the eigenvectors of H:

```
    [T,D]  =  spec(H);
```

Since H is a 2 by 2 matrix, it has two eigenvalues (D(1,1) and D(2,2)) while T is a 2 by 2 matrix that defines two eigenvectors:

```
    T1  =  T(:,1)
    T2  =  T(:,2)
```

These eigenvectors and eigenvalues allow us to separate the motion of this dynamic system into the two individual oscillatory components that generate the complex pattern shown in Figure 5.8. Their motion is given by the following uncoupled equations of motion:

$$d^2 p_1/dt^2 = -D(1,1)\, p_1$$
$$d^2 p_2/dt^2 = -D(2,2)\, p_2$$

The variables p_1 and p_2 are referred to as the normal coordinates of the system. They correspond to the amplitude of two different modes that oscillate at the frequencies `sqrt(D(1,1))` and `sqrt(D(2,2))`. It can be shown that

```
D = inv(T)*H*T
```

We can combine the variables p_1 and p_2 into a vector **P** that is related to the vector **Q** as follows:

$$\mathbf{Q}(t) = \underline{\mathbf{T}} \, \mathbf{P}(t)$$

Substituting this into the undamped equation of motion then gives the following:

$$\underline{\mathbf{T}} \left(d^2 \mathbf{P}/dt^2 \right) = -\underline{\mathbf{H}}\,\underline{\mathbf{T}}\,\mathbf{P}$$

so that

$$d^2 \mathbf{P}/dt^2 = -\underline{\mathbf{D}}\,\mathbf{P}$$

We can force the pendulum to oscillate at the frequency `sqrt(D(1,1))` by releasing it from initial conditions (q_1 and q_2) that correspond to the first eigenvector (`T1`). The resulting oscillation is shown by the upper plot in Figure 5.9. The solid curve represents the angular position (q_1) of the upper pendulum while the dashed curve is that of the lower pendulum. The upper and lower sections of the pendulum are moving together, so the two pendulums behave nearly like a rigid body. With initial conditions corresponding to the second eigenvector, the oscillation is much faster, as shown in the lower plot. The upper and lower masses are moving in antiphase, so $\sin(q_2-q_1)$ is effectively doubled.

5.4.4 Structural vibrations in an aircraft

The linearized state equations for the double pendulum are similar to the equations that describe the vibration of a mechanical structure. Such flexible structures often have a very large number of degrees of freedom, making an exact analysis virtually impossible. A reasonable approximation may often be obtained by reducing the degrees of freedom by ignoring vibration modes that occur at frequencies above the band of interest. This can generally be done by breaking down the structure to a finite number of point masses that are attached to one another by weightless links. The links are assumed to have the same elastic properties as the physical structures that they replace.

Consider the bending of the wings on an aircraft that is flying straight and level. Suppose that the body of the aircraft is rigid, so it can be reduced to a single point mass (m_0). If we can neglect the rigid body motion, the mass (m_0) will remain stationary. If we assume that the bending of the wings is symmetrical, we can reduce

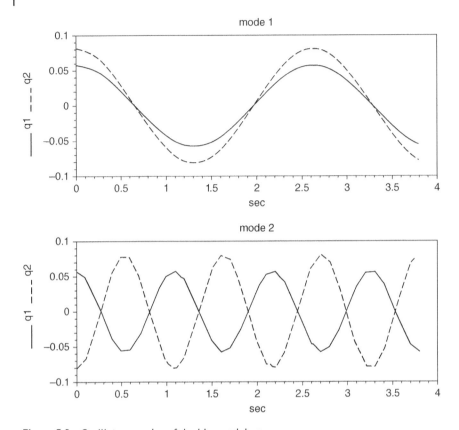

Figure 5.9 Oscillatory modes of double pendulum.

the model to the bending of a single wing about the fixed body. We could further reduce the model by assuming that the wing can be replaced by an inboard mass (m_1) and an outboard mass (m_2). We can then measure their motion relative to the body, and define the following generalized coordinates:

q_k = the vertical deflection of the mass (m_k)

$w_k = dq_k/dt$

The potential energy of the system is made up of two parts. We firstly have the gravitational potential energy U_g resulting from the change in height as the wing bends up and down:

$$U_g = m_1 g\, q_1 + m_2 g\, q_2$$

Its derivatives correspond to the constant gravitational forces ($m_k g$) that bend the wing:

$$\partial U_g / \partial q_k = m_k\, g$$

The wing can be regarded as a beam whose stiffness is defined as a matrix ($\underline{\textbf{C}}$) of coefficients [c_{ij}]. The deflection at point i due to a unit load applied at point j is given by c_{ij}. The internal strain, potential energy is then given by

$$U_s = 1/2\, \textbf{Q}'\underline{\textbf{K}}\,\textbf{Q}$$

where

Q is a column vector with components {q_1 ; q_2}
Q′ is a row vector with components [q_1, q_2]
$\underline{\textbf{K}}$ = inv($\underline{\textbf{C}}$) is a symmetric 2 by 2 matrix of influence coefficients [k_{ij}]

The partial derivatives $\partial U_s / \partial q_1$ and $\partial U_s / \partial q_2$ can then be grouped into the column vector, given by $\underline{\textbf{K}}\textbf{Q}$. The kinetic energy of the system is given by:

$$T = 1/2\left[m_1 w_1{}^2 + m_2 w_2{}^2\right]$$

Its derivatives correspond to the momentum of the individual masses (m_k):

$$\partial T / \partial w_k = m_k\, w_k$$

The rate of change of momentum is then given by:

$$d(\partial T / \partial w_k)/dt = m_k\, dw_k/dt$$

The kinetic energy is independent of the position of the masses, so

$$\partial T / \partial q_k = 0$$

Substituting these quantities into Lagrange's equation provides the equation of motion for the wing:

$$\underline{\textbf{M}}\, d^2\textbf{Q}/dt^2 + \underline{\textbf{K}}\,\textbf{Q} = 0$$

In this case the generalized mass is a diagonal matrix ($\underline{\textbf{M}}$) with coefficients [m_k] while inv($\underline{\textbf{M}}$) is a diagonal matrix with coefficients [$1/m_k$]. We can again determine the modes of oscillation by finding the eigenvalues and eigenvectors of the matrix inv($\underline{\textbf{M}}$)$\underline{\textbf{K}}$. We can also write the state equations of the system in terms of its normal coordinates:

$$d^2\textbf{P}/dt^2 + \underline{\textbf{D}}\,\textbf{P} = \text{inv}(\underline{\textbf{T}})\,\textbf{F}$$

We have added generalized external forces (**F**) to these equations. These could model the aerodynamic forces that act on the wing. The model represents them as point forces that act on the masses (m_k). We can take the Laplace transform of this equation in order to find the transfer function (see Section 6.3.3) that describes the response of the wing to external forces:

$$s^2 \mathbf{P}(s) + \underline{\mathbf{D}} \, \mathbf{P}(s) = \mathrm{inv}(\underline{\mathbf{T}}) \, \mathbf{F}(s)$$

5.5   Discussion

This chapter has shown how we can model the motion of bodies that can be approximated by point masses. The first requisite for success was to understand the physical laws that determine their behavior. We could then use Newton's laws of motion to model them mathematically by means of differential equations. Computer models could then be created by using the techniques that were developed in Chapter 4. It was also demonstrated how Lagrange's equations could help to derive differential equations that describe the motion of more complex mechanical systems.

We should perhaps remark that the derivation of a mathematical model depends on the physical laws that are assumed to determine the behavior of the object. The case studies that are presented here were based on axioms that had been made by Newton. If we wished to model the orbit of the planet Mercury we may have used the space–time formulation developed by Einstein, which would have given somewhat different results.

We have once again used mathematics to arrive at analytical solutions that allowed us to do cross-checks against the numerical results given by the computer. At the end of Chapter 4 we presented arguments as to why it is essential to verify our computer models by whatever means we have at our disposal. We were able to verify the planetary model by somewhat complex mathematical analysis. In the case of the pendulum model, we did not find a complete analytical solution, but we could find a mathematical expression for isoclines that could be plotted in the phase plane. These could then be used as a cross-check by comparing them with the slopes of the state trajectories. The models that appear in later chapters will be more complex, making it even more important to verify them by independent methods.

Exercises

Readers can create their models on the platform of their choice, where the chosen platform will include its own operating and plotting tools.

1   Create and test the planetary model shown in Figure 5.1 with different values of H and M.
     How are these related to the mass of the sun?
     Also plot the variables r and Q vs. time.

2 Create and test the pendulum model shown in Figure 5.3 with different values of the length (L).

What is the relationship between L and the period of the pendulum?
What happens when we vary the mass (m) and the damping (Z)?
Simulate the pendulum by means of the program shown in Section 5.3.2.

3 Create and test the double pendulum model shown in Figure 5.7 where the matrix (H) is calculated by means of the program shown in Section 5.4.1.

What happens when we vary the masses ($m1$ and $m2$) and the lengths ($L1$ and $L2$)?
What initial conditions produce sinusoidal oscillations?
Simulate the double pendulum by means of the program shown in Section 5.4.2.

Bibliography

Davis, H.F. (1967). *Introduction to Vector Analysis*. Boston: Allyn and Bacon.

Karplus, W.J. (1958). *Analog Simulation*. New York: McGraw Hill.

Korn, G.A. and Korn, T.M. (1956). *Electronic Analog Computers*. New York: McGraw-Hill.

Rogers, A.E. and Connoly, T.W. (1960). *Analog Computation in Engineering Design*. New York: McGraw Hill.

Rubin, O. (2016). *Control Engineering in Development Projects*. Boston: Artech House.

Shearer, J.L., Murphy, A.T., and Richardson, H.H. (1967). *Introduction to System Dynamics, Reading*. MA: Addison-Wesley.

Soroka, W.W. (1954). *Analog Methods in Computation and Simulation*. New York: McGraw Hill.

Tomovic, R. and Karplus, W.J. (1962). *High Speed Analog Computers*. New York: Wiley.

6

Flight simulators

The history of aviation began with myths and legends, such as those of Icarus and Wayland the Smith. These personify our desire to fly like birds.

> There be three things too wonderful for me, yea, four which I know not:
> The way of an eagle in the air; ...

Proverbs 30: 18,19

Computers can be used to simulate the flight of an aircraft, or even that of a bird. By these means we can learn more about the laws of motion that govern their way through the air.

6.1   Introduction

The last chapter has set the scene for us, by showing how the motion of physical objects can be described by differential equations. This chapter extends these ideas by studying the creation of computer models for use in the aircraft industry as flight simulators or to assist with the design of flight control systems. The simulation engineers will need to understand some basic aerodynamics. This can be obtained by attending courses in aeronautics or by studying textbooks on the subject. Flight control goes hand in glove with aircraft design. We can gain some appreciation of the immensity of the field when we realize that some countries have established national offices to administrate their activities in aeronautics, which involve armies of engineers, technicians, scientists, and mathematicians. Massive wind tunnels have been built to measure the behavior of aircraft, while much effort has been expended in creating computer models that simulate the airflow around the aircraft, and others that model the dynamic behavior of the aircraft. Flight test centers have been established to verify the performance of the aircraft themselves. Large data bases have been created to store and collate experimental results.

Computer Models of Process Dynamics: From Newton to Energy Fields, First Edition.
Olis Rubin.
© 2023 The Institute of Electrical and Electronics Engineers, Inc.
Published 2023 by John Wiley & Sons, Inc.

We will firstly consider the derivation of the equations that describe the motion of the aircraft in all 6 degrees of freedom, as is typically used in a flight simulator. When flight control systems are being designed the engineers will often work with a reduced model that concentrates on a particular mode of motion. We will follow this trend by studying the creation of a computer model that concentrates on the pitch motion of an aircraft.

6.2   The motion of an aircraft

The flight of an aircraft exhibits many modes of motion that may give problems to the pilot. Consider the situation where the ailerons are used to produce a roll moment that rotates the aircraft to a given bank angle. The ailerons will be trimmed to zero when the desired bank angle is reached, but the roll rate will take a finite time to settle back to zero. This time constant is referred to as the "roll subsidence" mode. The actual objective is to bank the aircraft and turn to a new heading. The wings will be levelled when the desired heading is reached but the heading and bank angle will slowly diverge from the steady condition. This phenomenon, called "spiral divergence," is an unstable exponential motion with a time constant of several minutes. There may also be an oscillation, called "Dutch roll," with a period of a few seconds, which may be relatively lightly damped.

With the advent of high-performance jet aircraft, the so-called "short period pitch" oscillations have become visible. Some jet fighters have a stability problem at high angles of attack where the short period pitch becomes unstable and the angle of attack then increases until the aircraft stalls. In addition to the short period pitch mode, nearly all aircraft have a long period oscillation called the "phugoid mode," where it tends to fly a sinusoidal path in the vertical plane. This is primarily due to an exchange of potential and kinetic energy, much like the oscillation of a pendulum. In the case of the pendulum, it was the tension in the suspension that opposed the force of gravity, whereas it is now the lift force that performs this function. As the aircraft proceeds from the highest point of the flight path to the lowest point it increases speed, thus increasing the lift of the wing. When the lift exceeds the force of gravity the dive slope will start reducing, and eventually the dive becomes a climb. The speed of the aircraft then reduces and the climb becomes a dive at the highest point of the flight path. The period of the phugoid oscillation is generally several minutes, and in the next section we will simplify the model of pitch motion by neglecting the phugoid mode.

The flight in three dimensions can be modeled in MATLAB-Simulink, as shown in Figure 6.1. The lift and drag are tied to the velocity vector, the weight is fixed to the local vertical, and the thrust is tied to the body of the aircraft. The orientation of the aircraft and its flight path is represented by the following symbols:

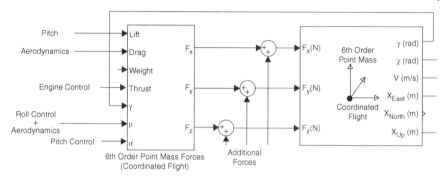

Figure 6.1 Simulation model of 3D flight.

μ = the bank angle of the wings from the horizontal
α = the angle of attack (a)
γ = the flight path angle (climb or dive)
χ = the heading angle (equals zero when the aircraft flys due east and γ is zero)
X_{East}, X_{North}, X_{Up} = the Cartesian position of the aircraft in local earth coordinates

These are calculated in the blocks marked 6th Order Point Mass.

We will show later how the angle of attack is changed by pitch control, while the resulting lift and drag on the aircraft will then depend on its aerodynamics. The bank angle is changed by roll control, and again depends on the aerodynamics. The engine control varies the thrust on the aircraft.

Suppose that we are flying due north, straight, and level. We turn to the east by banking the aircraft so that the right wing is down. The lift vector will then have a horizontal component $L \sin(\mu)$ that turns the aircraft to the east. The vertical component of lift reduces to $L \cos(\mu)$. We can avoid going into a dive as we bank the aircraft by increasing the lift force to compensate for this. We will then go into what is known as a coordinated turn.

6.2.1 The equations of motion

The equations of motion for an aircraft with 6 degrees of freedom will be derived, with the assumption that the aircraft behaves like a rigid body. We will begin by considering the motion in three dimensions of its center of mass. Appendix B discusses the use of vector analysis to describe the kinematics, and then applies Newton's laws to derive the equations of motion. The equations will be defined in "body axes" that rotate with the aircraft, while the origin moves with its center of mass. The X axis points forward along the center line of the aircraft, the Y axis points along the right wing, while the Z axis points down. We will define the unit vectors ($\mathbf{i}, \mathbf{j}, \mathbf{k}$) in the X, Y, Z directions. The velocity vector ($\mathbf{V}$) of the aircraft is taken with respect to inertial space, where the Earth is taken as the inertial reference. The equations have the following form:

$$\mathbf{F} = m\,d\mathbf{V}/dt = m\,[\mathbf{T}d\mathbf{V}/dt + \mathbf{\Omega} \times \mathbf{V}]$$

where

$\mathbf{F}$	=	resultant of the forces acting on the aircraft
m	=	the mass of the aircraft
$\mathbf{V}$	=	the velocity of the aircraft with respect to inertial space
$\mathbf{T}$	=	a unit vector in the direction of $\mathbf{V}$
$\mathbf{\Omega}$	=	angular velocity of the aircraft with respect to inertial space

Appendix B also shows how vectors can be used to describe Euler's equations of motion for a rigid body in the following form:

$$\mathbf{M} = d\mathbf{H}/dt = \underline{\mathbf{I}}\,d\mathbf{\Omega}/dt + \mathbf{\Omega} \times (\underline{\mathbf{I}}\,\mathbf{\Omega})$$

where

$\mathbf{M}$	=	resultant of the moments about its center of mass
$\underline{\mathbf{I}}$	=	a matrix containing the moments and products of inertia
$\mathbf{H}$	=	the moment of momentum

The sixth-order model shown in Figure 6.1 would implement the above equations. The following conditions apply to unaccelerated straight and level flight: $\mathbf{F}$, $\mathbf{M}$, and $\mathbf{\Omega}$ are all equal to zero.

$$\mathbf{V} = \mathbf{i}\,U_0 + \mathbf{j}\,0 + \mathbf{k}\,W_0$$

where U_0 and W_0 are constant.

The angle of attack a_0 is given by

$$a_0 = \text{arc tan}\,(W_0/U_0)$$

This must give a lift force equal to the weight of the aircraft while the engine thrust must equal the drag.

Consider small perturbations in the forces and velocities around these flight conditions. These are defined to have the following forward, right, and downward components:

$$\mathbf{F} = \mathbf{i}\,F_x + \mathbf{j}\,F_y + \mathbf{k}\,F_z$$

$$\mathbf{V} = \mathbf{i}\,u + \mathbf{j}\,v + \mathbf{k}\,w$$

The moments and angular velocities are defined to have the following roll, pitch, and yaw components (about the X, Y, Z axes):

$$\mathbf{M} = \mathbf{i}\,\mathcal{L} + \mathbf{j}\,\mathcal{M} + \mathbf{k}\,\mathcal{N}$$

$$\mathbf{\Omega} = \mathbf{i}\,p + \mathbf{j}\,q + \mathbf{k}\,r$$

The equations for force perturbations can thus be written as

$$F_x = m \left[du/dt + w q - v r \right]$$
$$F_y = m \left[dv/dt + u r - w p \right]$$
$$F_z = m \left[dw/dt + v p - u q \right]$$

For an aircraft that is symmetrical about the XZ plane, the products of inertia J_{xy} and J_{yz} are zero. Thus the moment of momentum and the vector product can be written as

$$\mathbf{H} = \underline{I} \, \Omega = \mathbf{i} \left[I_x p - J_{xz} r \right] + \mathbf{j} \, I_y q + \mathbf{k} \left[I_z r - J_{xz} p \right]$$
$$\Omega \times \mathbf{H} = \mathbf{i} \left[H_z q - H_y r \right] + \mathbf{j} \left[H_x r - H_z p \right] + \mathbf{k} \left[H_y p - H_x q \right]$$

The moment equations can thus be written as

$$\mathcal{L} = I_x \, dp/dt - J_{xz} \, dr/dt + q r \left(I_z - I_y \right) - p q J_{xz}$$
$$\mathcal{M} = I_y \, dq/dt - p r \left(I_x - I_z \right) - \left(p^2 - r^2 \right) J_{xz}$$
$$\mathcal{N} = I_z \, dr/dt - J_{xz} \, dp/dt + p q \left(I_y - I_x \right) - q r J_{xz}$$

6.3 Short period pitching motion

The designer of a pitch autopilot finds it useful to have a simplified model that simulates the short period pitch motion of the airframe about its Y axis. Most aircraft are designed to be aerodynamically stable about the pitch axis, so that they settle to a steady angle of attack when the controls are at a particular position. Figure 6.2 shows a drastically simplified side view of an aircraft that is flying in the horizontal plane while its body is pitched in a nose-up attitude, where:

$\mathbf{A}$ = vector that lies on the axis of the aircraft
$\mathbf{V}$ = velocity vector, in the horizontal plane
a = angle between $\mathbf{A}$ and $\mathbf{V}$, known as the angle of attack
$\mathbf{W}$ = force of gravity, which acts vertically downward on the mass of the body

The force of gravity acts on the body through its center of mass. Its magnitude (W) is equal to mg, where

m = the mass of the body
$g = 9.81 \text{ m s}^{-1}$

The motion of the aircraft produces a pressure field in the air that varies over its surface. The pressure increases proportionally with $(\frac{1}{2}\rho v^2)$, where v is the airspeed and ρ is the air density. These pressures produce forces that are normal to the surface at any point on the wings and the body. All these aerodynamic forces can be

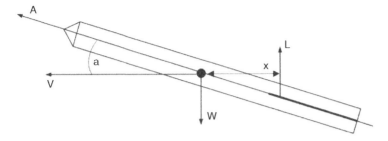

Figure 6.2 Aerodynamic stabilization of pitch motion.

consolidated into a single force that acts on the body in a line that passes through the center of pressure. One way of measuring this resultant force is to mount a model of the aircraft in a wind tunnel, on a special spring balance that allows us to determine the magnitude and direction of the force, as well as its line of action. The component in the opposite direction to the velocity vector is called the *drag*. This has a longer-term effect of slowing down the aircraft, but generally has a lesser effect on its short-term motion. There are components normal to the velocity vector that are called the *lift* and the *sideforce*.

The side view in Figure 6.2 shows:

L = the lift force
x = horizontal distance between the center of mass and the lift line

The lift force will produce a pitching moment about the center of mass:

$$\mathcal{M} = x\,L$$

Figure 6.2 depicts the situation where the center of mass is in front of the center of lift. When the body is rotated to an angle of attack, the moment ($\mathcal{M}$) tries to pull the axis (**A**) back into alignment with the velocity vector (**V**). This behavior can be compared with that of a weathercock that points into the wind or a pendulum that swings back to the vertical. The lift force (**L**) depends on the angle of attack (a). We will model this by a function $L(a)$. For small angles this function is nearly linear, but it becomes highly nonlinear when the lifting surfaces eventually stall. We will similarly model the pitching moment ($\mathcal{M}$) by a function $-M(a)$ where the minus sign indicates that it is a restoring moment. The aerodynamic forces and moments are proportional to the pressure ($\frac{1}{2}\rho v^2$).

Consider the free settling from an initial disturbance giving a perturbation in the pitch rate $q(t)$. This will provoke a short period pitch oscillation where the axis (**A**) oscillates about the velocity vector (**V**). We will simplify the short period pitch model by ignoring the phugoid oscillation. This is generally far slower than the period of a pitch transient, so we can assume that the aircraft has a constant

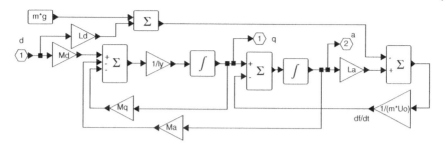

Figure 6.3 Pitch simulation model.

forward speed (U_o). Figure 6.3 shows a simulation in Scilab Xcos of the settling from an initial pitch rate.

The pitch rate (q) creates a damping moment $-M(q)$ while the angle of attack (a) causes a lift force $L(a)$ and a pitching moment $-M(a)$. These functions also depend on the flight conditions ($\frac{1}{2}\rho v^2$). We have linearized the aerodynamic forces, so the damping moment is modeled by $-M_q q$, the lift force is modeled by $-L_a a$, and the pitching moment by $-M_a a$. For the moment we will ignore the external input (d).

The roll and yaw rates (p and r) are both assumed to be zero, so the moment equation about the Y axis becomes

$$I_y \, dq/dt = \mathcal{M} = -M_a a - M_q q$$

This equation of motion for the pitch rate (q) is implemented as shown in Figure 6.3. The pitch rate then causes perturbations on the angle of attack and the lift force. The sideslip and the roll rate (v and p) are zero and we assume that the deviations from the level flight are small, so the Z-axis force equation becomes

$$m \, [dw/dt - U_o q] = F_z = L_a \, a - m \, g$$

The equation of motion for the angle of attack (a) is then given by

$$a = \text{arc tan} \, (w/U_o)$$
$$da/dt \approx (dw/dt)/U_o = q - (L_a a - mg)/(U_o m)$$

It is implemented as shown in Figure 6.3. The above equation can be interpreted as follows. We assume that the deviations from level flight are small, so the vertical acceleration of the aircraft is approximately equal to

$$G \approx (L_a a - m \, g)/m$$

This will cause the velocity vector (**V**) shown in Figure 6.2 to rotate, where the change in its angle (f) relative to the horizontal is given by

$$df/dt = G/U_o$$

The angle of attack (a) is the angle between the axis of the body and the flight path, so we have

$$da/dt = q - df/dt$$

6.3.1 Case study of short period pitching motion

Consider a four-engine jet transport flying straight and level at 40 000 feet, where the flight parameters are as follows (see Blakelock, 1965):

$$m = 80\,000 \text{ (kg)}$$

$$Iy = 350\,000 \text{ (kg m}^2)$$

$$Uo = 200 \text{ (m s}^{-1})$$

The aerodynamicists have calculated the dimensionless stability derivatives $C_{l\alpha}$, $C_{m\alpha}$, C_{mq}, etc., and calculated the lift and moment coefficients as shown in the following examples:

$$L_a = \tfrac{1}{2}\, \rho v^2\, S\, C_{l\alpha}$$

$$M_a = \tfrac{1}{2}\, \rho v^2\, S\, c\, C_{m\alpha}$$

$$M_q = \tfrac{1}{2}\, \rho v^2\, S\, c\, C_{mq}$$

$$S = \text{the wing area}$$

$$c = \text{the mean aerodynamic chord}$$

We will assume that they obtained the following values:

$$M_q = 70\,000 \text{ (Nm per rad s}^{-1})$$

$$M_a = 350\,000 \text{ (Nm rad}^{-1})$$

$$L_a = 7\,000\,000 \text{ (N rad}^{-1})$$

When the model defined by Figure 6.3 is run with these values, the free settling of the pitch rate that results from an initial error in angle of attack is shown in Figure 6.4.

The aircraft has elevators to control its longitudinal motion. In level flight they are trimmed to give a lift force equal to the weight of the aircraft. If they are now deflected nose down, the airflow over their surfaces will produce a downward change in their lift. Since the elevators are behind the center of mass, this creates a positive pitching moment on the airframe. The airframe then pitches upwards, increasing the angle of attack to produce more lift on the wings and the aircraft goes into a climb. Suppose that the aerodynamicists have calculated the lift and moment coefficients due to an elevator deflection (d) to be

$$M_d = 350\,000 \text{ (Nm rad}^{-1})$$

$$L_d = -2\,100\,000 \text{ (N rad}^{-1})$$

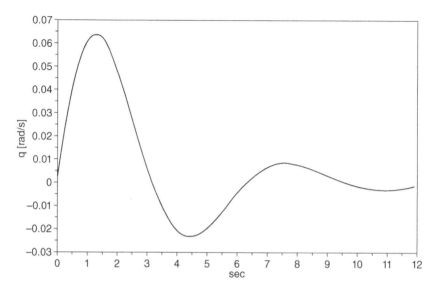

Figure 6.4 Pitch rate response to disturbance.

The elevator is much smaller than the wing but its moment arm is proportionately larger. The calculations of M_d and L_d must allow for rotation of the elevators together with the pitching of the aircraft. They must also allow for the downwash from the wings, which changes the airflow around the elevator surfaces.

The elevator deflection is added as an external input that acts through the coefficients (M_d and L_d), shown in Figure 6.3. We see that a deflection $d > 0$ firstly gives a negative acceleration of the aircraft, after which there is a positive acceleration as the airframe pitches nose up.

6.3.2 State equations of short period pitching

The repetitive nature of computer programs makes them ideal for performing matrix operations. This has contributed to the increasing use of state equations to model dynamic systems. Scilab and MATLAB both use many matrix operations, and many functions that are based on matrix state equations.

Suppose that the model shown in Figure 6.3 is saved in a file pitchAircraft. zcos. When it is run it creates a diagram data structure called scs_m. The following Scilab functions can then be used to determine the parameters of a matrix state equation that describes the evolution of the linearized model:

```
sys = lincos(scs_m);
[A,B,C,D] = abcd(sys);
```

This produces a matrix (A) and a column vector (B):

```
A  =  [ - 0.203   - 1.015
            1.     - 0.425 ]
B  =  [   1.015
          0.1275 ]
```

The integrators are directly connected to the outports, thus C is a unit matrix:

```
C  = [ 1.          0.
       0.          1. ]
```

D is a matrix of zeros and can be neglected.

Using the vector notation given in Appendix B, the outputs of the two integrators can be grouped into a column vector that defines the state of the model:

$$\mathbf{X} = [q; a]$$

while the derivative of the state vector is

$$d\mathbf{X}/dt = [dq/dt; da/dt]$$

The gain blocks in Figure 6.3 define the coefficients of the state equations. We can also group them into the following row vectors.

$$\mathbf{A}_1 = [-Mq/Iy, \ -Ma/Iy]$$
$$\mathbf{A}_2 = [1., \ -La/(m * U_o)]$$

which allows us to write the state equations of the model as follows:

$$dq/dt = \mathbf{A}_1 \mathbf{X} + [Md/Iy] \, d$$
$$da/dt = \mathbf{A}_2 \mathbf{X} + [Ld/(m * Uo)] \, d$$

We can now explain the meaning of the matrix (A) and the column vector (B) that were computed by Scilab. The first and second rows of the matrix (A) correspond to the row vectors: $\mathbf{A}_1$ and $\mathbf{A}_2$, while the column vector (B) corresponds to

```
B  = [ Md/Iy
       Ld/(m*Uo)  ]
```

Expressing A as the matrix $\underline{\mathbf{A}}$ we can combine the two state equations into a single matrix equation:

$$d\mathbf{X}/dt = \underline{\mathbf{A}} \mathbf{X} + \mathbf{B} \, d$$

We can also simulate the settling of **X** from a given initial condition by the following program:

```
dt  =  0.1;
for  k=1:K
     X(:,k+1)  =  X(:,k)  +  dt*A*X(:,k);   // rectangular
                                            // integration
     t(k+1)  =  t(k)  +  dt;
end
```

The following statement will display the eigenvalues of the matrix (A):

```
{T,  D]  =  spec(A)
```

D is a diagonal matrix that contains the eigenvalues:

```
D(1,1)   =   - 0.314 + 1.00i
D(2,2)   =   - 0.314 - 1.00i
```

which indicates the lightly damped oscillation at approximately 1 rad s^{-1} as shown in Figure 6.4.

6.3.3 Transfer functions of short period pitching

We can take Laplace transforms of the variables in the above state equation, where we will use $X(s)$ to represent the Laplace transform of $X(t)$.

Appendix A.3.1 states that the Laplace transform of d**X**/dt can be expressed as $sX(s)$. Thus, we now obtain an algebraic equation:

$$s\,X(s) = \underline{A}\,X(s) + B\,d(s)$$

This can be rearranged to determine the transfer function of the system:

$$\underline{F}(s) = (s\underline{I} - \underline{A})^{-1}\,B$$

where $\underline{I}$ is the same unit matrix as C, which was shown in the last section.

We can find the transfer function of the system that was found by lincos (scs_m). This is done by the Scilab statement:

```
[Ds,num,den]=ss2tf(sys)
```

If the pitch model shown in Figure 6.3 has a single outport from the pitch rate (q), this will display the following polynomials:

```
den  =   1.1 + 0.628s + s²
num  = 0.3 + 1.0s
```

The transfer function between the elevators and the pitch rate will thus be:

$$H(s) = (0.3 + s)/(1.1 + 0.628s + s^2)$$

The poles of the system (roots of den) are equal to the eigenvalues of the matrix (A). The Scilab function lincos (scs_m) does not allow for the source block [m*g] in Figure 6.3.

6.3.4 Frequency response of short period pitching

We may wish to design a pitch autopilot that uses feedback from a rate gyro to damp the pitch oscillations. It would then be useful to know the frequency response of $H(s)$. Appendix A gives a brief introduction to such techniques. If we are working in Scilab, we can use the following function to directly create the Bode plot that is shown in Figure 6.5:

```
bode(sys,fo,fn);
```

where the frequency range is specified by (fo, fn) in Hz. This computes $H(j\omega)$ as a complex function of $j\omega$, whence it derives the gain and phase as is shown in Appendix A.2.

The elevator is deflected by a servo that has a given frequency response to commands from the autopilot. Before we add this to Figure 6.3, we can use the following Scilab functions to investigate its behavior. We can firstly create a continuous transfer function by using the following instructions:

```
s = poly(0,'s');        //  s = seed to define polynomials
                        //  with the symbol "s"
sysC = syslin('c',[n0+n1*s+n2*s^2], ...
            [d0+d1*s+d2*s^2]);
```

We can plot the frequency response of the transfer function as follows:

```
subplot(2,1,1);         gainplot(sysC,fo,fn)
subplot(2,1,2);         phaseplot(sysC,fo,fn)
```

We can convert the above continuous system to a discrete system as follows:

```
sysD = ss2tf(dscr(tf2ss(SysC),0.1));
```

We can also create a discrete transfer function by using the following instruction:

```
sysD = syslin('d',[n0 + n1*s + n2*s^2], ...
            [d0 + d1*s + d2*s^2]);
```

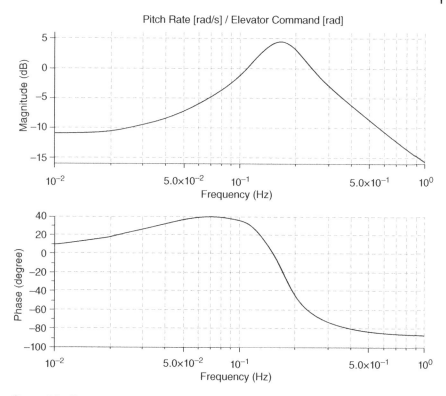

Figure 6.5 Frequency response of pitch rate $Q(j\omega)$ to elevator command $D_c(j\omega)$.

The Wright brothers used control surfaces (called canards) that were placed near the nose of the aircraft. When the pilot moves the stick in order to climb, the canards are deflected to produce upward lift. Because they are well ahead of the center of mass, this causes the airframe to pitch upwards, and the acceleration continues to increase as the angle of attack builds up. Canards have the disadvantage that their angle of attack is larger than that of the wing, so they generally stall before the wing can reach its maximum capability.

This case study has considered a reduced model to describe the longitudinal motion of the aircraft. We can add the phugoid motion, the effect of drag, and the thrust produced by the engine. The elevators and engine can be used to control aircraft speed and flight level. We can use separate models to study pitch, yaw, and roll, where these can then be linked to form more complex models to study the interactions between their functions. Finally, there can be a full 3D flight simulator, such as that shown in Figure 6.1, to test the whole system under all flight conditions. Designers have to weigh up many factors before deciding on an aircraft layout. In an ideal situation the flight control engineers would participate in the design team, where the flight control requirements are traded off against other considerations. Simulation models can be of assistance at the beginning of a project, by serving as prototypes for doing "what-if" studies where the design team tries to anticipate everything bad that could happen.

6.4 Phugoid motion

We have considered the short period pitching motion of the aircraft while ignoring the slower change in speed and height. We can now do the converse, and model the long period phugoid motion by assuming that the aircraft is being flown at a constant angle of attack (a_o). If the lift force at a nominal speed (U_o) equals the weight of the aircraft, its longitudinal acceleration is zero. This implies that:

$$\tfrac{1}{2} \rho \, U_o^2 \, L_a \, a_o/m = g$$

When the aircraft flies at a speed $U_o + u$ its longitudinal acceleration is given by:

$$a = A(U_o + u)^2 - g$$
$$A = g/U_o^2$$

The flight path angle (f) then changes at the following rate:

$$df/dt = a/U_o$$

We thus have

$$df/dt = F \, (U_o + u)^2 - g/U_o$$
$$F = g/U_o^3$$

Suppose that the thrust from the engines exactly cancels out the drag force. When the aircraft climbs at an angle (f) its speed will reduce due to gravity:

$$du/dt = -g \sin (f)$$

These equations are modeled by the following program:

```
g  = 9.81;                // m s⁻²
Uo = 200;                 // m s⁻¹
F  = g/Uo^3;
dt = 1;                   //  steplength
u  = -10;
f  = 0;
t  = 0;
for k=2:100
        u(k)  = u(k-1)  - dt*g*sin(f(k-1));
        f(k)  = f(k-1)  + dt*F*(Uo+u(k))^2 - dt*g/Uo;
        t(k)  = t(k-1)  + dt;
end
```

This produces a phugoid oscillation with a period of 90 seconds. We can also calculate the oscillation in height by adding the following statement within the loop:

```
h(k) = h(k-1) + dt*u(k)*sin(f(k));
```

We can also simulate actions that pilots may take to counteract the fall in speed or height. They open the throttle to increase speed but are limited by the engines; alternatively, they could decide to increase speed by pitching the aircraft into a dive.

We could modify the simulation to include the effect of drag on aircraft speed, and add transfer functions to model the response of engine thrust to throttle and the aircraft pitch response to the elevators. We can then use these additions to investigate their effect on the frequency and damping of the phugoid oscillation.

6.5 User interfaces

Up to now we have concentrated on the creation of computer models that can be used by engineers and scientists to investigate problems that occur in the course of their professional work. The case studies have presented the "engine room" where the actual computation is done. There are many market areas where the user interface is of paramount importance. This is the "shop window" seen by less informed users.

Flight simulators can be built to interface with the actual cockpit instruments and controls. In some cases, it may be acceptable to mimic the instruments on computer screens. These may be used together with motion simulators that physically "rotate" the cockpit and apply g-forces to the pilot's seat.

Commercial simulators often include very sophisticated video packages that display animated views of the outside world as seen from the cockpit as the aircraft flies, banks, and turns. The programming of such animated images is a subject on its own, which uses specialized software to create an illusion of reality.

This goes beyond the scope of this book, where the figures have been created by the graphics that come with the simulation packages. No attention has been given to the creation of user interfaces. It is possible to create a rather crude form of computer animation by means of the simulation graphics. The basic principles are illustrated by the following simple Scilab program that creates an animated picture of a circular disc that moves along a ballistic trajectory, and spins while it moves:

```
xh = [0,0,600,600];
yh = [0,10,10,0];
xs = [290,297,300,303,310,303,300,297,290];
ys = [390,393,400,393,390,387,365,387,390];
t = [0:.01:1]*2*%pi;
x = -50*cos(t);  y = 50*sin(t);
X = [x(15),x(65)]
Y = [y(15),y(65)]
h = 50:10:550;
v = 300 - 9*[-5:.2:5].^2;
fig1=scf(1); clf;
plot(xh,yh,'m',xs,ys,'c')
for k=1:51
    w = cos(k/8);
    plot(w*x+h(k),y+v(k),'k',w*X+h(k),Y+v(k),'k')
    sleep(1)
    plot(w*x+h(k),y+v(k),'w',w*X+h(k),Y+v(k),'w')
end
```

At each simulation step the image of the object is erased before plotting its new position in the plane. This is done by following the instruction:

```
plot(w*x+h(k),y+v(k),'w',w*X+h(k),Y+v(k),'w')
```

The program can be extended to represent the rotation of a simple three-dimensional object, where we could use a wire frame model to delineate the edges between its faces. Its rotation can then be represented by changing its isometric projection. The programming of commercial simulator images requires an effort that is orders of magnitude greater than this example.

6.6 Discussion

Computer models can be an invaluable resource for engineers and designers throughout every phase of a project. They can be used to demonstrate the feasibility of new proposals, and in the course of a project they can assist the designers with making expensive decisions. When an aircraft is being commissioned and qualified, they can be used to simulate hazardous tests and to determine safety limits and emergency procedures. There is also a thriving industry that produces flight simulators to train pilots.

The very creation of simulation models forces everyone to delve deeper into the characteristics of the aircraft, which can give a valuable insight into its behavior.

The simulation engineers should work closely with the aircraft designers by studying design data, test results, and data from similar aircraft.

This chapter has given no more than the barest impression of the work that is required to create a flight simulator. The equations of motion are based on the principles that were developed by Newton, Euler, and others, but the interactions with the aerodynamic forces substantially increases the challenges to the simulation engineer. The user interfaces also demand a significant expenditure of labor.

Two examples are given to show how simplified simulation models can describe particular motions of an aircraft, where the aerodynamic forces and moments were linearized in order to make the results more comprehensible to the reader. There will be more complex models when it is necessary to study phenomena such as Dutch roll or coordinated turns.

Actual flight control models will generally involve nonlinear aerodynamic data. The aerodynamic coefficients will initially be estimated by specialists, who will generally make use of wind tunnels and computational fluid dynamics. In the later stages of a project the performance of the aircraft will be verified by flight testing. This is an iterative process, which involves predictions from a computer, testing by a pilot, updating the computer model, new predictions, and further flight tests.

The reader should have gained an impression of the work that is involved in a challenging field. All singing, all dancing digital simulators may be necessary at times, but a simplified model will often be a more useful tool for the design engineer.

Exercises

1   Create the aircraft simulation model shown in Figure 6.3. This defines the pitch response to elevator deflections The gains (including the linear approximations of the aerodynamic functions) can be set to the values given in Section 6.3.1.

   Verify that the aircraft responds to a step pitch disturbance as shown in Figure 6.4.

   Plot the response to a step produced by moving the elevators.

   Plot the free settling from an initial angle of attack.

2   Create the program given in Section 6.4 and verify the frequency of the phugoid motion.

   Plot the effect of moving the throttle (and the elevators) on the phugoid motion.

3   The phenomenon called "Dutch roll" is caused by an interaction between the yaw and roll motions of an aircraft, where the angle of sideslip (b) produces a

rolling moment while the roll rate (p) produces a yawing moment. The response of roll rate (*p*) and angle (*P*) to yaw sideslip is given by an equation of the form:

$$I\, dp/dt + M_p\, p = M_d\, b$$

$$dP/dt = p$$

There is then a weathercock yaw motion given by an equation of the form:

$$J\, d^2b/dt^2 + M_r\, db/dt + M_b\, b = M_P\, P$$

Compare a model of Dutch roll motion with the model of phugoid motion that you created in Exercise 2.

Can you propose how to break up the Dutch roll model into subsystems?

If the Dutch roll takes the form of an oscillation, what can you deduce regarding the polarity of the cross-coupling terms.

Bibliography

Ashley, H. (1974). *Engineering Analysis of Flight Vehicles*. Addison Wesley: MA, Reading.

Blakelock, J.H. (1965). *Automatic Control of Aircraft and Missiles*. New York: Wiley.

Etkin, B. (1959). *Dynamics of Flight*. New York: Wiley.

Rogers, A.E. and Connoly, T.W. (1960). *Analog Computation in Engineering Design*. New York: McGraw Hill.

Rubin, O. (2016). *Control Engineering in Development Projects*. Boston: Artech House.

7

Finite element models and the diffusion of heat

We will now go from the motion of bodies in space to the flow of heat. This is described by the second law of thermodynamics. There is a musical version of this scientific law:

> "Oh, you can't pass heat from the cooler to the hotter
> You can try it if you like but you'll only look a fool-er
> 'Cause the cold in the cooler will get hotter as a ruler."
>
> Flanders and Swann
> (*Source:* Rights Managed)

We are now dealing with a much more complex physical phenomenon, and will begin to have some doubts as to how we should model its behavior. We can fortunately combine our models with theoretical analysis in order to improve our confidence in the results.

7.1 Introduction

When we went from Chapter 2 to Chapter 4 we made the transition from systems that implemented discrete operations to models that simulated continuous variation with time. We showed in Chapters 5 and 6 that the state of the model can be described by a vector and its evolution can be described by a differential equation. We will now consider how to describe the internal state of a solid body and go on to derive equations that define its continuous evolution with time. This will be done without regard for the theories that matter consist of billions of atoms that move around in empty space, where its internal heat causes the kinetic energy of these atoms to increase. We will rather regard a solid body as continuous matter with a given density, while the heat that is stored in the body occupies a similar

Computer Models of Process Dynamics: From Newton to Energy Fields, First Edition.
Olis Rubin.
© 2023 The Institute of Electrical and Electronics Engineers, Inc.
Published 2023 by John Wiley & Sons, Inc.

continuum in space. Its temperature is then defined as the quantity of heat that is stored divided by its heat capacity. If the heat is unevenly distributed, this gives rise to a temperature profile. Now consider the temperature (T) at a point that is defined by its Cartesian coordinates (x, y, z). Its value at a given instant (t) can be described by a function of the form $T(x, y, z, t)$. The temperature profile may then be mathematically represented by a three-dimensional scalar field of the type that is discussed in Appendix C. Heat can then flow from a hotter area to its neighbors at a rate that is determined by the conductivity of the material. The rate of flow is also determined by the temperature gradient at that point. It is shown that such a gradient is a vector field, which is given by the partial derivatives of T with respect to x, y, and z. It is shown in Appendix C that the evolution in time of $T(x, y, z, t)$ is described by a partial differential equation (known as the *diffusion equation*). In order to simplify the analysis we will consider the evolution of a one-dimensional thermal system where the temperature profile is a function of the form $T(x, t)$. The diffusion equation is then reduced to the following form:

$$\partial^2 T / \partial x^2 = A \left(\partial T / \partial t \right)$$

Now suppose that we represent the continuous temperature profile by its values $T1(t)$, $T2(t)$, ... at a finite number of points. Instead of going back to the atoms themselves we will break up the solid body into finite elements, represented by the series of points: $x1, x2, ...$ The heat flow between the points is then determined by the material between them. This can be modeled by means of an electrical ladder network such as that shown in Figure 7.1, where the voltages $V1$, $V2$, ... at the network nodes can be used to represent the values of $T1$, $T2$, ..., while the currents $I0$, $I1$, $I2$, ... represent the heat flow between these points. The impedances (Z) then represent the resistance to heat flow, while the admittances (Y) from the nodes to earth represent the heat capacitance. This is a useful analogy for analyzing the behavior of a physical system that can be modeled by one-dimensional scalar and vector fields, and will also be used to explain the behavior of a continuous temperature profile. Suppose that we have a solid body that has a nonuniform temperature profile, which is also isolated from its environment. Heat will then flow from a higher temperature to a lower one. The ultimate result is that the temperature profile becomes flat, where

$$T1 = T2 = \text{etc.}$$

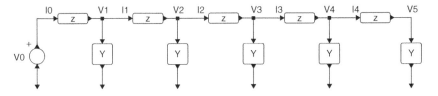

Figure 7.1 An electrical ladder network.

In this chapter we will create a finite element computer model that approximates the one-dimensional diffusion equation. These models are derived from such a ladder network. We will do cross-checks by comparing the answers from the computer model with analytical results.

Fourier introduced the series that bears his name for the purpose of determining the diffusion of heat, which he first recorded in his *Mémoire sur la propagation de la chaleur dans les corps solides* of 1807. This approach is outlined in Appendix C.2 and is used to verify the finite element model under specific conditions. The application considered in this chapter is primarily concerned with the transfer function that defines the response of the temperature at one point to the change in temperature at the other end. Appendix C.3.2 derives such a transfer function for a specific situation that is obscurely related to that of the finite element model. One may well ask whether we are using the analysis to verify the simulation or are we using the simulation model to verify the analysis?

7.2 A thermal model

Consider a nuclear reactor that produces energy which is used to drive a power plant. We will assume that the reactor core is surrounded by a wall of graphite which reflects stray neutrons back into the core so as to sustain the nuclear chain reaction. The energy released by the nuclear fission in the core is converted into heat that is removed by a coolant that flows from the core into a turbine where it does physical work. However, some of the heat flows from the core into the graphite wall. We will look at the creation of a thermal model to simulate the heat flow through the graphite wall. Appendix C.1 discusses the use of scalar and vector fields to analyze a heat-transfer process. The temperature distribution within a solid body is described by a three-dimensional scalar field $T(x, y, z)$ while the heat flow through the body is described by a vector field $\mathbf{Q}(x, y, z)$.

We will suppose that the reactor consists of a relatively long cylindrical core surrounded by an annular wall, and restrict our attention to a region where there is only radial heat flow through the wall, giving circular isothermal surfaces. If the diameter of the core is much greater than the thickness of the wall its outer circumference will be very nearly equal to its inner circumference. We can then approximate the wall by a flat plate with sides that are normal to the X axis in a Cartesian system X, Y, Z. An analytical thermal model for such a configuration is discussed in Appendix C.1. If the isothermal planes (of constant temperature) within the wall are normal to the X axis the heat flow will then be along the X axis. This allows us to analyze the three-dimensional temperature field $T(x, y, z)$ by means of a one-dimensional function $T(x)$. A partial differential equation (known as the *diffusion equation*) that describes the evolution of the temperature $T(x)$ is derived in Appendix C.1.1:

$$k\left(\partial^2 T/\partial x^2\right) = c\left(\partial T/\partial t\right)$$

where

$c =$ the heat capacity (joules per K per m^3) of the material

$k =$ the thermal conductivity (watts per K per m) of the material

$x =$ the distance from a point on the surface between the reactor core and the graphite wall

The heat flow (watts) within the wall is along the X axis, so that

$$- \mathbf{i}\, Q(x) = k\, \partial T/\partial x$$

$\mathbf{i} =$ a unit vector along the positive directions of the X axis

7.2.1   A finite element model based on an electrical ladder network

Such a thermal system is analogous to the electrical ladder network shown in Figure 7.1, where the impedances (Z) are pure resistances (R) and the admittances (Y) are pure capacitances (C). The currents ($I0$, $I1$,...) flowing through the resistors then represent heat flows, while the voltages ($V1$, $V2$,...) at the network nodes represent temperatures. (The nodes will be called by the same names as their associated voltages.) This analogy represents a finite element approximation of the above partial differential equation. We justify this by observing that the derivation in Appendix C.1.1 of the distributed system started with infinitesimal elements, so we hope that this approximation will approach the behavior of a distributed system as we increase the number of elements in the ladder. Also, the structure of the ladder elements was derived by following the same reasoning as was used in Appendix C.1.

We will use the analogy of an electrical ladder network to analyze the response of the thermal system to heat inputs. This allows us to use the extensive analytical tools based on electrical network theory. A capacitor (C) can be represented by its impedance ($1/sC$). The transfer function from the voltage $V4$ to $V5$ in Figure 7.1 can then be derived to be the following first-order lag:

$$F(s) = V5/V4 = (1/sC)/[R + 1/sC] = 1/(1 + sT)$$

$T = R\,C =$ the time constant (s)

Now $V3$ and $V5$ both feed into node $V4$ through equal resistors (R). They thus combine to give an equivalent voltage source ($V3 + V5$)/2 with an output impedance ($R/2$). We thus have

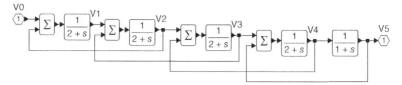

Figure 7.2 Finite element model.

$$V4 = [(V3 + V5)/2] (1/sC)/[R/2 + 1/sC] = (V3 + V5) E(s)$$
$$E(s) = 1/(2 + sT)$$

Similarly:

$$E(s) = V3/(V2 + V4) = V2/(V1 + V3) = V1/(V0 + V2)$$

All the state variables ($V1$, $V2$, $V3$,...) in this model have the same physical units (volts). They can equally well represent some other quantity such as temperature or pressure. We can also normalize their units, so that one normalized simulation unit could represent 1 mV or 1 V. We can also normalize simulation time, so that one time unit could represent 1 ms or 1 s. It could also represent T seconds, in which case the time constant (T) is equal to 1 s in normalized simulation time.

The network is then simulated in Scilab, as shown in Figure 7.2.

7.2.2 Free settling from an initial temperature profile

Figure 7.3a shows a finite element model of the thermal field where the temperatures $T0$ and $T6$ of the inner and the outer surfaces of the graphite wall are both pinned to zero. The outputs $T1$, $T2$, $T3$, etc. represent temperatures $T(x, t)$ at the centers of the elements, where the heat flow is along the X axis. We will normalize the units of distance so that the thickness of the wall equals six units. We then have that $T1$, $T2$, $T3$, etc. are the temperatures at $x = 1, 2, 3,...$.

Figure 7.3b shows how transfer function blocks [1/2 + s] are realized by implementing differential equations, such as the following:

$$C \, dT3/dt = Q23 + Q43$$

where

$Q23 = K \, (T2{-}T3) =$ the heat flow (watts) from node $T2$ to node $T3$
$Q43 = K \, (T4{-}T3) =$ the heat flow (watts) from node $T4$ to node $T3$
$K =$ the thermal conductivity (watts per K) from any node to its neighbor
$C =$ the heat capacity (joules per K) of the material around the node

(a)

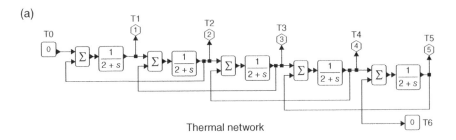

Thermal network

(b)

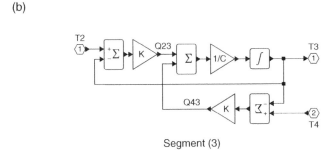

Segment (3)

Figure 7.3 (a, b) Finite element model with fixed endpoints.

We again normalize the units of time (t) so that KC equals one unit. Finally, we choose the cross-sectional area of the finite elements, so that $C = 1$ joule per K, whence $K = 1$ watt per K.

We can then rewrite the above equations as

$$dT3/dt = (T2 + T4) - 2T3$$

The model has five integrators that can be set to give a desired initial temperature profile. We will set these to follow the sinusoidal function that is indicated by the **O** symbols in Figure 7.4:

$$T(x, 0) = \sin(x\, w/2)$$
$$w = 2\pi/6$$

The symbols (**v**) in Figure 7.4 show how the temperature profile settles with time, corresponding to $T(x, t)$, where $t = 2, 4, 6$ and $x = 1, 2, 3,....$ These again follow a sinusoidal function, dropping to zero at the surfaces of the wall.

Appendix C.2 shows how to find the evolution of a temperature profile $T(x, t)$ in an infinite thermal field. We can calculate the settling from an initial sinusoidal temperature profile, indicated by the **O** symbols in Figure 7.4:

$$T(x, t) = \exp(-t/u)\, \sin(x\, w/2)$$

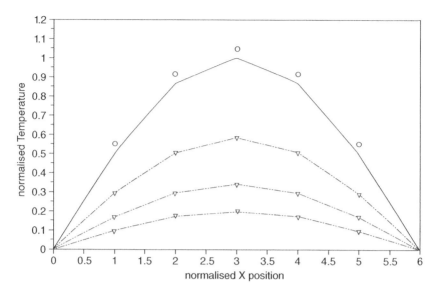

Figure 7.4   Free settling of temperature profile

where
$$u = (1/w)^2$$

We find that this analytical result agrees up to the seventh decimal place, with the temperature profiles generated by the finite element model. This cross-check should satisfy us that the finite element model is valid under the specified conditions. We may have to use more elements and give careful consideration as to how we simulate the end effects that apply to a particular application.

7.2.3   Step response test

The step response of the model defined by Figure 7.2 is shown as a solid line in Figure 7.5. The voltages $V1$ to $V5$ were initialized to zero, while the figure shows the response of $V5$ to an input $V0 = 1$. The dash-dotted curve in Figure 7.5 shows how the response of the model in normalized time can be approximated by a time constant of 13 seconds plus a time delay of 2 seconds.

As discussed in Section 6.3.2, the diagram data structure (scs_m) of the model shown in Figure 7.2 can be converted into a linear state-space system, sys=lincos(scs_m), and the Scilab instruction bode(sys,fo,fn) will plot its frequency response. This is shown in Figure 7.6.

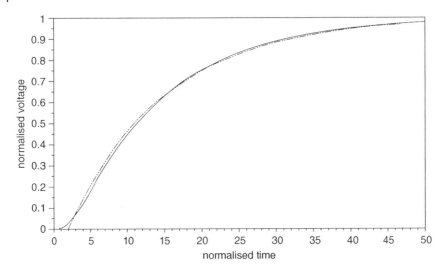

Figure 7.5 Step response of finite element model.

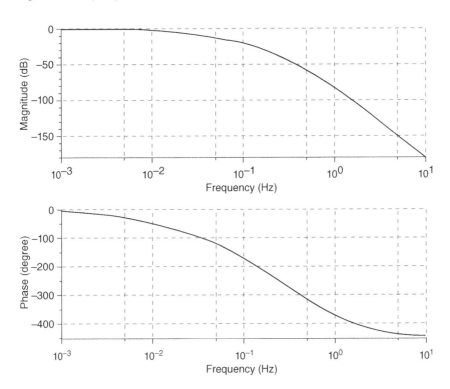

Figure 7.6 Frequency response of finite element model.

The following Scilab instruction can then find the transfer function from the input $V0$ to the output $V5$:

```
[Ds,num,den] = ss2tf(sys);
```

which is then found to be

$$H(s) = num/den = 1/(1 + 15s + 35s^2 + 28s^3 + 9s^4 + s^5)$$

The following Scilab instruction then finds the time constants of $H(s)$:

```
Ts = -1 ./[roots(den)]
Ts = [ 12.3 1.44 0.58 0.35 0.27 ]
```

We can cross-check this by deriving $H(s)$ by algebra, from the relationships between $E(s)$ and $F(s)$ that were given in Section 7.2.1. The transfer function is thus dominated by a time constant of 12.3 seconds, which confirms the above approximation by a time constant of 13 seconds.

Appendix C.3.2 determines the transfer function that describes the propagation of temperature within an infinite one-dimensional thermal field. This is given by a transcendental function: $\mathbf{H}(s) = \exp(-x\sqrt{s})$, whereas the model has a rational transfer function. It is also not certain whether we can make a valid comparison, since the analytic expression is for an infinite field while the model describes a finite body. $\mathbf{H}(s)$ can be used to determine the frequency response:

$$\mathbf{H}(j\omega) = \exp[-P(\omega)] \exp[-j\,P(\omega)]$$

$$P(\omega) = \left(x/\sqrt{2}\right)\sqrt{\omega} = \text{phase lag in radians}$$

The following Scilab program plots the frequency response shown in Figure 7.7:

```
frq=logspace(log10(fo),log10(fn),frN);
W = 2*%pi*frq;
x = 5;                          //   distance
P = (x/sqrt(2)) * sqrt(W);      //   phase in radians
mag = -20*log10(exp(1))*P       //   gain [dB]
phs = -P*180/%pi;               //   phase lag in degrees
bode(frq,mag,phs)
```

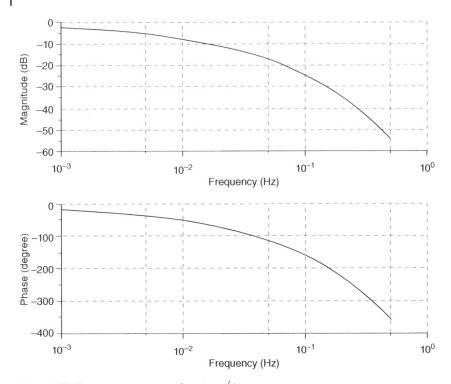

Figure 7.7 Frequency response of $\exp(-x\sqrt{s})$.

The time response $h(t)$ is given by the inverse Laplace transform of $\mathbf{H}(s)$. Conventional methods fail in this case, so we will go back to the general definition of inverse Laplace transform:

$$h(t) = (1/2\pi j) \int H(\sigma + j\omega) \exp[(\sigma + j\omega)t] \, d\omega,$$

where the integral is from $-\infty$ to $+\infty$

If the system is stable we can reduce this to

$$h(t) = (1/2\pi j) \int H(j\omega) \exp(j\omega t) \, d\omega$$

We will then restrict our attention to the imaginary part of $\exp(j\omega t)$ and replace the integral by the sum of odd Fourier components. This gives

$$h(t) = H(j\omega)A_1 \sin(\omega t) + H(j3\omega)A_3 \sin(3\omega t) + H(j5\omega)A_5 \sin(5\omega t) + \cdots$$

This describes the response of $\mathbf{H}(s)$ to an input $\mathbf{To}(s)$, which is made up of Fourier components, where $n\omega$ is the frequency of the nth harmonic and A_n is its magnitude. If A_n equals A_1/n, this gives a square wave that switches between -1 and $+1$. The amplitudes of its harmonics are proportional to $1/\omega$, so $h(t)$ corresponds to the inverse Laplace transform of $H(s)/s$.

The following Scilab program plots the response $H(t)$ to this input signal $To(t)$:

```
t = 0:.2:50;
x = 5;
w1 = %pi/(5*x^2);                  //  fundamental frequency
for n=1:2:99
      dTo = sin(n*w1*t)/n;
      To = To + dTo;
      P = (x/sqrt(2)) * sqrt(n*w1);
      dH = exp(-P)*sin(n*w1*t - P)/n;
      H = H + dH;
end
plot(t,(4/%pi)*To,'k',t,(4/%pi)*H,'k')
```

The vector (H) that corresponds to the signal $h(t)$ is plotted in Figure 7.8. We see that it resembles the step response that was plotted in Figure 7.5 when we realize that the input signal is now a square wave.

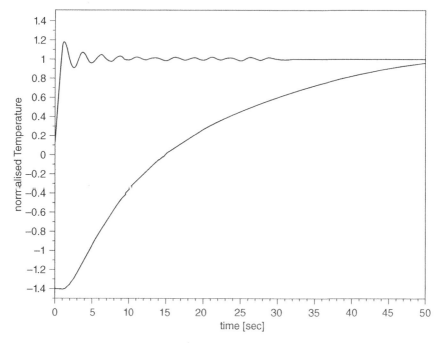

Figure 7.8 Step response of $\exp(-\sqrt{(sU)})$.

The highest harmonic in the input **To**(s) is limited to 15.6 Hz. The vector (To) that corresponds to the square wave signal *To*(t) is also plotted in Figure 7.8. We see that it has a superimposed Gibbs oscillation. **H**(s) attenuates the high-frequency components, so that H shows negligible oscillation.

7.2.4   State space model of diffusion

We can describe the state of the computer model shown in Figure 7.2 by a vector:

$$\mathbf{T} = [T5; T4; T3; T2; T1]$$

We can increase the number of elements in the model to seven by defining the state vector to be

$$\mathbf{T} = [T7; T6; T5; T4; T3; T2; T1]$$

The differential equations describing the model can then be written as a state equation:

$$\mathrm{d}\mathbf{T}/\mathrm{d}t = \underline{\mathbf{A}}\,\mathbf{T} + \mathbf{B}\,T0$$

where

```
A =  [  -K      1       0       0       0       0       0
         1    -2*K      1       0       0       0       0
         0      1     -2*K      1       0       0       0
         0      0       1     -2*K      1       0       0
         0      0       0       1     -2*K      1       0
         0      0       0       0       1     -2*K      1
         0      0       0       0       0       1     -2*K ] / C
B =   [ 0;     0;      0;      0;      0;      0;      1 ]
```

This can be implemented by means of the model shown in Figure 7.9, where the gain block [*A*] gives an output $\underline{\mathbf{A}}\,\mathbf{T}$, while the gain block [*B*] gives an output **B**T0.

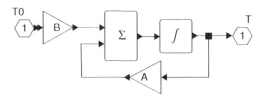

Figure 7.9   State space model of diffusion equation.

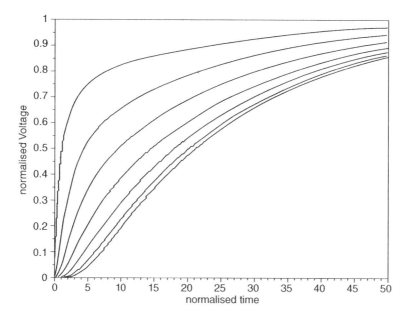

Figure 7.10 Step response of state space model.

This can also be simulated by the following program, where T is the state vector:

```
dt=0.1;
t(1) = 0;
T(1) = [0;0;0;0;0;0;0];
T0 = 1;
for k=1:499
    t(k+1) = t(k) + dt;
    T(:,k+1) = T(:,k) + dt*A*T(:,k) + dt*B*T0;
end
```

Figure 7.10 shows the step response of the model to the input (T0). T1 is the quickest to respond, followed by T3, T3,... in sequence. The response of T5 can be compared with Figure 7.5, bearing in mind that the heat still diffuses through two more sections before reaching the end of the body.

We can create a symmetrical model, such as that shown in Figure 7.3, by changing A to

```
A(1,1) = -2*R;
```

We can add a temperature T8 at the other end of the body by modifying B to

```
B = [[0; 0; 0; 0; 0; 0; 1],[1; 0; 0; 0; 0; 0; 0]]
```

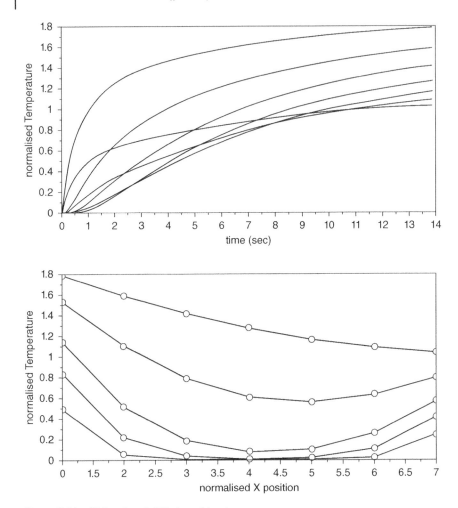

Figure 7.11 Bidirectional diffusion of heat.

The input to the model is now a vector [T0 ; T8] that defines the temperature at the two ends. Figure 7.11 shows the response of **T** to a step of two units in *T0* and one unit in *T8*. The upper plot shows how the addition of a heat sink at *T8* significantly alters the response of the body to a step temperature change at either end. The temperatures *T1* and *T7*, which are nearest to the ends, are the quickest to approach their steady states. The lower plot shows how the heat diffuses inwards from both ends causing the internal temperatures to rise. The eventual temperature profile will be a straight line between T0 and T8. The internal temperatures are slower to approach their steady states. The curves in the lower plot can be compared with those shown in Figure 7.4. In this case we have a mixture of harmonic modes that settle exponentially at different rates, causing the shape of the temperature profile to change as it approaches the steady state. These plots illustrate a link that exists between harmonic analysis and transfer functions. The differences between the step responses shown in the upper plot and those shown in Figure 7.10 illustrate how the character of the thermal field also depends on the coupling between the body and its environment.

7.3 A practical application

Consider a nuclear reactor with a cylindrical core that is surrounded by a graphite wall. This is encased in a steel pressure vessel that is in a citadel made of reinforced concrete. Suppose that we wish to determine the operating temperature within the reactor core, but that conditions are too severe to take such measurements. We can perhaps build thermocouples into the graphite wall and determine the relationship between these measurements and the temperature inside the core itself. One way of addressing this challenge is to create a model that predicts the temperature profile in the graphite wall produced by conditions within the core. We will assume that the core exactly determines the temperature of the inside surface of the wall. We then have to consider the physical phenomena that determine the heat loss at the outside surface of the wall. Suppose that the steel pressure vessel can be modeled as a perfect conductor that loses heat from its outer surface by convection and radiation. The heat transfer coefficients may be quite complex, but for the purpose of demonstration we will assume that they can be modeled by a thermal conductivity connected to a constant ambient temperature. These arguments lead us to create a model such as that shown in Figure 7.12, where the final element $[1/1.3 + s]$ is based on the assumption that this conductivity equals 0.3 K. The input to this block is modeled as K T4 + 0.3 K T6.

The frequency response of this finite element model is shown in Figure 7.13. The equivalent transfer function of `lincos(scs_m)` is dominated by a time constant of six seconds, where

$$H(s) = 0.64\,(1 + s1.7)(1 + s0.37)/$$
$$(1 + s5.95)(1 + s1.27)(1 + s0.56)(1 + s0.35)(1 + s0.27)$$

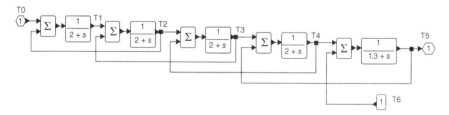

Figure 7.12 Simulation of physical hardware.

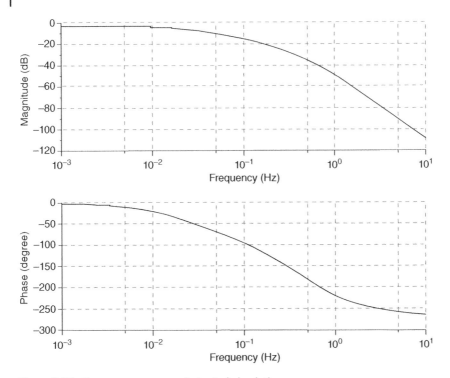

Figure 7.13 Frequency response of physical simulation.

The phase lag is less than 10 degrees for frequencies up to 0.004 Hz, which should be ample for following changes in reactor power. We note in passing that we could estimate the temperature of the core from a measurement at the pressure vessel. We could then compensate for the thermal lag of the wall by implementing an inverse filter of the form:

$$F(s) = (1 + s6)(1 + s1.3)/Q(s)$$

The denominator, $Q(s)$ can be designed to act as a lowpass filter, while not introducing excessive lag on the estimated temperature.

Suppose that the temperature within the cylindrical reactor varies with the radial distance (r) from the axis of the core, giving circular isothermal surfaces. We also suppose that the heat flows horizontally through the wall. Appendix C.4.3 derives the form of the div(grad( )) operator in polar coordinates, whence we see that the evolution of a temperature field $T(r)$ is given by

$$(1/r)\partial T/\partial r + \partial^2 T/\partial r^2 = (c/k)\partial T/\partial t$$

We can modify the one-dimensional finite element model shown in Figure 7.12 to describe the radial heat flow. The wall can be segmented into concentric annular elements, each having an inner radius (r), an outer radius ($r + d$) and a height equal to unity. The parameters of the elements will vary since their volumes and surface areas will increase as we move further from the center.

7.4 Two-dimensional steady-state model

The evolution of a three-dimensional temperature field is determined by a diffusion equation:

$$\partial^2 T/\partial x^2 + \partial^2 T/\partial y^2 + \partial^2 T/\partial z^2 = (c/k)\,\partial T/\partial t$$

whereas a one-dimensional scalar field can be represented by a vector with n finite elements, a two-dimensional field must be represented by a matrix with m by n elements, and a three-dimensional field must be represented by a three-dimensional array of elements. The complexity of a finite element model that describes the evolution of the field increases rapidly as we increase the number of dimensions. We will not tax the reader by describing the laborious construction of a three-dimensional model, but will rather illustrate how to plot a two-dimensional steady-state field $T(x, y)$, where $\partial T/\partial t$ is equal to zero. The diffusion equation then reduces to the *Laplace equation*:

$$\partial^2 T/\partial y^2 = -\partial^2 T/\partial x^2$$

A particular solution to this equation is found in Appendix C.4.1. Its shape is composed of Fourier components, which restricts our choice to fields that are fixed at the ends of a finite region. This limits its use as a model for typical physical systems. However, it is useful for verifying the behavior of a computer model by means of a simple cross-check. The solution was further simplified by assuming that at all points the heat flows in the positive x direction. This simplifies it to the following form:

$$T(x, y) = \exp(-x\pi/B)\,\sin(y\pi/B)$$

We can use this to model a temperature field within a rectangular plate where two sides that are parallel to the X axis are kept at temperature zero. These will be on the lines given by $y = 0$ and $y = B$, where we will assume that B equals eight. We will further assume that the side that lies on the Y axis ($x = 0$) is in contact with a heat source that gives a sinusoidal temperature profile, while the fourth side, $at = 14$, is in contact with a heat sink.

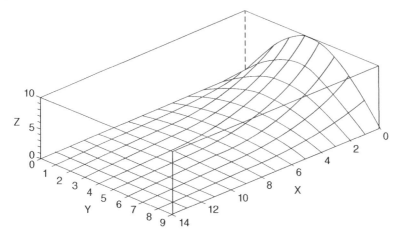

Figure 7.14 Temperature field within a rectangular plate.

We can use the following Scilab program to plot $T(x, y)$ vs. x and y, as shown in Figure 7.14:

```
X = [0:14]';
Y = 0:9;
Z = 10*exp(-X*%pi/9) * sin(Y*%pi/9);    //  Z = T(x,y)
  plot3d(Y,X,Z)
f=gcf();
f.color_map=whitecolormap(3)
```

The matrix (Z) corresponds to the two-dimensional temperature field.

We must acknowledge that this analysis is somewhat synthetic and that the system was tailored to approximate the mathematical solution. We could possibly approximate real applications by increasing the number of modes, but would then have to verify the answer by other means.

7.5   Discussion

We have considered the conduction of heat through a homogeneous solid body. This presented challenges that were unlike anything that we have hitherto encountered. Most of the study was concerned with a one-dimensional thermal field, where it was possible to approximate the temperature profile in a cylindrical wall to give a purely radial heat flow, which is one-dimensional. In many applications we will be forced to consider two- and three-dimensional fields, which will increase our effort and the required computing power by orders of magnitude. It is a much more daunting challenge to create realistic computer models that simulate natural phenomena, such as a meteorological model of the Earth's atmosphere. Such a project would involve questions that go far beyond the contents of these pages, and the author is unable to recommend a textbook that will provide the answers. We also have opportunities to create engineering models that simulate conditions inside large chemical plants, aerodynamic models that look at airflow around a wing, and others too numerous to mention. It takes true wisdom to decide how realistic a model must be, and what is enough to satisfy our needs.

The case study that occupied most of this chapter examined a physical object that could be described by a linear one-dimensional diffusion equation. A finite element model was created and evaluated by comparing its behavior with the results of two different theoretical approaches. Even though the model contained only five elements, its results compared very well with theory. While it is generally not possible to find an analytical solution to a nonlinear diffusion equation, nonlinear components *can* be used in finite element models. For example, the nuclear reactor model created in Section 7.3 could have used a nonlinear function $F(T6 - T5)$ to simulate the convective heat transfer from the outside surface of the pressure vessel to the atmosphere.

The basic approach that was used in this chapter can be adapted to model many physical phenomena, such as the diffusion of gases or of a liquid through a porous medium. A one-dimensional thermal system is analogous to the transmission of electrical signals through a coaxial cable, since this is dominated by the capacitance between the central wire and the sheath and the resistance of the wire itself. In the next chapter we will go on to consider the propagation of current and voltage in an electrical transmission line, where the system includes the effect of the induced magnetic field. In this chapter it was discovered that the model is sensitive to the way in which its boundary conditions are simulated. We will find that this effect becomes even more acute in the next chapter, where propagation is governed by the wave equation.

We should by now begin to understand that computer models of variable fields in a continuous space do not replace theoretical analysis. No single approach is likely to produce an entirely satisfactory solution for such cases. We generally need to exploit the synergy that can be achieved between computer simulation, mathematical analysis, and physical prototypes. We should also be guided by the following thought:

"The purpose of computing is insight, not numbers"

R.W. Hamming (1962)

Exercises

Readers can create their models on the platform of their choice, where the chosen platform will include its own operating and plotting tools.

1 Create the thermal model shown in Figure 7.2 and plot the responses of $V1$, $V2$, $V3$, $V4$, $V5$ when a step input is applied at $V0$.

   Determine the frequency response of $V5$.

   How would you simulate a nonuniform solid, where the material changes between $V3$ and $V4$?

2 Modify the model by adding a fixed input $V6$ at the end of the node $V5$. What does this represent?

   With $V0$ and $V6$ equal to zero, plot the evolution from different initial profiles of $V1 \dots V5$.

   With $V1 \dots V5$ initially equal to zero, plot their evolution for various unequal values of $V0$ and $V6$.

   Repeat this with a model that has twice the number of finite elements.

3 Write a computer program that uses a `for` loop with rectangular integration between discrete time steps (`dt=0.1`) to simulate a single thermal segment such as that shown in Figure 7.3b.

   Use constant input temperatures T2 and T4 and compute the temperature $T3$ as a vector `T3(k)`.

   Plot the evolution of `T3(k)` from the initial condition `T3(1)=0`.

   Experiment with various inputs T2 and T4.

   Draw a block diagram that shows how `T3(k+1)` is calculated from `T2, T4`, and `T3(k)`.

   Use a Z-transfer function block $[z^{-1}]$ to represent a delay of `dt`.

   When such a block has an input `T3(k+1)` it produces an output `T3(k)`.

   Redraw the block diagram with discrete integrators that have the Z-transfer functions: $1/[z-1]$.

   Compare the result with the segment shown in Figure 7.3.

   Can you now create a computer program that represents the discrete equivalent model shown in Figure 7.3a?

   Try experimenting with various values of d*t*.

4 Create the state space program given in Section 7.2.4 with a state vector containing 20 elements that are all initialized to zero. Plot their responses when the input to the vector **B** equals unity.

   Modify the vector B to take an input at both ends. How must you modify the matrix A to produce responses similar to Figure 7.11? You can now experiment with different initial state profiles.

5 Create a two-dimensional temperature matrix (T) with 15 by 10 elements that corresponds to the two-dimensional temperature shown Figure 7.14.

Create the `grad()` function given in Appendix C.1 and use it to calculate the components `Gx` and `Gy` of the gradient of the temperature profile.

Create the `div()` function given in Appendix C.1.1 and use it to calculate the divergence of the gradient `Gx` and `Gy`.

Create the `curl()` function given in Appendix C.4.2 and use it to calculate the curl of the gradient matrix. What do you obtain?

Can you create a vector field that has a non-zero curl?

6 Describe how you would create a two-dimensional diffusion model, using an augmented version of the nodal element shown in Figure 7.3b.

How many heat flow paths would there be from a particular node?

How would you define the interfaces between a square element and its neighbors?

Bibliography

Cheng, D.K. (1958). *Analysis of Linear Systems*. Reading: Addison-Wesley.

Davis, H.F. (1967). *Introduction to Vector Analysis*. Boston: Allyn and Bacon.

Jordan, E.C. (1953). *Electromagnetic Waves and Radiating Systems*. London: Constable.

Starkey, B.J. (1958). *Laplace Transforms for Electrical Engineers*. London: Iliffe & Sons.

8

Wave equations

As we create models that describe more and more complex physical phenomena, we will begin to have more and more doubts as to how we should model its behavior.

> "Mysterious even in the light of day,
> nature will never let her veil be stolen,
> and what she will not show your mind
> you'll not get out of her with screws and levers"

> Goethe's Faust
> (*Source:* In the Public Domain, Rights Holder Harvard University)

In many ways this chapter presents us with the ultimate challenge that we will venture to address. We now need a combination of computer modeling and mathematical analysis in order to obtain an adequate understanding of the physical process.

8.1   Introduction

It was stated at the outset that this book was written with an important objective, of taking you along a learning curve that goes from the basics to subjects of increasing complexity. We started this process in Chapter 3, where we saw how the building blocks of MATLAB and Simulink could be fitted into programs that performed various functions. Chapter 4 went on to use such discrete operations to simulate differential equations, while Chapters 5 and 6 showed how to apply this technique to model the motion of physical objects. Chapter 7 took this further by considering the diffusion of energy through a solid body. This chapter represents the last lap on the path to greater technical complexity, by looking at the propagation of waves through space. Even when we consider one-dimensional space there is still a significant challenge to reconcile computed results with mathematical analysis.

Computer Models of Process Dynamics: From Newton to Energy Fields, First Edition.
Olis Rubin.
© 2023 The Institute of Electrical and Electronics Engineers, Inc.
Published 2023 by John Wiley & Sons, Inc.

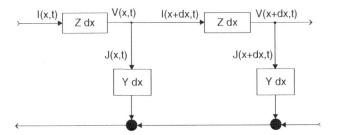

Figure 8.1 Simulation of a single wire transmission line.

The first study considers the propagation of a voltage down a transmission line that is modeled as a wire that carries an electric current from a transmitter to a receiver. It is assumed that the return current flows back to the transmitter through an Earth plane that has zero resistance. The voltage of the wire relative to the Earth plane can thus be represented by a profile $V(x, t)$, where x is the distance from the transmitter. The concept of an impedance that was developed in circuit theory is used to model the transmission line.

Figure 8.1 represents the change in voltage over an infinitesimal length (dx) of the wire. This will have an infinitesimal series impedance (Z dx), where

$$V(x - dx, t) - V(x, t) = -I(x, t) Z \, dx$$

and $I(x, t)$ represents the current flow down the wire at the point (x). For example, if Z dx is a pure resistance (R dx), the above equation is an expression of Ohm's law.

There will typically be a current that flows from the wire to earth through an admittance Y dx:

$$I(x + dx, t) - I(x, t) = V(x, t) Y \, dx$$

This could be a leakage current through a conductance G dx.

We will begin by showing how this network can produce a diffusion equation similar to that found in Chapter 7, and can then be expanded to produce a wave equation.

Cheng (1958) and Jordan (1953) use a slightly more complex network that models two identical parallel wires. The current flows out through one wire and back through the other so the series impedance ($Z/2$ dx) is divided between them. The final result is the same as that obtained with the network shown in Figure 8.1.

8.2 Energy storage mechanisms

Chapter 7 considered the storage of heat energy in a solid body that caused its temperature to rise. In a one-dimensional thermal system the *energy density* at a point Q (x, t) was the quantity of heat per unit length. Now consider a coaxial cable that consists of a central wire that is surrounded by dielectric material and an outer conducting sheath which is earthed. The central wire typically has a resistance

(R) per unit length while the sheath can be approximated by a perfect conductor. We can regard the cable as a one-dimensional object that conducts electric charge and characterize its state at any instant by the profile $Q(x, t)$ of its charge density. There will typically be a capacitance (C) per unit length between the central wire and earth so the charge will produce a voltage on the wire. This is given by

$$V(x,t) = Q(x,t)/C$$

This is analogous to a thermal system, where the temperature to $T(x, t)$ is proportional to the energy density.

When a voltage source is connected to the cable this will produce a voltage gradient along the wire. We can represent the change in voltage over an infinitesimal length (dx) of the wire by the network shown in Figure 8.1. In a coaxial cable we can approximate $Z\,dx$ by a pure resistance ($R\,dx$) so the voltage gradient produces the following current:

$$I(x,t) = -(dV/dx)/R$$

The state of the cable can thus be characterized by a voltage profile $V(x, t)$ that produces a current profile $I(x, t)$. This is again analogous to the thermal system, where $I(x, t)$ corresponds to the heat flow.

The thermal system and the coaxial cable both have a single mechanism for storing energy (heat in the one case and charge in the other) whence the energy propagation can be mathematically modeled in both cases by a diffusion equation. In the case of a coaxial cable the propagation of signals can be described by the following equation:

$$\partial^2 V/\partial x^2 = RC\,(\partial V/\partial t)$$

Now consider a transmission line with parallel wires that form a circuit that includes a transmitter and a receiver. We will again simplify our model by postulating that there is a single wire that carries an electric current (I) from the transmitter to the receiver while the return current flows through a hypo thetical earth. We will consider the line voltage at any point to be the voltage (V) of the single wire relative to the earth. The current will induce a magnetic field that is determined by the permeability that surrounds the wire. Electromagnetic induction opposes any change in current by generating a back emf. We can again use the network shown in Figure 8.1, where the impedance ($Z\,dx$) now consists of a resistance ($R\,dx$) in series with an inductance ($L\,dx$), where L is the inductance per unit length. The inductance then gives the following infinitesimal back emf:

$$E(x,t) = -L\,dx\,(\partial I/\partial t)$$

whence

$$V(x - dx, t) - V(x, t) = -I(x, t)R\,dx - (\partial I/\partial t)L\,dx$$

The effect of the impedance (Z) per unit length thus gives the following voltage gradient:

$$\partial V/\partial x = -RI - L(\partial I/\partial t) \tag{8.1}$$

The voltage (V) can cause a leakage current to flow from the wire to earth. The admittance ($Y\,dx$) in Figure 8.1 will then consist of a capacitance ($C\,dx$) in parallel with a conductance ($G\,dx$). The conductance (G) per unit length then gives the following infinitesimal leakage current:

$$J(x, t) = V(x, t)\,G\,dx$$

As the current flows down the line it is reduced by leakage (GV) through the conductance, and there will be a further current ($C\,\partial V/\partial t$) that flows through the capacitance. The combined effect of these is to give the following current gradient:

$$\partial I/\partial x = -C(\partial V/\partial t) - GV(x, t) \tag{8.2}$$

This transmission line has two mechanisms for storing energy. There is the electric field that determines its capacitance and the magnetic field that determines its inductance. There can be an interchange between the energy in the electrical and magnetic fields that can cause a resulting oscillation. This phenomenon is similar to the oscillation of a pendulum, where the model given in Figure 5.3 shows how the potential energy (as determined by the angular position Q) can be interchanged with its kinetic energy (as determined by the angular velocity W). The interchange between them is shown in Figures 5.4 and 5.5.

8.2.1 Partial differential equation describing propagation in a transmission line

Differentiating Equation (8.1) with respect to x then gives

$$\partial^2 V/\partial x^2 = -R\,\partial I/\partial x - L\,\partial^2 I/\partial t\partial x$$

From Equation (8.2) we then have

$$\partial^2 V/\partial x^2 = RGV + RC\,\partial V/\partial t - L\,\partial^2 I/\partial t\partial x \tag{8.3}$$

Differentiating Equation (8.2) with respect to t then gives

$$\partial^2 I/\partial x\partial t = -G\,\partial V/\partial t - C\,\partial^2 V/\partial t^2$$

Substituting this expression for $\partial^2 I/\partial x \partial t$ into Equation (8.3) gives the following partial differential equation:

$$\partial^2 V/\partial x^2 = LC\,\partial^2 V/\partial t^2 + (RC + GL)\,\partial V/\partial t + RGV$$

This is known as the *telegraphist's equation* for the voltage along a line. Define the *propagation velocity* of voltage and current along the line as

$$c = 1/\sqrt{[LC]}$$

Consider the case of a distortionless transmission line, where

$$R/L = G/C$$

and define a damping coefficient (a) that satisfies the following:

$$a = \sqrt{[R\,G]}$$

whence

$$a/c = \sqrt{[RGLC]}$$

We can then show that the partial differential equation simplifies to

$$\partial^2 V/\partial x^2 = \left(1/c^2\right)\partial^2 V/\partial t^2 + (2a/c)\,\partial V/\partial t + a^2 V$$

If the causes of energy dissipation are removed, the propagation is given by the following wave equation:

$$\partial^2 V/\partial x^2 = \left(1/c^2\right)\partial^2 V/\partial t^2$$

The energy will then travel down the line without any losses. This can give problems when we attempt to model a finite transmission line, where the energy wave will generally be reflected when it encounters a discontinuity at the end of the line. It then travels back along the line and interferes with the incoming energy wave. This chapter will consider limited situations that are not too clouded by such effects. The voltage propagation along the length of a coaxial cable is also affected by a mismatch at its end.

8.3 A finite element model of a transmission line

The network shown in Figure 8.1 describes infinitesimal changes in the voltage profile $V(x, t)$ and the current profile $I(x, t)$. We can approximate the transmission line by dividing it into finite sections. This is shown in Figure 8.2 as a ladder network where there are discrete changes in voltage and current over each section. The voltages ($V1$, $V2$, ...) at the network nodes represent the line voltage at distances (x_1, x_2, ...) along its length, while the currents ($I01$, $I12$, ...) represent the currents that flow between the nodes. The impedances (Z) between nodes represent the combined effect of resistance and inductance over the lengths (x_1) (x_2-x_1)

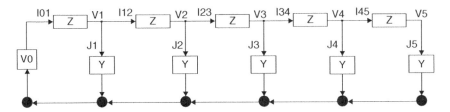

Figure 8.2 Transmission line simulated by a ladder network.

(x_3-x_2), etc., while the admittances (Y) represent the conductance and capacitance to earth of the same lengths. Their values differ from the impedance Z and admittance Y per unit length that were used before.

Figure 8.3 shows a computer simulation of the following network equations that determine the voltage V3 at node 3, which is at a distance $x3$ along the line:

$$V2 - V3 = R\,I23 + L\,\partial I23/\partial t$$
$$V3 - V4 = R\,I34 + L\,\partial I34/\partial t$$

Combining these equations and taking Laplace transforms, we obtain:

$$V2(s) + V4(s) - 2\,V3(s) = (R + sL)\,J3(s) \tag{8.4}$$

where the current from node 3 to earth is given by

$$J3 = I23 - I34$$

Since $J3$ equals the net current flowing into node 3 we have

$$J3(s) = (G + sC)\,V3(s) \tag{8.5}$$

Equations (8.4) and (8.5) define the inner feedback loops around the two integrator blocks that appear in Figure 8.3. Their open-loop transfer functions are given by $R/sL = G/sC$. If these are the same:

$$R/L = G/C = A$$

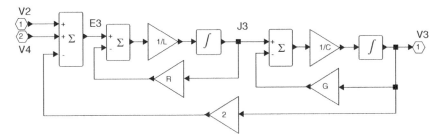

Figure 8.3 Simulation of a ladder network, section 3.

where the ladder network will approximate a distortionless transmission line.

The following computer program implements the above differential equations to calculate the variables `V(k,1)`, `V(k,2)`, `V(k,3)` ... `V(k,80)` that represent ladder voltages $V1$, $V2$, $V3$, ... $V80$. The computation time is given by `k*Ts`. The variable `V0` represents a constant input voltage $V0$ which simulates a step input at `k = 1`.

```
L=1; C=1;
A = 0.01;                           // attenuation factor
K = 8000;
N = 80;                             // number of nodes
Ts = .02;                           // time step
t = [0:K]*Ts;
V0 = 1;                             // step input at k = 1
V = zeros(K+1,N);
J = zeros(K+1,N);                   // current flow to earth
for k=1:K
    E = V0 +V(k,2) -2*V(k,1);
    J(k+1,1) = J(k,1) - Ts*A*J(k,1) +(Ts/L)*E;
    V(k+1,1) = V(k,1) - Ts*A*V(k,1) +(Ts/C)*J(k+1,1);
    for n=2:N-1
        E = V(k,n-1)+V(k,n+1)-2*V(k,n);
        J(k+1,n) = J(k,n) - Ts*A*J(k,n) +(Ts/L)*E;
        V(k+1,n) = V(k,n) - Ts*A*V(k,n) +(Ts/C)*J(k+1,n);
    end
    E = V(k,N-1)-V(k,N);
    J(k+1,N) = J(k,N) - Ts*A*J(k,N) +(Ts/L)*E;
    V(k+1,N) = V(k,N) +(Ts/C)*J(k+1,N);
end
```

The ladder network has an open circuit at the end so the last node is given by

$$V79(s) - V80(s) = (R + sL) J80(s)$$
$$J80(s) = (G + sC) V80(s)$$

The step responses of $V35$, $V40$, and $V45$ are shown in Figure 8.4.

We can cross-check these against analytical results. Appendix C.3.3 shows that the transfer function of an infinite distortionless transmission line corresponds to a time delay (x/c), where c is the speed with which the signal travels to a distance x. Any line losses ($A>0$) would attenuate the signal exponentially with distance.

Figure 8.4 shows how the signal is delayed as it travels down the line. The parameter (A) is slightly positive, so there is some attenuation of the voltage wave

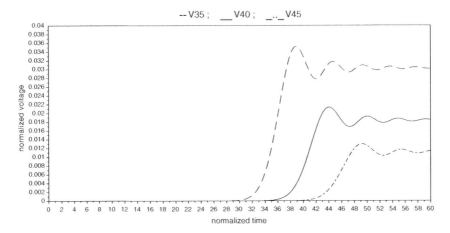

Figure 8.4 Step response of a line with 80 sections.

as it moves from node to node. The computer model produces an unwanted oscillatory response at the frequency $1/\sqrt{LC}$. Figure 8.3 shows that increasing the values of R and G further damps the oscillation but this will give unwanted attenuation of the wave.

It is shown in Appendix C.3.1 that the wave can be reflected at the far end of a finite transmission line, causing it to travel back at the same speed towards the sending end. The wave can be further reflected at the sending end, causing it to travel to and fro between the ends. The model has an open circuit at node 80, which causes such a reflection. If we were to increase the simulation time in Figure 8.4 we would find that the interference between the incoming and the reflected waves grossly aggravates the unwanted oscillation that is caused by the finite element approximation. The reflections at the ends can be reduced by the use of matched terminations.

Appendix C.3.3 shows that the frequency response of an infinite distortionless transmission line corresponds to a transcendental transfer function. One way of determining the transfer function of the finite element computer model is to create its matrix state equation in the form:

$$dV/dt = \underline{A}\,V + \underline{B}\,V0$$

The state matrix ($\underline{A}$) will have 2N by 2N terms, which include 2 by 2 blocks that model elements such as that shown in Figure 8.3, which have resonant peaks at the frequency $1/\sqrt{LC}$. We can create the matrix (A), the vector (B), and define a row vector (C) that selects a chosen node V(k). The state-space system can then be created as sS=syslin('c',A,B,C), and its transfer function is then found by the instruction `ss2tf()`. This will differ significantly from the theoretical solution, since it includes resonant peaks.

We may have demonstrated that it is feasible to create a computer model to simulate one-dimensional wave propagation, but the unwanted oscillation in the responses shown in Figure 8.4 raises serious questions. If we were to divide a given length of line into twice the number of elements, we will halve the values of L and C, which will double the frequency of the oscillation. We may possibly obtain an adequate model if we increase the number of nodes by orders of magnitude, where we would have to reduce the time step accordingly. Due to the imperfections of the present model, we will do no further frequency response calculations.

Over the years engineers and scientists have developed a mature methodology for designing transmission lines by exploiting theoretical results that are based on the telegraphist's equation. Readers can find an introduction to this technology in Cheng (1958) and Jordan (1953).

We will now proceed to more fruitful fields and study a standing wave in a body with finite length.

8.4 State space model of a standing wave in a vibrating system

By plucking the string on a musical instrument we can cause it to vibrate. We will assume that the string is stretched between two points that lie on the X axis, and that the vibrations take place in the XY plane. The deflection (y) of the string from the X axis is then given by a profile $y(x)$. It can be shown that the resulting motion $y(x, t)$ of the string satisfies a one-dimensional wave equation:

$$\partial^2 y/\partial x^2 = \left(1/c^2\right) \partial^2 y/\partial t^2$$

The term $(1/c^2)$ is equal to m/F, where F is the tension in the string, while m is its mass per unit length.

This is the same wave equation that described the behavior of a lossless transmission line, but the present object is significantly different from the system that was simulated in the last section. The reason for this difference is the way in which the string is attached at its ends.

We will model such deflections by a vector with seven elements, whose motions are described by the above differential equations. These can then be written as the following second-order state equation:

$$d^2 \mathbf{Y}/dt^2 = \underline{\mathbf{A}}\,\mathbf{Y}$$

The state matrix is then given by

$$
A = \begin{bmatrix}
-2 & 1 & 0 & 0 & 0 & 0 & 0 \\
1 & -2 & 1 & 0 & 0 & 0 & 0 \\
0 & 1 & -2 & 1 & 0 & 0 & 0 \\
0 & 0 & 1 & -2 & 1 & 0 & 0 \\
0 & 0 & 0 & 1 & -2 & 1 & 0 \\
0 & 0 & 0 & 0 & 1 & -2 & 1 \\
0 & 0 & 0 & 0 & 0 & 1 & -2
\end{bmatrix} / c^2
$$

We can set $c = 1$ and implement the state equation by the following program. Rather than simulating the way in which the string is plucked we will run the program from an initial profile $Y(:,1)$ that forms part of a half-sine wave, between two ends that are held at zero.

```
dt=0.1;
t = 0;
Y(:,1) = sin([1:7]'*%pi/8) // initial profile = y(x, 0)
V(:,1) = zeros(7,1);       // initial velocity profile = 0
for k=1:199
      t(k+1) = t(k) + dt;
      V(:,k+1) = V(:,k) + dt*A*Y(:,k);
      Y(:,k+1) = Y(:,k) + dt*V(:,k+1);
end
```

Figure 8.5 shows the settling of the model from the initial deflection that has the profile of a half sine wave. The left-hand plot shows how this profile maintains its shape as the string vibrates. We can check this result by analysis. Appendix C.2.1 shows how a system that satisfies a one-dimensional wave equation can oscillate with a sinusoidal mode shape. The fundamental vibration mode of a string has nodes at its ends. For a string of length L, the mode shape $\sin(wx/c)$ must satisfy the relationship $w = \pi c/L$.

The frequency of the vibration is shown by the right-hand plot in Figure 8.5. Appendix C.2.1 also shows that the mode oscillates at a frequency w that is determined by the length L. This is not related to the frequency that was observed in Figure 8.4, where the state of the model was free at the one end. The **o** symbols in the right-hand plot of Figure 8.5 indicate the times where the snapshots of the mode shape were taken.

Similar vibrations will occur in the column of air that resonates in an organ pipe, in other wind instruments, or in a concert hall. Vibration analysis is also important in mechanical structures, machinery, aircraft, and other vehicles.

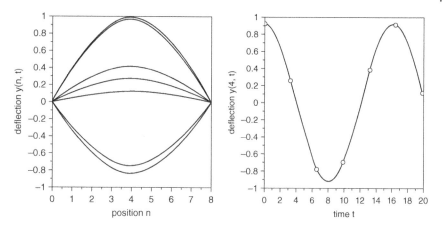

Figure 8.5 Vibration of an elastic string.

8.4.1 State space model of a multiple compound pendulum

The vibration of a string can be compared with the swinging motion of a pendulum, such as that which is shown in Figure 5.4. In both cases the oscillation is caused by a restoring force that pulls the system back towards its rest position. In the case of a pendulum this is the force of gravity while in this case the force is due to the tension in the string. When the string is deflected, the tensile force is rotated to point inwards, so it now has a component that pulls the string back towards the X axis. In practice there will be friction or air resistance that slowly dissipates the kinetic energy within both systems, so the oscillation will settle with time.

The above program can be implemented by means of an X cos model that has the structure shown in Figure 5.7. To simulate a vibrating string the gain block will have the matrix (A) as a parameter while the integrator blocks will be set to the initial conditions $Y(:,1)$ and $V(:,1)$. This illustrates the versatility of the state-equation model. In Section 5.4.1 it is used to model a double pendulum. It can equally well model the multiple compound pendulum that will be considered below. Section 5.4.1 considered the motion of a compound pendulum. This consisted of an upper pendulum that was suspended from a fixed point, while a lower pendulum was suspended from the upper pendulum. Lagrange's equations were used to derive the following second-order matrix equation that modeled the motion of the system:

$$d^2\mathbf{Y}/dt^2 = -\underline{\mathbf{A}}\,\mathbf{Y}$$

The matrix $\underline{\mathbf{A}}$ was a function of the masses and lengths of the two pendulums.

Consider a rope that is suspended from one end. When it is at rest it will hang vertically below its suspension point and when it is disturbed we can define its deviation from the vertical by a profile $Y(z)$, where z is the distance below the suspension point. The motion of the rope is analytically defined by a wave equation:

$$\partial^2 Y / \partial t^2 = g\,(L - z)\,\partial^2 Y / \partial z^2 - g\,\partial Y / \partial z.$$

If the rope is not too rigid, we can approximate its motion by a finite element model that consists of n sections that hang from one another, where each section can be modeled as a pendulum. Such a system can be described by the above matrix equation, where $\underline{\mathbf{A}}$ is an n by n matrix that can be derived by means of Lagrange's equations. We can modify the model defined by Figure 5.7 to simulate the motion of such a rope. The motion of the suspension point can be modeled by a scalar input (u) that feeds into the model through a vector $\mathbf{B}$. The state vector ($\mathbf{Y}$) could now represent the angles that the individual pendulums are deflected from the vertical. The above model can be adapted to simulate the motion of the in-flight refueling line that is released by a tanker aircraft, while other aeronautical applications include models of a tether to tow a glider or other payloads. Such simulations must also include the drag forces that act on the rope and the payload.

Similar finite element models are used to analyze the vibration of complex structures that consist of flexible elastic links that can be described by a stiffness matrix ($\underline{\mathbf{K}}$). Lagrange's equations can then be used to derive a higher-order matrix equation that describes the interaction of the links with the masses within the structure, much in the same way as was described in Section 5.4.4.

8.5 A two-dimensional electromagnetic field

Section 3.4.3 derived a wave equation that determined the evolution of a three-dimensional electromagnetic field. Whereas a one-dimensional scalar field can be represented by a vector with N elements, a two-dimensional field must be represented by a matrix with M by N elements and a three-dimensional field must be represented by a three-dimensional array of L by M by N elements. The complexity of a finite element model that describes the evolution of the field increases rapidly as we increase the number of dimensions. We will not tax the reader by describing the laborious construction of a three-dimensional model, but will rather consider how to reduce the dimensions of the model. In Section 7.2 we were able to reduce a three-dimensional cylindrical thermal field to a one-dimensional model by ignoring the axial and angular distribution. By a similar argument we could reduce the propagation of a radio wave through free space in spherical coordinates, to a one-dimensional model that depends only on the radial distance from a single source.

Our everyday experience tells us that a ray of light travels in a straight line without any deviation on its sides. Newton saw that it is not very easy to understand how this could happen if light is considered as a form of wave motion. However, closer examination has shown that sideways spreading becomes very small and difficult to detect if the width of the ray is much larger than its wavelength. This is fortunate for our sense of vision. Things become different with a diffraction grating, where the distance between the lines is very small and the reflected rays interfere with one another to separate the colors. The classical way of visualizing this interference is to imagine monochromatic light to be emitted from a series of point sources that are equispaced along a line. The wave field is often drawn as a series of circles with different radii, where the spacing between circles represents the wavelength of the light. If such circles are drawn around each source, they generate a series of fairly straight wave fronts that are hidden inside a complex circular pattern. The computer can help to plot the interference pattern in a more understandable way. Consider a row of 21 sources along the X axis spaced one wavelength apart. Each source emits sine waves that spread out radially like ripples in a pond. We can use the following program to simulate the instantaneous field as a function $W(x, y)$:

```
for g=0:20
    for j=1:200
        for k=1:200
            G = g / (2*%pi);
            r = sqrt( y(k)^2 + (x(j)-G)^2 );
            W(j,k) = W(j,k) + 5*sin(2*%pi*r);
        end
    end
end
e = W. *W;
I = abs (W);
```

`I(x,y)` represents the limits to which the electromagnetic oscillation at point (x, y) will go in one time period. Figure 8.6 is an isometric plot of `I (x,y)` for 18 values of y in close proximity to the X axis, where there is significant interference. Each line is a plot of `I (x)` at a fixed value of y. The Y axis proceeds diagonally upward from the bottom left corner, while each "corrugated row" is parallel to the X axis. The sources lie along the bottom of the plot, from $x = 0$ to $x = 20$. The large ripples represent the main beam and show a cyclic variation with a half wavelength of $4\pi \approx 12$ samples.

Since the eye responds to the mean luminous power over time, the program has computed the instantaneous power (e) of the electromagnetic wave at each point. Since we have not computed the time variation of the field, we will have to estimate the mean power by taking the average of the signal (e) over the neighborhood of x, y. Figure 8.7 shows a series of plots of `e (x)` at $y = 0$, 50, 100, 150, and 200 wavelengths. This is a pseudo-isometric projection of `e (x,y)` where seven neighboring values have been superimposed to simulate the variation of luminous intensity with time that would be produced by projecting the beam

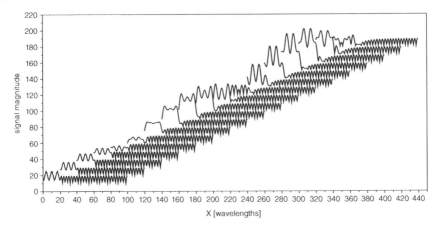

Figure 8.6 Plot of an interference field.

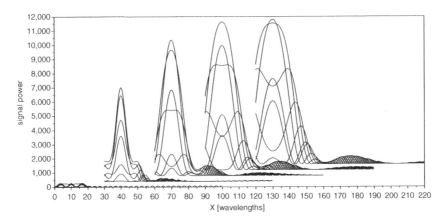

Figure 8.7 Projection on discrete planes.

on a screen that lies in the *XZ* plane at the corresponding value of *y*. These are plotted as functions of *x*, where the plot at the bottom left corresponds to the first seven values shown in Figure 8.6. This example illustrates how a computer can model the main beam of light plus the sidelobes that are produced by a discrete array of sources. It can similarly be applied to model radio waves that are produced by a discrete array of antennas. We see that the pattern becomes more regular as we move out along the *Y* axis. In actual fact, the program did not model the wave propagation; the solution was found analytically while the computer calculated the numbers and did the plotting. This is a good time to note that we could find an analytical solution to the wave equation because it is linear, otherwise we would be forced to simulate the electromagnetic field by means of a finite element model. This would require an enormous amount of computing power. Figures 8.6 and 8.7 are plots of an instantaneous state of the electromagnetic field, which is not a steady state. We cannot really reduce the dimensions of the system by replacing the wave equation with Laplace's equation.

8.6 A two-dimensional potential flow model

We will now return to Section 3.5.1 that described a study that was done by Lord Rayleigh to explain how aerodynamic lift is produced on a spinning body. We will apply the mathematical properties of flow fields to analyze two-dimensional steady flow at right angles to an infinitely long cylinder. The flow can be described in cylindrical coordinates (r and θ). It is possible to create an analytical model of incompressible and irrotational aerodynamic flow by using the potential function $P(r, \theta)$ that was introduced in Section 3.5.1. We can then write Laplace's equation as follows:

$$(1/r)\partial P/\partial r + \partial^2 P/\partial r^2 + (1/r^2)\partial^2 P/\partial\theta^2 = 0$$

Appendix C.4 showed how to find a harmonic solution to this equation. We will consider a single mode shape, which varies radially as $R(r)$ and tangentially as $S(\theta)$. The functions $R(r)$ and $S(\theta)$ are again given by separate ordinary differential equations. We have:

$$d^2 S/d\theta^2 = -c\, S(\theta)$$

Since we can assume that the far upstream and downstream flows are the same, this implies that $c = 1$ and therefore the solution of the equation is

$$S(\theta) = \cos(\theta)$$

The differential equation for $R(r)$ then becomes

$$r(dR/dr) + r^2(d^2 R/dr^2) = R(r)$$

which has the following solution:

$$R(r) = r + (a^2/r)$$

We can show this by substituting the derivatives of $R(r)$ back into the differential equation.

The streamlines follow the gradient of the potential function, so we can take partial derivatives in order to find algebraic expressions for the radial and tangential velocities of the flow:

$$Vr = \partial P/\partial r = Vo\, S(\theta)\, dR/dr = -Vo\, \cos(\theta)\left[1 - (a/r)^2\right]$$

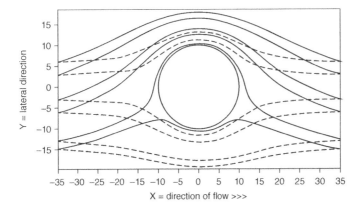

Figure 8.8 Potential flow around a cylinder, without and with circulation.

$$V\theta = - (Vo/r)\,\partial P/\partial\theta = - Vo\,[R(r)/r]\,dS/d\theta = Vo\,\sin(\theta)\left[1 + (a/r)^2\right]$$

The following program uses these expressions to plot the streamlines that are shown as dashed curves in Figure 8.8:

```
a = 10;
dx=0.1;
X = -35:dx:35;
for k=1:K
    t = atan(Y(k),X(k));
    r = sqrt(X(k)^2+Y(k)^2);
    Vr = - cos(t) * (1-(a/r)^2);
    Vt =   sin(t)*(1+(a/r)^2);
    Vx = (Vr*cos(t)) - (Vt*sin(t));
    Vy = (Vr*sin(t)) + (Vt*cos(t));
    dy = dx*Vy/Vx;
    Y(k+1) = Y(k) + dy;
end
```

The program commences at $X(1) = -35$, while the value of $X(k)$ is then stepped in fixed increments (dx) of 0.1 unit until it reaches the right-hand edge of the figure, at $X(1) = +35$. This could be done since the velocity vector always has a positive component in the X direction. Particular streamlines could be generated by starting $Y(1)$ from various chosen values. The streamlines are generated by a technique that can be compared with the method of isoclines that was used in Section 5.3.1 to generate trajectories that describe the motion of a pendulum. The current Cartesian coordinates of a streamline, X(k) and Y (k), are converted into cylindrical coordinates (r and t). The above algebraic expressions for the radial and tangential velocities are then used to compute Vr and Vt, while these allow us to compute the horizontal and vertical velocities (Vx and Vy). The slope of the streamline (Vy/Vx) is then used to determine the increment (dy) corresponding to the fixed increment (dx). The streamline is then advanced from the point [X(k), Y(k)] by an increment (dx, dy). The step length (dx) must be made small enough to limit truncation errors. The program also becomes unstable when the streamline is too close to the surface of the cylinder.

Van Dyke (1982) and von Karman (1954) show images of similar flow patterns around a cylindrical body, which were produced in water tunnels, wind tunnels, and tests with viscous flow. These do not truly validate the potential flow model used here, but they do give us confidence that it may be used as a conceptual tool. We could equally well use a potential flow model to simulate the effect of a moving cylinder in stationary air. We see that the flow pattern has both horizontal and vertical symmetry about a circle that is drawn as a solid line. This has a radius of 10 units, as determined by the parameter (a). The chosen potential function gives a flow field with streamlines that follow the surface of a cylindrical body, represented by this circle.

The radial velocity is thus zero on the surface of the body. The dynamic pressure on the surface of the cylinder is thus proportional to $V\theta$ squared. Since $\sin(\theta) = \sin(\theta + \pi)$, the forces on opposite sides of the cylinder are equal, and so the air resistance is zero. This confirms the result obtained by d'Alembert.

We can simulate the effect of a spinning cylinder by superimposing a clockwise circulatory motion on the above flow pattern. Such circulatory motion can be defined by a potential function of the form:

$$Q(\theta) = G\theta$$

The relation $\mathbf{V} = \mathbf{gradp}(Q)$, defined in Appendix C.4.3, then corresponds to the following tangential velocity at the radius r:

$$T(r) = (1/r)\, dQ/d\theta = G/r$$

The mass of a ring of fluid at radius (r) is proportional to $2\pi r$ and thus the circulatory momentum of such a ring of fluid is the same at all radii. The constant (G) can be chosen so that G/a corresponds to a desired tangential velocity at the surface of the cylinder.

Consider the flow field produced by the following potential function:

$$P + Q = V_0 \cos(\theta)\left(r + [a^2/r]\right) + G\theta$$

The radial flow field is the same as before, but the tangential velocity at a point (r, θ) is now given by

$$V\theta = -(1/r)(\partial P/\partial\theta + dQ/d\theta) = V_0 \sin(\theta)\left[1 + (a/r)^2\right] + (G/r)$$

This circulatory motion is superimposed in the above program by modifying the variable Vt, which is now calculated as follows:

```
Vt = (sin(t)*(1+(a/r)^2)) + (G/r);
```

This produces the streamlines shown as solid curves in Figure 8.8. Aerodynamicists refer to this pattern as "circulatory flow" although none of the streamlines actually encircle the cylinder. Rebuffet (1962) shows an image of a similar flow pattern that was experimentally produced by rotating a cylinder in a uniform flow field. It may be supposed that the friction on the surface of the rotating cylinder drags the fluid behind, and thereby superimposes circulatory flow on the fluid. The superimposed circulatory motion causes some of the streamlines that would have passed below the cylinder to bend upwards and flow over the top, after which they bend downwards to reach their original level. As a result, the streamlines are "bunched up" above the upper surface of the cylinder and rarified below it. The mass flow rate per unit area is thus greater in the region above the upper surface, so the velocity of flow must increase, while the velocity below the cylinder must decrease. The dynamic pressure (q) above the cylinder thus decreases while it increases on the lower surface. There is a resulting upward force on the rotating cylinder, known as the Magnus effect. This confirms the result that was obtained by Rayleigh, while the existence of this force was proved practically by Flettner. The use of the model as a conceptual tool is thus amply justified.

Rebuffet (1962), Van Dyke (1982), and von Karman (1954) show images of analogous flow patterns around airfoils, where the shape of the streamlines are distorted to follow the surface of the particular wing profile. These shapes can be approximated by potential flow fields with multiple terms such as those used in the above program. The coefficients of such elements can then be varied to more or less match the wing profile. The pressure profile on the upper and lower surface of the wing can then be computed, whence the lift can be estimated.

Many years have been spent by a veritable army of engineers, technicians, scientists, and mathematicians who have used the results of wind tunnel tests and theoretical analysis to create such computer models. The books that appear in the bibliography at the end of this chapter give extensive references to literature on the subject. Flow visualization is a specialized field in itself, that makes use of wind tunnels, water tunnels, and other setups. There are extensive images of flow patterns that have been produced around various wing profiles. As explained in the literature, there are many other side effects that may cause significant deviations from potential flow.

The creation of "circulatory flow" around a non-rotating wing can be roughly explained as follows. We would expect a pressure difference between the lower and upper surfaces to cause an upward flow of air at the back of the wing. However, the inertia of the air causes it to be left behind the moving wing, so this upward flow causes a free vortex in its wake. Since angular momentum must be conserved, there must be circulatory flow attached to the wing. We reiterate that no streamlines actually encircle the wing.

We can visualize this effect by dragging our hand through still water. After some experimentation with the angle that the hand is held, we will be able to create a small whirlpool on the surface of the water that continues to rotate after the hand is removed.

8.7 Discussion

The challenges that appeared in Chapter 7 have become more pronounced in this chapter. The finite element model that is used to simulate a linear one-dimensional wave equation requires a number of sections that exceed those used in Chapter 7 by orders of magnitude. Whereas we encountered some difficulty with end effects in the model of a diffusion process, the end effects in the model of a transmission line gives critical problems due to the phenomenon of wave reflection. These problems disappeared when we modeled a standing wave in a vibrating system where the ends were held fixed. The results were then confirmed by harmonic analysis. This model can be adapted to study other one-dimensional physical systems that are governed by the wave equation, and can also include nonlinear effects and an inhomogeneous medium.

The chapter then went on to show how two-dimensional systems could be studied by using a combination of mathematical analysis and computation. The phenomenon of diffraction was visualized in two dimensions by modeling a monochromatic electromagnetic wave that radiates from a point source to produce a series of spherical wavefronts. The computer modeled the two-dimensional field as concentric circles radiating from multiple sources, and produced a plot of an instantaneous electromagnetic field that is shown in Figure 8.6. This model can also be applied in the engineering design of phased array radio antennas.

A two-dimensional aerodynamic flow field was modeled by the scalar potential function that was mathematically derived in Chapter 3. The computer could then generate the streamlines of a flow pattern by following the gradient of the potential function.

The creation of a three-dimensional field was avoided because of the sheer volume of work that this would entail. Two-dimensional models have given us considerable insight as to how waves propagate by spreading energy into the surrounding area. In a three-dimensional medium this process would give different numbers, but the basic principle is likely to remain the same. The models were also limited to linear processes because we could use the mathematical tools to check the results. Although these models were based on questionable approximations, they were good examples of the following sentiment:

"The purpose of computing is insight, not numbers"

R.W. Hamming (1962)

Exercises

Readers can create their models on the platform of their choice, where the chosen platform will include its own operating and plotting tools.

1   Modify the program shown in Section 8.3 to simulate a single transmission line segment such as that shown in Figure 8.3. Use constant input voltages V2 and V4 and compute the voltage V3 and the current J3 as vectors V3(k) and J3(k).
    Plot the evolution of V3 (k) and J3 (k) from the initial condition V3 (1) = 0 and J3 (1) = 0.
    Experiment with various inputs V2 and V4, and various values of the attenuation factor (A).
    Draw a block diagram that shows how J3 (k+1) and V3 (k+1) are calculated from J3 (k), V3 (k), V2, and V4.
    Use a Z-transfer function block $[z^{-1}]$ to represent a delay of Ts.
    For example, such a block can have an input V3 (k+1) and an output V3 (k).
    Redraw the block diagram with discrete integrators that have the Z-transfer functions:

$$1/[z-1]$$

   Compare the result with Figure 8.3.

2   Add a second segment to the program that you created in the previous exercise. This computes the voltage V4 (k) and J4 (k) from V3 (k) and a constant input voltage (V5).
    Plot the evolution of V3 (k) and V4 (k), J3 (k), and J4 (k) from the initial conditions.

   V3 (1) =V4 (1) =0 and J3 (1) =J4 (1) =0 .

   Experiment with various inputs and parameters, and compare the results with the previous exercise.

3 Create the transmission line program shown in Section 8.3 and plot the step responses of V40 ... V50 to an input V0. Experiment with different values of *A* and different numbers of elements.

4 The transfer function of an infinite lossless transmission line is exp(−*sT*), which corresponds to a time delay of *T* seconds.
 Appendix A.7 simulates this by a first-order Padé approximation

$$(1 - sT/2)/(1 + sT/2)$$

Create a delay line by connecting several Padé elements in series and plot its step response.
 The Z-transfer function block $[z^{-1}]$ that represents a discrete delay element is programmed by the following difference equation:

```
x(k+1, n)  =  x(k, n-1)
```

Create a program that includes several discrete delay elements and plot its step response.
 What is the salient difference between these two structures and a transmission line?
 What physical processes can be simulated by them?
 What physical processes can be usefully simulated by finite element wave equation models?

5 Create a finite element model of a transmission line using transfer function blocks to satisfy the following equations:

$$V1(s) = H(s)\,[V0(s) + V2(s)]$$
$$V2(s) = H(s)\,[V1(s) + V3(s)]$$
$$V3(s) = H(s)\,[V2(s) + V4(s)]$$
$$V4(s) = H(s)\,[V3(s) + V5(s)]$$
$$V5(s) = G(s)\,V4(s)$$

The transfer function *H*(*s*) can be derived from Figure 8.3, while its parameters can be taken from the program shown in Section 8.3. The voltage *V*0 is fed into the model from an inport, while the voltage *V*5 goes to an outport. The transfer function *G*(*s*) is given by the equations:

$$V4(s) - V5(s) = (R + sL)\,J5(s)$$
$$J5(s) = (G + sC)\,V5(s)$$

If the model is created in Simulink as a file `fem.mdl` or in Scilab as a file `fem.zcos` you can use the function `linmod()` to import it into the applicable workspace.

Plot its frequency response using the procedure given in Sections 6.3.2 to 6.3.4 for Scilab and Section 10.4.1 for MATLAB. Compare this with the oscillatory step response shown in Figure 8.4.

Now compare it with the frequency response $G\exp(-j\omega T)$ of an infinite distortionless transmission line, whose phase lag varies linearly with frequency while its attenuation is the same at all frequencies.

Plot the frequency responses of $V1$, $V2$, $V3$, and $V4$ to see how the finite element model affects the frequency components of the signal as it is transmitted through the segments.

6 Create the standing wave program shown in Section 8.4 and plot the resulting vibration.

The state vector (Y) does not include the ends of the string, $Y0$ and $Y8$, which are held at zero.

Change the initial profile $Y(:,1)$ to the third harmonic and plot the vibration mode.

Create a model similar to that in Exercise 5, using seven transfer function blocks, where the first block includes $Y0$ as an input and the seventh block includes an input $Y8$.

7 The interference effect between electromagnetic waves can also be described by drawing a series of concentric circles to represent the individual wavefronts that emanate from each of the sources.

Draw this geometric construction where the spacing between the circles equals the wavelength of the radiation. Then draw lines that are tangential to a set of these circles.

These represent wavefronts produced by the diffraction effect.

This can be done at various angles that are given by the wavelength of the radiation and the distance between the sources, see Bragg (1933).

8 Create the potential flow program described in Section 8.6 and plot the streamlines without and with circulatory motion.

Try modifying the flow pattern by adding a second vortex behind the first. Reduce the strength of the vortices by about a third and separate them by about 20 units.

Experiment with the Y position of the second vortex.

A similar technique is used by aerodynamicists to estimate the lift force on an aircraft wing.

Bibliography

Bragg, S.W. (1933). *The Universe of Light*. London: G. Bell & Sons.

Cheng, D.K. (1958). *Analysis of Linear Systems*. Reading: Addison-Wesley.

Davis, H.F. (1967). *Introduction to Vector Analysis*. Boston: Allyn and Bacon.

Jordan, E.C. (1953). *Electromagnetic Waves and Radiating Systems*. London: Constable.

Maxwell, J.C. (1888). *An Elementary Treatise on Electricity*, 2e. Clarendon Press: Oxford.

Rebuffet, P. (1962). *Aérodynamique Expérimentale*. Paris: Librairie Polytechnique Ch. Béranger.

Starkey, B.J. (1958). *Laplace Transforms for Electrical Engineers*. London: Iliffe & Sons.

Van Dyke, M. (1982). *An Album of Fluid Motion*. Stanford: The Parabolic Press.

von Karman, T. (1954). *Aerodynamics*. New York: McGraw-Hill.

9

Uncertainty and softer science

We will now discuss challenges of a different nature. How do we create a computer model that describes a badly defined phenomenon?

> "If all economists were laid end to end, they would not reach a conclusion."
> George Bernard Shaw
> (*Source:* In the Public Domain)

Many of the so-called softer sciences must rely on expert opinion that is based on contradictory data. The challenge is to draw conclusions from such confusing information.

9.1   Introduction

The previous chapters illustrate the creation of computer models that describe physical objects with increasing complexity. Later examples presented us with significant challenges that we overcame by making some questionable approximations. This reduced our confidence in the computed results, which we sought to mitigate by supplementing our models with mathematical analysis. This chapter will introduce us to further sources of uncertainty.

Section 9.2 will consider the perplexing problem that arises when we wish to create a computer model of a physical object without making full use of its underlying physics. The first example illustrates the case where we have imperfect knowledge of its microscopic behavior, while the second example considers the extreme case where we have no information that can be used to derive equations that model the behavior of a plant. We then treat the plant as a "black box," where we characterize its dynamic behavior by its response to an input signal. We then go further and show the use of test signals to identify such an impulse response.

Computer Models of Process Dynamics: From Newton to Energy Fields, First Edition.
Olis Rubin.
© 2023 The Institute of Electrical and Electronics Engineers, Inc.
Published 2023 by John Wiley & Sons, Inc.

Section 9.3 will then address the computer modeling of random behavior. It firstly discusses the creation of a random variable using a machine that is by nature precise. It then goes on to show how a computer can be used to estimate the mean and variance of a batch of random numbers and how to find an algebraic model that best fits the data. This leads on to techniques for estimating the state of a given system from external measurements that are contaminated by noise.

Section 9.4 goes on to consider some softer sciences, where it pays some attention to a business model. In economic science the emphasis is on data collection and statistical analysis. The physical outcome of any action is generally so influenced by environmental factors beyond our control, and outside our scope, that it is easy to gain an impression that the process behaves in an entirely random manner.

The next study is concerned with digital images from a surveillance camera, where it is wished to determine whether a human is present. The problem involves yet another type of uncertainty, where we wish to recognize a pattern that characterizes a human, but we do not as yet possess a template that performs this function.

9.2   Empirical and "black box" models

"As far as the laws of mathematics refer to reality, they are not certain, and as far as they are certain, they do not refer to reality"

Albert Einstein
(*Source:* Rights Managed)

We often strive to advance the credibility of a model by stating that it is "based on the laws of physics." We have already hinted at the fallacy that accompanies this statement. Thus Chapter 5 presented models that were based on Newton's laws of motion while Chapter 3 discussed the validity of Newton's axioms. As shown above, Einstein was well aware that physics is composed of questionable theories. Chapters 7 and 8 started to raise doubts as to whether we can adequately model all physical phenomena. Whereas conventional aerodynamics approximates the lift forces on an aircraft by a continuous pressure field, the kinetic theory of gases models this by the random collisions of billions of atoms. Thermodynamics similarly approximates the kinetic energy of billions of atoms by a continuous temperature field. By similar arguments, Newton made a gross approximation when he modeled the mass of a body as a single quantity that exists at its center of gravity. The point kinetic model of a nuclear reactor involves a similar simplification, where a cloud of randomly moving neutrons is modeled by a single number that effectively exists at a point. These types of assumptions basically rely on the law of averages, which we believe to become more accurate when we deal with very large numbers. The next section illustrates how we meet a significant challenge when we strive to apply the law of averages in order to create a model which describes the physical behavior of a fairly common object.

9.2.1 An imperfect model of a simple physical object

Consider a coil consisting of a number of turns (N) that are wound around a soft iron core. If we pass an electric current (i) through the coil, this will create a magnetomotive force $F = N i$ that produces a magnetic flux, most of which will pass through the core. We can model the behavior of the core by assuming that the microscopic structure of the iron is composed of magnetic areas called domains. One possibility is to model these domains as a finite matrix of magnetic elements. When the iron is in a pristine condition the domains are all "jumbled up," so the material shows no sign of being magnetic. When we pass a current through the coil, the magnetomotive force will cause the domains to align themselves with the magnetic field. This occurs in much the same way as iron filings would align themselves around a magnet. We can attempt to simplify this microscopic effect by considering a point kinetic model where the alignment of the domains is represented by the total magnetic flux (ϕ) through the iron. The slope ($d\phi/dF$) is initially quite small, possibly because the domains are initially so randomly aligned that it takes a relatively large magnetomotive force to produce a significant change in flux. The change in magnetic flux that is caused by passing an electric current through the coil can similarly be expressed as the following slope:

$$d\phi/di = N\, d\phi/dF$$

As the current through the coil is increased the slope becomes larger. It seems as if the domains are acting like small magnets that exert a pull on one another, so that they are aiding the magnetic field to pull them in line. A model of the physical process will have to include the interactions that pull the domains in and out of line and the "friction force" that resists their "rotation."

As we continue increasing the current through the coil, the domains will eventually be fully aligned and the flux will then saturate. If the current is now reduced, the magnetic pull of the domains continues to hold them in alignment and the slope as the current reduces is smaller than it was when the current was increasing. This phenomenon is known as hysteresis. A plot of flux versus current will thus take the form of a loop. We can express this by defining $\phi(i)$ to denote the flux when the current is increasing while $\Phi(i)$ denotes the flux when the current is decreasing, where $\Phi(i)$ is larger than $\phi(i)$ at the same current. The behavior of the iron is even more complicated than this. If di/dt is reversed before the flux saturates, the resulting hysteresis loop will be smaller. There are in fact a multiplicity of hysteresis loops that depend on the way in which the current varied with time. We will need a very complex computer model if we wish to reproduce this behavior. The magnetic flux will be a nonlinear function of the electric current, but this function must also include memory. If we wish to create a computer simulation of this function, we may decide to include a large finite element model that simulates the magnetic domains.

We now come to the electrical behavior of the coil. Faraday's induction law implies that a change in flux produces a voltage:

$$e = N\,(d\phi/dt) = N\,(d\phi/di)\,di/dt$$

For the moment let us write the above equation as

$$e = L(\phi, di/dt)\,di/dt$$

where $L(\phi, di/dt)$ is analogous to an inductance.

Now suppose that a voltage source (v) is connected to a circuit that includes a resistance (R) in series with the coil. The growth in current is then given by the following differential equation:

$$L(\phi, di/dt)\,di/dt + R\,i = v$$

However, we must remember that $L(\phi, di/dt)$ is a function of both ϕ and the way in which the current varied with time. If we wish to create a computer simulation of this differential equation, we may decide to include a large finite element model that simulates the interactions that pull the domains in and out of line and the "friction force" that resists their "rotation." It is perhaps surprising that such a "simple" physical device could have introduced so much uncertainty in the creation of the model.

9.2.2 Finite impulse response models

There are plants, particularly in the process control industry, that are difficult to describe by proven mathematical equations. This presents us with another form of uncertainty if we wish to model a plant under these challenging circumstances. One solution may be to reduce the model to an exercise in data processing. We can then model the plant by operating on its input signals u (k), which are sampled at the instant $t = k*Ts$, to calculate its output y (k). We start by using the following computer program to collect the input data stream u (k) into a vector (X) of length n:

```
for k=1:K    // K determines the duration of the simulation
    for m=n:-1:2
        X(m)  =  X(m-1);
    end
    X(1)  =  u(k);
end
```

At each cycle the outer `for` loop stores the last n samples `u(k)` in the vector:

```
X = [u(k) u(k-1) ... u(k-n)]
```

Such programs have been used to simulate pure transport delays. In the case of a conveyor belt, u would be used to represent the quantity of material that is being loaded onto the one end of the belt, while `X(n)` represents the quantity of material arriving at the other end. The vector X represents the profile of the material that lies on the belt at any sample instant.

Suppose that X is initially empty and a quantity `u(1)` is loaded at the first cycle (`k=1`). If there are no further inputs `u(k)`, after this the output `X(n)` would remain at zero for n-1 cycles and jump to `u(1)` at the nth cycle, and then go back to zero for the remaining cycles. This sequence represents the impulse response of the discrete model.

We also see that an intermediate element `X(m)` would jump to `u(1)` at the mth cycle while remaining at zero at all other times. This observation leads us to consider using the above program to model the impulse response of a more general plant by taking the weighted sum of the elements `X(m)` each time the vector X is updated. This can be done by adding a further statement just before the end of the outer `for` loop:

```
y(k+1) = sum(H.*X);
```

where H is a vector `[H(1) H(2) ...H(n)]`. The output `y(n)` would respond to the single input `u(1)` as follows:

```
y(1) = 0
y(2) = H(1)*u(1)
y(3) = H(2)*u(1)
...
y(n) = H(n)*u(1)
y(n+1) = 0 ...
```

The vector H thus represents the response of the model to an impulse. It is limited to a finite interval of n cycles and is commonly known as a finite impulse response.

An arbitrary input signal `u(k)` can be built up as a string of such impulses. If we neglect initial conditions, the output of the model is given by the following convolution sum (Tou, 1959):

```
y(k+1) = sum(H.*X);
       = H(1)*u(k) + H(2)*u(k-1) + H(3)*u(k-2) + ...
```

There are some conditions that must be satisfied before we can use this approach to model a plant. The plant behavior must be reasonably linear and time invariant.

It must also settle to a stable steady state within the finite interval of n cycles. We assume that the input u (k) is zero for all negative time, so that the initial state of X can be set to zeros (1, n).

Before we can model a plant in this way, we need to determine its finite impulse response. Instead of measuring its response to a large pulse, we can use a pseudo-random binary sequence as a test signal. The generation of such signals is discussed in Section 2.4.1. It is shown there that the signal is spread over time, but can then be "gathered into a pulse" by cross-correlation. This technique has the advantage that we may possibly test a plant under operational conditions with a low-level signal that persists over a longer time and then extract its response by cross-correlation.

An example of such a signal, which switches between the values +1 and -1 is shown in the top plot of Figure 2.1. We can regard it as defining a series of discrete pulses: s (1), s (2), s (3). We can then sample the resulting output of the plant to obtain a corresponding series of discrete values: q (1), q (2), q (3). If the plant is reasonably linear and time invariant, its response can be approximated by

$$q(k) = P(1)*s(k) +P(2)*s(k-1) \ldots + P(n)*s(k-n) \ldots$$

Now consider the cross-correlation C (n) between q (k) and the delayed signal s (k-n). This is given by the mean value of

$$P(1)*s(k)*s(k-n) +P(2)*s(k-1)*s(k-n) \ldots +P(n)*s(k-n)*s(k-n) \ldots$$

Section 2.4.1 shows that the product s (k-n) *s (k-n) is equal to a constant (1) at all times, while the other products, s (k) *s (k-n), are signals that switch between +1 and -1, and have mean values equal to -1/255. The cross-correlation C (n) is thus approximately equal to P (n) with a reasonably small error.

We can thus estimate the impulse response of the plant by cross-correlating its output (q) with a bank of pseudorandom signals that can be generated as shown in Section 2.4.1. If the plant is perturbed by external disturbances or the output sensor is contaminated by noise, the resulting effects will generally be suppressed by the cross-correlation.

9.3 Randomness within computer models

Human affairs are beset with random events. Financial forecasters and economists practice their professions with great trepidation. In these situations, randomness is somewhat synonymous with unpredictability.

When throwing dice, we think that we are producing random integers between one and six, where there is an equal probability that their values are any one of these six numbers. We are thus describing their amplitude distribution to be uniform.

Appendix D gives an introduction to the laws of chance and the subject of statistical analysis. This represents an attempt to take the randomness out of unpredictable phenomena. Whereas it may be of interest to insurance companies that the average lifetime of a given population group is Y years, this is not quite so reassuring to spouses of individuals within this group.

An aircraft that flies through turbulence, a vehicle that travels over rough terrain, or a ship at sea are all subjected to random forces. These forces are possibly unpredictable, but we have found means to describe their power spectra. In Chapter 10 we will describe the simulation of a system that undergoes random disturbances, where we can record the applicable random data and read it into the simulation workspace.

When we create a computer model to simulate a "random" variable we would generally like a small sample to represent the characteristics of a large population. We can then use it to test the performance of a system in a random environment with some confidence that it may perform as well in the real world. Once we have created the model, we can no longer say that it is really unpredictable. All we have to do is to run the model, and we will know what the "random" variable is going to do! With these cautionary thoughts we will go on to describe some programs that may be described as "random."

9.3.1 Random number generators and data analysis

We will first go back to the binary machine described in Section 2.4.1. This was used to produce a sequence $x(k)$ that switched between $+1$ and -1. This was "pseudorandom" in the sense that the correlation between $x(k)$ and its future value, $x(k + n)$ was very small. The sequence was cyclic, but its period could easily be made so large that it would not repeat in a simulation study. We then showed that this property could be exploited in several ways.

There are other simple systems that can behave in a "chaotic" manner. For example, consider the following program:

```
for k = 1:K
    x(k+1) = (1-R)*x(k) + R*x(k)^2;
end
```

If R is small, $x(k)$ behaves quite regularly, but at $R = 3$ and above, the behavior is "chaotic."

The Scilab function `rand()` generates "uniform random" numbers using a method described in Malcolm and Molar (1973). The following program uses this method to produce "random" numbers:

```
x = 1253476594;
a = 843314861;
```

```
C = 453816693;
for k=1:K
    x(k+1) = modulo(a*x(k)+c, 2^31)
end
```

The Scilab function `x=modulo(N,D)` generates the remainder (x) of a modulo D division (N/D) of the integers N and D. The variable (x) is fairly uniformly distributed between zero and 2e9. We can subtract the mean value to center it about zero, and change its amplitude by a multiplication factor. We can then produce an approximately Gaussian distribution as follows:

```
for h=12:12:K
    g(h/12) = sum(x(h-11:h))/12;
end
```

We can also import physical measurements that are contaminated by noise into a computer. Suppose that such a variable has been sampled and stored in a vector (v). The following MATLAB or Scilab functions will compute its mean value and variance:

```
meanV = sum(V) / max(size(V))
x = V - meanV;
varx = sum(x^2) / max(size(x))
sigma = sqrt(varx)
```

We may also remove "outliers" greater than 3 sigma (standard deviations):

```
iOut = find( abs(x)>3*sigma );
x(iOut) = [];
```

and use the Scilab function `histplot(n,x)` to plot a histogram of the data (x).

9.3.2 Statistical estimation and the method of least squares

Suppose that we have taken several measurements of a physical constant, but found to our dismay that they differed from one another. We could model the situation by assuming that the ith measurement is given by

```
yi = C + ni
```

where C is the true value of the constant while ni is an error that is introduced by the measuring instruments. If we have taken n measurements we can hopefully combine them to obtain an estimate of C that is closer to the true value. If we assume that the measuring instruments are unbiased, and we have equal confidence in each measurement, we can regard the errors (ni) to behave like a random variable with zero mean value.

One way of estimating C from the measurements y1, y2, ...yn is known as the method of *least-squares*, where an estimate D is found that minimizes the following function:

```
S(D)  =  (y1-D)^2 + (y2-D)^2 + ...(yn-D)^2
```

This is given by dS/dD = 0, where

```
dS/dD  =  2*(y1-D) + 2*(y2-D) + ... 2*(yn-D)
```

The least-squares estimate thus corresponds to the mean value of the measurements.

The least-squares approach can also be used to fit an algebraic model that describes the relationship between two variables. This can be illustrated by the following example. Suppose that two variables have been sampled and stored as the column vectors U and V shown in Table 9.1, where we believe that the values of the variable V(k) depend on the values of the variable U(k).

Suppose that we normalize U by creating a column vector x that has zero mean value:

```
x = U - meanU;
```

and we wish to model the dependence of V(k) on x(k) as an algebraic function.

Table 9.1 Data and analysis.

U	V	x	Y
0	41.49	-6.7083	41.5900
0.5	43.07	-6.2083	42.9648
1.	44.	-5.7083	44.2652
2.	46.61	-4.7083	46.6519
3.	49.09	-3.7083	48.7691
4.	51.05	-2.7083	50.6354
5.	52.1	-1.7083	52.2699
8.	55.81	1.29167	55.9695
11.	57.38	4.29167	58.2588
13.	60.09	6.29167	59.2522
15.	60.09	8.29167	59.9949
18.	60.81	11.2917	60.9684

Since there may be noise on the measurements, we will use the method of least-squares to find an algebraic function that approximates the data. For example, we can find a third-order polynomial that has the following form:

```
Y(k) = C(1) + C(2)*x(k) + C(3)*x(k)^2 + C(4)*x(k)^3
```

where the coefficients C(k) minimize the variance = sum((Y-V).^2). We will examine a procedure to estimate these coefficients.

First compute a matrix (X) whose elements X(k,n) are the powers x(k)^n:

```
X = ones(x);
for n=1:3
    X = [X,x.^n];
end
```

Then compute the matrix product:

```
Cxv = X'*V;
```

This is a column vector with the following components:

```
Cxv(1) = sum(V)
Cxv(2) is the cross-correlation between V(k) and x(k)
Cxv(3) is the cross-correlation between V(k) and x(k)^2
Cxv(4) is the cross-correlation between V(k) and x(k)^3
```

Now compute a matrix (IXX) that is the pseudoinverse of X'*X:

```
XX = X'*X;
IXX = inv(XX)
=    0.266743    -0.006047    -0.006743     0.000432
    -0.006047     0.012549     0.000835    -0.000193
    -0.006744     0.000835     0.000286    -0.000027
     0.000432    -0.000193    -0.000027     0.000004
```

We can then compute the matrix product:

```
C = IXX*Cxv
=    54.579211
      1.1880432
     -0.0905058
      0.0031352
```

The elements of C are the coefficients C(k) of the above third-order polynomial. We can then compute the least-squares fit to the data (V and U) by the instruction:

```
Y = X*C
```

This is a column vector whose *k*th component is

```
Y(k) = C(1) + C(2)*X(k) + C(3)*X(k)^2 + C(4)*X(k)^3
```

The output `Y(k)` of the polynomial model is shown together with `V(k)` in Table 9.1. The residual error (V-Y) has zero mean and a variance = 0.16.

We can combine this into a "hat matrix" (H) and compute Y by a single operation:

```
H=X*IXX*X';
Y = H*V;
```

9.3.3 A state estimator

Appendix D.4 relates how Gauss estimated the orbit of a planetoid from somewhat imprecise astronomical observations. In the process of doing so he developed a technique called the method of least squares, which was used in the previous section to find an algebraic function that modeled the relationship between a batch of observations (V) and a variable (U). This section extends these ideas, to estimate the state of a dynamic system from an input signal that consists of noisy measurements. It uses a model of the actual system to predict its future motion and then uses the measurements to correct the predictions. The resulting structure behaves like a filter that is related to the frequency response of the physical system. This is based on the premise that most of the measurement noise is in a frequency band that is higher than the bandwidth of the physical system. There is a compromise between removing the noise and tracking the desired signal. The noise in the measurement is not completely removed while the estimated state lags the actual state. This device, which is known as a Kalman filter, differs from the batch process described in the previous section in that the state estimate is revised recursively, each time that a new measurement is available.

We will use a simple example to illustrate the process. Consider a radar which scans the vicinity for possible aircraft. It has an antenna that rotates through 360 degrees every two seconds. Since the radar echos are embedded within clutter, we need a filter to extract aircraft position from the noise. We will simulate its performance in a tracking test where an aircraft is flying in a circle around the radar at a radial distance of 5 km. At each scan of the antenna the radar will receive an echo from the aircraft and can compute its position from the measured bearing and range. Suppose that the radar is at the center of an XY plane while the motion of the aircraft is simulated as follows:

```
X = 5*[cos(k*Ts*w); sin(k*Ts*w)];
```

The two-dimensional vector (X) represents the position of the aircraft that is sampled at the period `Ts` = 2 seconds, where `k*Ts` is a vector of sample instants while `w` determines the time to fly a full circle.

The flight path of the simulated aircraft is shown in Figure 9.1 by the * symbols that indicate the position given by the radar echos. Its speed is 125 m s^{-1}, while its turning radius is 5 km. It is thus flying with a constant centripetal acceleration, unknown to the filter, of 3.125 m s^{-2}. It flies through a simulated clutter band to the west of the radar, where the * symbols deviate from the circular path.

The burst of clutter is simulated as a burst of noise which is created by the following Scilab instructions:

```
rand("seed",5369);
noise = zeros(2,100);
noise(1,60:68) = noise(1,60:68) + rand(1,8+1,'normal')*.5;
```

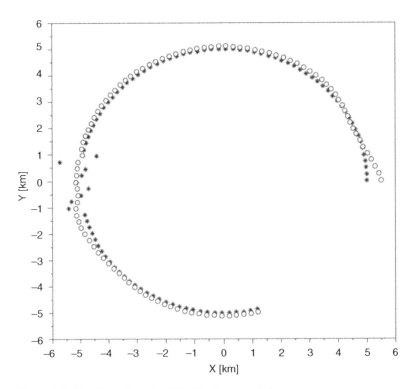

Figure 9.1 Tracking of an aircraft in the horizontal plane.

The radar echo is corrupted by the clutter, which affects the computed position of the aircraft, and is simulated as a noisy measurement that is the input to the state estimator:

```
Xi = X + noise;
```

We now come to the implementation of the state estimator. Firstly, consider the model of aircraft motion. The state of the system at any instant is given by its position (X) and velocity (V) that is again a two-dimensional vector. Suppose that at the sample instant (k*Ts) we have estimated the aircraft position to be a two-dimensional vector Xe(:,k) and its velocity to be Ve(:,k). Thus its estimated *X* position is Xe(1,k) while its estimated *Y* position is Xe(2,k).

If we could obtain an estimate Ae(:,k) of aircraft acceleration, we could use it to predict its velocity at the next sample instant. However, since this is unknown, our best course of action is to assume zero acceleration. In this case we should use Ve(:,k) as the most likely velocity at the next sample instant, and then use rectangular integration to predict the position of the aircraft:

```
Xp(:,k+1) = Xe(:,k) + Ts*Ve(:,k);
```

The radar can reduce the effective background clutter by restricting the search for the next echo to a small tracking window that is centered around the predicted position Xp(:,k+1). When the new position information Xi(:,k+1) is sent as an input to the state estimator, it can use this data to correct the predicted position. We can regard the difference Xi(:,k+1)-Xp(:,k+1) as a tracking error signal that can be used in a feedback loop, to form a new estimate Xe(:,k+1) of aircraft position. If Xi(:,k+1) had been a perfect measurement we would simply have used it as our new estimate of the aircraft position. On the other hand, if Xi(:,k+1) had been of no value at all we would have continued to use Xp(:,k+1) as our estimate of aircraft position. If we have mixed feelings about the matter we can estimate Xe(:,k+1) to lie somewhere on the line between Xp(:,k+1) and Xi(:,k+1). Kalman showed that, if the noises within the system are Gaussian with zero mean, a least-squares estimate of position is given by an equation of the form:

```
Xe(:,k+1) = Xp(:,k+1) + Kp*(Xi(:,k+1)-Xp(:,k+1));
```

The state estimator must similarly revise the "predicted" velocity Ve(:,k) by assuming that the tracking error is partly due to aircraft acceleration, and thus use an equation of the form:

```
Ve(:,k+1) = Ve(:,k) + Kv*(Xi(:,k+1)-Xp(:,k+1));
```

The filter was implemented by means of the following program:

```
Xp = [5.5; 0];
Xe = Xp;
Ve = [0; 5.5*w];
for k=1:99
    Xp(:,k+1) = Xe(:,k) + Ts*Ve(:,k);
    Xe(:,k+1) = Xp(:,k+1) + Kp*(Xi(:,k+1)-Xp(:,k+1));
    Ve(:,k+1) = Ve(:,k) + Kv*(Xi(:,k+1)-Xp(:,k+1));
end
```

Kalman determined the gains Kp and Kv that produce the least-squares estimate of position and velocity. This calculation requires the designer to estimate the signal-to-noise ratio (SNR) of the incoming information, and is significantly more complex than the calculation of the matrix (H) described in Section 9.3.2. When the SNR is high the filter bandwidth is increased, to improve the tracking of an agile aircraft, while at low SNR its bandwidth is reduced to suppress the noise, and the filter relies more on past data to predict the future position of the aircraft. Rather than taxing the reader with complex mathematics, we will illustrate a heuristic approach whereby the gains can be designed to achieve a suitable bandwidth without undue resonant amplification.

The simulation assumes that the radar signal is exactly on the aircraft (Xi = X) except when it flies through the simulated clutter band. The transient response of the filter is tested by setting the initial estimates to range = 5.5 km and tangential velocity = 137.5 m s^{-1}. The settling of the filter with suitably chosen gains (Kp and Kv) is shown by the **o** symbols in Figure 9.1. There is an initial position error since Xp(1,1) is greater than Xi(1,1). This acts through the gain (Kv) to initially drive Ve(1,k) negative, which causes Xe(1,k) to move inwards and settle relatively quickly close to Xi(1,k). There is a significant oscillation in Ve (1,k) that takes 40 seconds to damp out. The perturbations in Xe(2,k) and Ve(2,k) are much smaller.

At 118 seconds the aircraft enters the clutter, as indicated by the * symbols in Figure 9.1. The perturbations to Xe(1,k) are significantly attenuated by the filter as shown by the **o** symbols in Figure 9.1, but there is a significant perturbation to Ve(1,k).

We can analyze the frequency response of the filter by considering the following continuous approximation:

$$dXe/dt = Ve + Kp\,(Xi - Xe)$$

$$dVe/dt = Kv\,(Xi - Xe)$$

where $Kp = $ Kp$/$Ts and $Kv = $ Kv$/$Ts.

Taking Laplace transforms of these gives algebraic equations with the Laplace variable (*s*):

$$s\,Xe(s) = Ve(s) + Kp\,[Xi(s) - Xe(s)]$$
$$s\,Ve(s) = Kv\,[Xi(s) - Xe(s)]$$

where *Xe*(*s*), *Ve*(*s*), and *Xi*(*s*) are the Laplace transforms of the corresponding variables.

These equations can be combined to give the transfer function of the filter:

$$Xe(s) = F(s)\,Xi(s)$$
$$F(s) = [Kv + Kp\,s]/[Kv + Kp\,s + s^2]$$

Appendix A discusses the frequency response of a given transfer function, while Chapters 6 and 10 give examples of frequency response plots. If *Kp* is relatively small, the filter will exhibit oscillatory behavior at a frequency that is close to the square root of *Kv*. This is then a good indication of its bandwidth. The discrete filter used in the simulation had a gain Kv = 0.05, so the bandwidth of the filter is close to 0.158 rad s^{-1}. The gain Kp = 0.18 was chosen to give reasonable damping of the oscillation. Increasing it introduces excessive sensitivity to the clutter.

9.3.4 A velocity estimator

Consider an aircraft that is fitted with a GPS receiver that gives accurate position measurements (Xi) and a strapdown navigation system that gives accurate measurements (Ai) of acceleration. We can use a state estimator, similar to that discussed in the last section, to determine the velocity of the vehicle from these measurements. Its performance can be improved by combining both sets of data (Xi) and (Ai). The program that was shown in the previous section is modified by using the acceleration information in the statement that updates the estimate (Ve) of velocity:

```
for k=1:99
    Xp(:,k+1)  = Xe(:,k) + Ts*Ve(:,k);
    Xe(:,k+1)  = Xp(:,k+1) + Kp*(Xi(:,k+1)-Xp(:,k+1));
    Ve(:,k+1)  = Ve(:,k) + Ts*Ai(:,k)...
                 + Kv*(Xi(:,k+1)-Xp(:,k+1));
end
```

This effectively blends the derivative of the measured position (Xi) with the integral of the measured acceleration (Ai) to estimate the velocity. By doing so, it can speed up the response of the filter without unduly compromising its susceptibility to measurement noise. The design of the gains (Kp and Kv) to achieve a desired transient frequency and damping will be the same as before.

The acceleration sample period (Ta) will probably exceed the GPS information by an order of magnitude, so that we can separate the velocity function of the filter into two operations. We can perform a prediction each time that we receive new acceleration information:

```
Vp(:,h+1)  = Ve(:,h) + Ta*Ai(:,h)
```

and then correct the velocity estimate when we receive new GPS information:

```
Ve(:,k+1) = Vp(:,k+1) + Kv*(Xi(:,k+1)-Xp(:,k+1));
```

If the filter uses n samples of acceleration per cycle, the effect of acceleration noise will be reduced by the square root of n.

9.3.5   An FIR filter

Signals are often sampled and then processed by a digital computer in order to extract the required information from high-frequency noise that corrupted the measurements. For example, a strapdown navigation system may receive a signal from a GPS receiver that corresponds to the X position of a vehicle. Suppose that this signal is sampled at the instants K*Ts and stored in a vector (U). A simple way to estimate the velocity of the vehicle is to form the finite difference:

```
d(k)   =   (U(k+1)-U(k)) / Ts
```

Whereas the vehicle may move very little between successive samples, the noise may change significantly, causing it to completely swamp the extracted velocity signal. This has led to the development of computational algorithms, that are referred to as digital filters, which will reduce the amplitude of the noise. Section 9.3.3 and Section 9.3.4 showed how a state estimator could determine the velocity from such measurements. Another design approach for digital band limited differentiator-filters is discussed by Kuo and Kaiser (1996). The idea is to approximate the frequency response $D(j\omega)$ of a pure differentiator for values of ω below a chosen frequency. Several algorithms are presented that approximate $D(j\omega)$ to varying degrees. We will simulate one of these, due to Martin (1962).

This differentiator-filter has a finite impulse response (FIR) that consists of the following 21 terms:

```
H = [ 0.983896
    - 0.468363
      0.28729
    - 0.191291
```

```
    0.13062
-   0.088958
    0.059197
-   0.038097
    0.025112
-   0.009885
    0.
    0.009885
-   0.025112
    0.038097
-   0.059197
    0.088958
-   0.13062
    0.191291
-   0.28729
    0.468363
-   0.983896  ];
```

The filter is implemented by the same program that was created in Section 9.2.2, where U is the input data from the GPS and the vector (x) contains the last 21 values of the position of the vehicle along the X axis. Its velocity (Y) in this direction is then determined as the sum:

```
Y = sum(H.*x);
```

It was tested with an input signal U(k) that is shown in the upper plot of Figure 9.2. This signal was chosen to verify performance rather than representing the expected motion of the vehicle. There is firstly a period of constant velocity to test the initialization of the filter. It takes 21 samples to fill its memory (x) with the data: U(1), U(2),…, U(21) before a valid estimate of velocity, Y(k) is obtained. This is shown in the lower plot of Figure 9.2. It must still be scaled to represent speed in m s^{-1}. There is then a period of constant acceleration to test the transient response of the filter. The output Y(k) of the filter takes 21 samples to settle to the correct velocity. The same lag occurs when Y(k) settles to a constant speed after the acceleration is removed. After these tests the noise rejection of the filter is tested by adding Gaussian noise to U(k), as can be seen on the upper plot. The filter is relatively sensitive to this noise, as shown by the disturbance on Y(k). The filter again takes 21 samples to settle after the noise is removed.

We can show by simulation and calculation that the signal-to-noise ratio of Y (k) as estimated by the differentiator-filter is 200 times better than that obtained

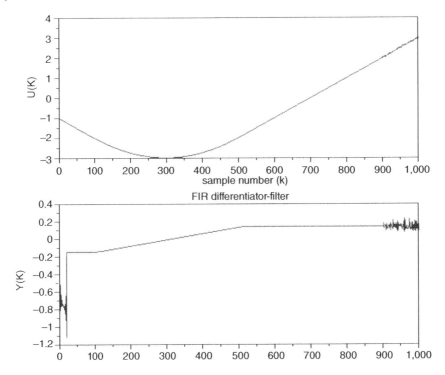

Figure 9.2 Response of FIR differentiator filter to position data.

by taking a finite difference $d(k)$. We can write a program such as the following to calculate the frequency response of the device:

```
C = H(1);
for n=2:21
    C = C + h(n)*exp(%i*n*w*T);        // complex gain
end
mag = abs(C);                          // real gain
```

This can then be run with a vector (w) of frequencies and a sample period (T) to find the gain. The determination of its phase lead is complicated by the time lag of the device.

FIR filters are also used to realize low-pass, band-pass, and band-stop functions.

9.4 Economic, Geo-, Bio-, and other sciences

"The purpose of computing is insight, not numbers"

R.W. Hamming (1962)

(*Source:* Rights Managed McGraw Hill Education)

All science begins with a process of observation and analysis. When a pattern begins to emerge from the data, the scientists can begin to propose theories that explain the behavior of the process that is being studied. In the case of the so-called "hard sciences," the data is reasonably repeatable over a large number of samples. The results can usually be explained by fairly simple formulae. Thus, Galileo could take measurements that could be explained by Newton's theories. It was pure good fortune that Galileo was dealing with quite small masses and velocities, which did not need the application of Einstein's theories.

The so-called "soft sciences" are not blessed with such good fortune. The processes being studied are significantly influenced by their environment so the data is often extremely variable. The scientists will spend much of their time tracking down the parameters that affect the results. When such parameters are neglected, they can give the impression that the process is varying unpredictably. The emphasis will then be on more data collection and statistical analysis. For example, geo-scientists have monitored CO_2 levels in the atmosphere over many decades. They may then fit a model of the following form, where the sinusoidal component represents seasonal variation while the exponential function is suggested by records of total world fossil fuel production from the mid-1960s:

```
for k=1:K
      y(k)   =   C(1)  +  C(2)*exp(C(3)*k)...
               +  C(4)*sin(C(5)*2*%pi/S);
end
```

The start date must be chosen to fit the seasonal variation, the constant (C) is chosen to fit the measurement period, and the coefficients C(n) may then be found by the method of least-squares.

Scientists who monitor geographic data often work with very large arrays that give quantitative data at given map coordinates. These can be compared with Section 9.5, where an array of 370 by 536 pixels is used to store the digital image shown in Figure 9.3. The map arrays can be orders of magnitude larger than this.

Figure 9.3 Digital image before and after enhancement. *Source:* Private and Fair Use, John Wiley & Sons

Many countries have departments of statistics that gather econometric data. For example, the Longley econometric data of the USA includes the following variables:

1) GNP deflator
2) GNP
3) Unemployment
4) Armed Forces
5) Population
6) Year
7) Employment

Economic science is heavily dependent on the accumulation and analysis of such data that can be statistically analyzed and correlated to assist with the creation of empirical models. Hopefully this can lead to a better understanding of the causal processes that are at work behind the models.

9.4.1 A pricing strategy

Commercial enterprises surely have a profit motive, but may price their products in various ways that depend on their temperament and their markets. They may price their products as a percentage markup on the cost of procurement, production, and the overheads needed to run the enterprise. They will also have to consider such questions as:

How much are clients prepared to pay?

How much more would it cost customers to switch to another supplier?

What do buyers regard as a fair price?

Suppose that we are in a business that is currently selling 2000 items a month at a price of US$10 each and wish to increase our turnover. It is fair to assume that the number of customers who decide to buy the product will increase if we reduce its price. It would be very helpful to know how sales will depend on price before we make any decision. If we have a database with relevant records, we can do some analysis using the techniques that were previously described. Otherwise, we will have to rely on expert opinion. We begin with a summary of some basic terms and formulae:

p: is the price per unit

R = k*p : is the total revenue from selling k units

C: is the total cost of producing k units

Suppose that we expect that sales will go up by approximately 20% if we reduce the price by 10%. We can express this feeling by a fairly simple function:

```
k = 2000 + 400*(10-p);
```

We will now rearrange this equation in the following form, known as a *demand function*:

```
p = (6000-k) /400;
```

This allows us to calculate the total revenue from selling k units as

```
R = (6000*k - k^2) / 400;
```

We then look at our book-keeping to find the fixed and running costs associated with production. Suppose that we estimate the cost of producing k items to be

```
C = 4000 + 5*k;
```

The total profit from selling k units will then be

```
P = R - C ;
```

We can then draw up a spreadsheet that shows the following:

p (US$)	k	R (US$)	C (US$)	P (US$)
12.	1200	14400	10000	4400
11.5	1400	16100	11000	5100
11.	1600	17600	12000	5600
10.5	1800	18900	13000	5900
10.	2000	20000	14000	6000
9.5	2200	20900	15000	5900
9.	2400	21600	16000	5600
8.5	2600	22100	17000	5100
8.	2800	22400	18000	4400

This leads us to believe that our current price is close enough to optimum, especially since there is significant uncertainty in our assumptions.

Economists may use differential calculus to solve the above problem. The modeling of a discrete process by continuous functions is somewhat specious, but allows the economist to exploit the considerable heritage of the calculus. This is done by considering the following derivative, known as the *marginal profit*:

$$dP/dk = dR/dk - dC/dk = 10 - k/200$$

The total profit is maximized at the price where the marginal profit is zero. We should not be surprised that this gives the same answer as we found with our spreadsheet:

$$k = 2000$$

"Few have heard of Fra Luca Parioli, the inventor of double entry book-keeping; but he has probably had much more influence on human life than has Dante or Michaelangelo."

H.J. Muller

The state of a business is measured by its finances and stock levels. The balance in a bank account can be modeled by a simple difference equation that includes the initial balance, the deposits, and the withdrawals. The variation of stock levels from month to month can be similarly modeled:

$$S(m + 1) = S(m) + Q(m) - K(m)$$

where

$S(m)$ = stock level at month m
$Q(m)$ = units produced between month m and month $m + 1$
$K(m)$ = units sold between month m and month $m + 1$

Price changes will have an effect on cash flow and stock levels. With effective advertising, a price reduction can have an almost immediate effect on the monthly sales figures. Stock levels will reduce until production can be increased to catch up with the extra sales. We can create a computer model that simulates the effect of a price change on the finances and stock levels. This model should come with a warning:

Danger! Here there be Dragons!

We are entering the domain of the soothsayer, with all its inherent dangers, when we plan our business on estimates of future sales. There was a time when popes and kings had astrologers at court to help them plan for the future. After all, if astronomers had success in predicting eclipses from star-gazing why should astrologers not have equal success in predicting more mundane matters? Nowadays governments have departments of statistics to perform the same role, with the same justification. If statistical analysis had success in predicting the orbits of planets and planetoids, why should it not have equal success in predicting economics?

The volume of sales can depend on the season. If we are selling ice-cream, there will be a huge peak in the summer sales. If we are selling bread, the effect will be negligible. We can correct for the number of days in the month. We may have heard that an important event, comparable with the Olympic Games is coming to our area. This can bring a large influx of customers, so how much can we increase our prices? What about an economic meltdown? Can we predict wars, volcanos, and virus plagues?We will enter the field of business modeling because it is very necessary, but will do so with considerable caution. Even having corrected for all foreseeable factors we still know that the actual sales figures will differ from our predictions. Consider a short list of reasons why this will occur:

The demand function that we used to price our product can be erroneous.

There could be changes in the economic environment. We may be able to extrapolate the trend from past figures, but business volatility is notoriously unpredictable.

There can also be an unpredictable "random" variation in the sales due to idiosyncrasies of the public.

How can we allow for errors in our predictions? Should we set up a *Monte Carlo* model by adding random numbers to the estimated sales figures? The Scilab random number generator `grand()`, referred to in Appendix D.1, could be used. Such methods require a large number of runs to generate a visible pattern. Alternatively, we could use algebraic probability functions to analyze the effect of random variations in sales. Such functions are described in Appendix D. Suppose that we wish to predict the effect on our business of changing the price of our product from US$12 to US$10 a unit. We assume that the mean monthly sales will go up to 2000, but guess that there is a 50% chance that they will lie between 2000 – 100 and 2000 + 100. We will still have to guess what probability function describes the random spread in sales figures. Each sale is an individual event, so we can use a binomial or Poisson probability distribution (see Appendices D.2 and D.3). The mean and variance of a Poisson distribution are equal to one another, and a binomial distribution with 2000 events will have the same properties. With a mean and variance equal to 2000, the standard deviation will be 45. If this was the only source of uncertainty in our predictions, the sales should lie between 2000 – 30 and 2000 + 30 with a probability of 50%. Perhaps our original guess was too pessimistic or perhaps there are other factors that contribute to the uncertainty in our predictions. We could decide that the Poisson distribution in sales is due to decisions by the public, but that it does not allow for business volatility, or errors that we made when defining the demand function. If we do not feel competent to distinguish between these factors, we can simply model their overall effect by a single random variable that has a variance V_N. As discussed in Appendix D, the variance of the sum of uncorrelated random variables is equal to the sum of their individual variances. We could describe them by a normal probability distribution (see Appendix D.4) that has a zero mean value while its variance can be suitably chosen. If we add a normally distributed variance V_N to the Poisson distributed random variable with variance 2000, the variance of their sum is given by:

$$V = 2000 + V_N$$

These sums have given us a slightly better feel for the numbers. Firstly, the relatively large monthly sales would imply that the effect of random discrete events would cause them to cluster more tightly about the mean than our original guess. If we believe that sales follow this statistical model, we must look for other reasons for our original uncertainty. The numbers also draw our attention to the fact that we must allow for other uncertainties that do not follow a discrete event statistical model.

We may decide to revise our initial guess, to give a 50% chance that monthly sales will lie between 2000 – 60 and 2000 + 60. This corresponds to a standard deviation = 89, and $V = 8000$. We thus require that the additional random variable (N) has a variance (V_N), which is three times larger than that due to random decisions by customers. Its standard deviation is thus increased by the square root of 3.

9.4.2   The productivity of money

Suppose that a manufacturer plans to start a new production plant and needs to know how best to employ the available capital. We will look at a simple mathematical model to predict the number (k) of units that can be produced by employing various amounts (x) on labor and on capital expenses (y). We can express this by the *Cobb–Douglas production function*:

```
k  =  c * x^a * y^(1-a);
c  =  a constant
0 < a < 1
```

We will not go into the reasoning behind the definition of this function but will assume that we have somehow arrived at the following *production function* for the particular product:

```
k  =  100 * x^(3/4) *  y^(1/4);
```

where x is scaled in dollars (at US$150 per labor unit) while y is scaled at US$250 per capital unit. The constant $c = 100$ then converts financial expenditure to a production level.

Any enterprise has limited resources. Suppose that the total expenditure on labor plus capital must not exceed US$50 000. This financial constraint can be expressed as

```
150*x + 250*y  =  50000
```

The manufacturer wishes to determine the best use of available resources in order to maximize the production level. The following computer program varies the labor cost (x) and then calculates the production level (k) when the rest of the available funds is used on capital expenses (y):

```
x = 200:25:300;
y = (50000-150*x) / 250;
k = 100*(x.^.75).*(y.^.25)
```

The following results show that maximum production is achieved when $x = 250$ and $y = 50$:

x =	200	225	250	275	300
y =	80	65	50	35	20
k =	15905	16495	16718	16425	15243

We can thus produce 16 718 units by spending US$37 500 on labor and US$12 500 on capital expenses.

Economic theorists can use calculus to find the optimum employment of resources. This can start by observing some properties of the *Cobb–Douglas production function*. They can plot contour lines (see Appendix C.4) in the *XY* plane, where each line represents a particular production level $k(x, y)$.

Consider the slope of $k(x,y)$ along a radial line given by $y = nx$. The production function can then be expressed as:

$$k = c\, x^a\, n^{1-a}\, x^{1-a} = c\, n^{1-a}\, x$$

If n is positive, the production rate increases with x where $dk/dx = c\, n^{1-a}$.

Readers can confirm these observations by doing Exercise 7 at the end of the chapter.

The gradient of production rate (see Appendix C.4) is given by

$$\mathbf{grad}(k) = \mathbf{i}\,\partial k/\partial x + \mathbf{j}\,\partial k/\partial y = \mathbf{i}\,75\,x^{-\frac{1}{4}}y^{\frac{1}{4}} + \mathbf{j}\,25\,x^{\frac{1}{4}}y^{-\frac{1}{4}}$$

The production rate increases if we move in the direction of $\mathbf{grad}(k)$. The gradient is normal to the production contour line at any point. This financial constraint can be expressed as a mathematical function:

$$g(x,y) = 150x + 250y = 50\,000$$

The financial constraint $g(x, y) = s$ is the equation of a straight line in the XY plane. If we could increase the available money (s), this line would move outwards from the origin of the plane, in the direction given by its gradient vector:

$$\mathbf{grad}(g) = \mathbf{i}\,\partial g/\partial x + \mathbf{j}\,\partial g/\partial y = 150\,\mathbf{i} + 250\,\mathbf{j}$$

Production will be maximized at a point (x_0, y_0) where the gradient vectors $\mathbf{grad}(k)$ and $\mathbf{grad}(g)$ are parallel. One of the production contour lines will just touch the constraint line at this point. This condition can be described by the equation

$$\mathbf{grad}(k(x_0, y_0)) = L\,\mathbf{grad}(g(x_0, y_0))$$

where L is a scalar, which is called the *Lagrange multiplier*.
Substituting the numerical values for $\mathbf{grad}(k)$ and $\mathbf{grad}(g)$ then gives

$$75\,x_0^{-\frac{1}{4}}y_0^{\frac{1}{4}} = 150\,L$$

$$25\,x_0^{\frac{1}{4}}y_0^{-\frac{1}{4}} = 250\,L$$

The first equation gives

$$L = \tfrac{1}{2}\,x_0^{-\frac{1}{4}}y_0^{\frac{1}{4}}$$

Substituting this in the second equation, we then find

$$x_0 = 5\,y_0$$

Replacing x_o by this expression in the financial constraint, we find that

$y_o = 50$ units of capital

and therefore:

$x_o = 250$ units of labor

Therefore,

$$L = \tfrac{1}{2}\, 250^{-\tfrac{1}{4}}\, 50^{\tfrac{1}{4}} = 0.334$$

The calculus thus gives the same result that was obtained by the simple computer program.

Lagrange (1736–1813) introduced this method in a paper on mechanics when he was just 19 years old!

Economists refer to L as the *marginal productivity of money*. This means that for each additional dollar spent on production, the additional units that can be produced are given by L. In actual practice, production and labor can only be changed in discrete units. We can seriously question whether the above analysis represents a theoretical or practical exercise. The above production function is somewhat of an oversimplification. The productivity of a given number of labor units will depend on the labor pool in the region. There will be a need for training and the trainers will probably have to be taken from the production line! We could start by modifying the production function to

$$k = c\,(e x)^a\, y^{1-a}$$

where e represents the effectiveness of the available labor.

Similar ideas are incorporated in the Solow–Swan model for a regional economy:

$$K(t) = [E(t)X(t)]^a\, Y(t)^{1-a}$$

$X(t) = X_o \exp(nt) =$ units of labor
$E(t) = E_o \exp(gt) =$ effectiveness of labor
$K(t) =$ the gross regional product

It is possible to derive a differential equation that describes the evolution of the regional economy when a given fraction of $K(t)$ is locally consumed while the rest is reinvested. Questions can again be asked regarding the validity of the model.

9.4.3 Comments on business models

Computers are widely used in business as working tools for data processing, calculation, record keeping, etc. The above examples give some idea of computer models that could assist with making business decisions. The illustrative models were oversimplified. It can be argued that further elaboration would not give more meaningful results unless we have a greater understanding of the underlying mechanisms that drive the system. Economic theory is one of the "soft sciences" where system behavior is not so easily described by hard equations. One approach that has been used is to collect as much data as possible and then strive to create a heuristic model that gives a statistical fit to the data, while hopefully satisfying a logical concept. Section 9.4.1 illustrated how meaningful models may have to include random behavior. Statistical analysis was used rather than the brute force method of Monte-Carlo simulation. Appendix D gives some background on the use of statistical analysis. Appendix D.5 discusses the use of statistical tables when sample testing is employed to determine product quality.

Section 2.5.1 gives an example of dynamic behavior where an investment grows with compound interest. The calculations are quite simple but involve inherent uncertainties. What is the probability that the interest rate could increase or decrease? What is the risk that we need to withdraw cash from the fixed deposit, and what loss will this incur? We can simulate the cash growth in the current account by implementing a difference equation that includes random variables:

$$X(n + 1) = [1 + A + a(n)]X(n) - W(n)$$

where

$X(n)$ = the balance in the account after the nth month
A = the nominal interest rate per month
$a(n)$ = a random change in the interest rate
$W(n)$ = a random cash withdrawal

It is easy to program this difference equation. The expertise lies in understanding the economic situation and the personal risk of finding ourselves in need of additional cash.

The production process described in the last section would operate according to a time schedule, where the completion times of various subassemblies need to be scheduled, so that they are available when they must be integrated within the product.

Inventory control models have been usefully employed in industry. An inventory control system is used to ensure that components are available when they are needed. There is a trade-off between keeping a small inventory so as to save expenses or a large inventory so as to avoid "outages" when some necessary item is not available. If we can measure the consequence of an outage in dollars, we have a direct basis for making this trade-off. The inventory control scheme is largely determined by the following:

1) At what stock level must a particular item be reordered?
2) How much must then be reordered?
3) What delays are caused by the buying office and incoming inspection?

Much is left to the reader to follow up on the ideas that have been presented and to venture further in the field of business modeling.

9.5 Digital images

The Python® programming language is extensively used for technical computing, where it has been expanded by many users. The Numpy extension contains many mathematical algorithms including matrix manipulation. The CV extension contains resources that allow the Python[1] platform to import image files as matrices that can then be processed by Numpy. There is then a plotting facility (matplotlib) that displays the matrices as visual images.

We will discuss the use of Python for manipulating digital images. The first thing to do when entering the Python platform is to import the above facilities by means of the commands:

```
import cv2
import numpy as np
import numpy.linalg as LA
from matplotlib import pyplot as plt
```

We can then import image files from the current directory by commands such as

```
img = cv2.imread("imName.jpg", 1)
```

This creates a matrix (img) whose elements correspond to the pixels that make up the image. Each element contains numbers that specify the intensities of the three primary colors (blue, green, red). Zero corresponds to black, while 255 corresponds to full intensity. The command (img.shape) displays the dimensions of the matrix. For example, an image with 536 rows, 370 columns, and three colors has a shape (536, 370, 3). The image is displayed by the command

```
cv2.imshow('aname', img)
```

or by the plotting facility

```
plt.imshow(img), plt.show()
```

A monochromatic copy of such a digital image is shown on the left-hand side of Figure 9.3. The actual image is in color.

---

1 Python is registered under the GNU General Public Licence (GPL) Copyright 2017 by Tutorials Point (I) Pvt. Ltd.

The contrast of the image depends on how the numbers in the elements are distributed over the range of intensities. A small variation of intensities will produce an image with little contrast. The numbers in the elements can be sorted into bins that cover the range from 0 to 255. We first rearrange the matrix (img) into a vector (imv) and then compute such a histogram as follows:

```
imv = img.flatten()
hist, bins = np.histogram(imv,256,[0,256])
```

The spread of the resulting histogram then tells us whether the variation in intensity is large or small. The CV extension contains resources that allow the Python platform to manipulate the histogram and thereby improve the contrast of the image. The enhanced image can then be stored in a matrix (imgE). The following command can then be used to reduce the colors in imgE to a gray scale:

```
imgray = cv2.cvtColor(imgE,cv2.COLOR_BGR2GRAY)
```

The matrix (imgray) has the shape (536, 370), indicating that there are no longer three colors. This image is shown on the right-hand side of Figure 9.3. The original image shown on the left-hand side of Figure 9.3 was similarly reduced to a gray scale to satisfy the restrictions of the printer.

There are many other resources that allow us to manipulate the image. For example, the matrix operation img[:,:,c] reduces the image to a single primary color, while the transposed matrix imgc.T rotates it through 90 degrees.

9.5.1   An image processor

Suppose that Figure 9.3 was taken by a camera that surveys an area in order to determine whether there is an intruder in its field of view. We wish to create a pattern recognition system that will "see" the human figure in this picture. Such a program is complex, so we will restrict this section to presenting a few operations that could help to achieve this objective.

We can regard the monochromatic image shown in Figure 9.3 to be a two-dimensional scalar field that defines an intensity profile such as that discussed in Appendix C.4. This appendix shows how we can create a function grad() that computed the components of a vector which approximates the gradient **grad( )** of a continuous scalar field.

Consider the matrix (imgray) that corresponds to Figure 9.3. The following Python function computes an array (gx) that is a smoothed gradient of intensity for the monochromatic image:

```
gx = cv2.Sobel(imgray, cv2.CV_32F, 1, 0)
```

The above Sobel function has been adapted to give better results for digital image processing. It uses the following algorithm to compute the element gx[y,x] of the array gx :

```
gx[y,x] =  imgray[y-1,x-1]  -imgray[y-1,x+1]  ..
           +2*imgray[y,x-1]  -2*imgray[y,x+1]  ..
           +imgray[y+1,x-1]  -imgray[y+1,x+1];
```

where imgray[y,x] is the intensity of the image at that pixel.

The elements of gx represent the gradients of intensity in the horizontal direction. We can also compute the gradients in the vertical direction by using the command:

```
gy = cv2.Sobel(imgray, cv2.CV_32F, 0, 1)
```

The horizontal gradient (gx) of the enhanced digital image is shown on the left-hand side of Figure 9.4, while the vertical gradient (gy) is shown on the right-hand side. A combination of the two approximates the gradient vector of a continuous scalar field.

Since the human figure is standing upright it is creating a predominance of vertical edges, which are shown in the matrix gx. The matrix gy shows considerably less contrast at these edges. On the other hand, the horizontal wall shows up

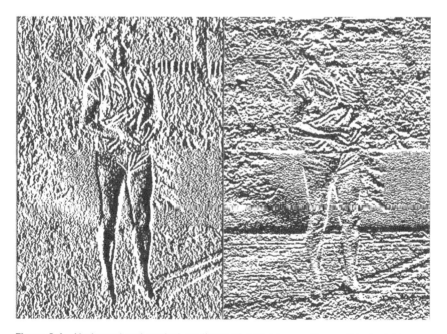

Figure 9.4 Horizontal and vertical gradients of digital image. *Source:* Private, John Wiley & Sons

very well in the matrix gy, while it has almost no effect on the matrix gx. We also see that the unclothed parts of the body produce a larger effect on the gradient than the clothed parts. The discrimination is also larger against the wall than against the vegetation. These differences between the human figure and the background have been used to create a numerical model of "humanness" that can form part of a computer program that searches for intruders within the image. We will firstly reduce the field of regard in Figure 9.3 to remove as much background as possible. We will also divide it into two windows, to distinguish between the lower and the upper half of the human figure. We will spend most of our attention on the lower window, since it stood out better from the background. It will be chosen to produce matrices img, imgE, imgray, gx, and gy that have 257 rows and 156 columns. We know from the calculus of vector fields that the intensity gradient is a maximum at the angle atan(gy,gx). Python can use the following command to compute matrices (mag and ang) that define the gradient at each pixel in polar coordinates:

```
mag, ang = cv2.cartToPolar(gx, gy)
```

For example, the sub-matrix imgray[101:103, 131:136] has the following elements:

```
array([[35, 38, 81,  158, 182],
       [34, 50, 115, 169, 182],
       [32, 62, 142, 180,  184]], dtype=uint8)
```

while the sub-matrix ang[102, 132:135] has the following elements:

```
array([[0.32181564, 0.33936396, 0.3687017],
dtype=float32)
```

The previous section showed how we could compute a histogram that described the amplitude distribution within a matrix. We can similarly compute a histogram (H) that describes the number of times that the elements of ang are within various angular sectors that each occupy a region of 45 degrees. These sectors define eight mean directions: 0, 45, 90, 135, 180, 225, 270, and 315 degrees. The vector (H) thus has eight elements. The histogram for the lower window has a large spike around 0 degrees and another around 180 degrees. Such a histogram could possibly serve as a numerical model of the human figure. Suppose that we scan the image from the surveillance camera with a similar window and use it to compute a histogram Hs. Section 9.3.2 showed how we can compute the correlation between the evolution of two different variables. We could use such an operation to determine how well the vector Hs correlates with the vector H. When the correlation is better than a pre-defined threshold value, we can decide that we have detected a human intruder. The threshold value should be chosen to give an acceptable probability of detection without producing excessive false alarms. It will require a great deal of further work to produce a practical pattern recognition system. Readers are invited to think about other modifications that can produce a more practical system. We see that such a histogram for the upper window has relatively little to distinguish it from the background. Is this due to the shape of the human body or the effect of clothing – or both? Should we compute histograms for many different humans in various situations? Is it then possible to combine their salient features to create a composite model that represents a typical human being? These are difficult questions that remain to be answered. The literature indicates that there are other options that are being considered in the field of pattern recognition.

9.6 Discussion

We must be prepared to meet up with uncertainty as we delve deeper into the study of even the most commonplace object. Take the example of water. We drink it every day, we wash in it, it is indispensable for life, but it will take a very complex computer model to explain its properties. Engineers use extensive tables (Cooper and LeFevre, 1969) that describe how its density, enthalpy, entropy, and specific heats vary with temperature and pressure. How do we model its miraculous properties that are necessary for life on this planet? Why does it contract as the temperature reduces down to 4 °C and then start expanding as it goes down to freezing point? The biologist may answer that it does so because marine life in the polar regions needs it to do so! Perhaps one of the readers will write a computer model that explains how it does it. There are a myriad of such questions, but let us restrict ourselves to just one more. How do we write a computer model that simulates capillary attraction? Must the model go down to a molecular level to describe the electrostatic forces between its positive and negative ions?

We should expect to be confronted by many different forms of uncertainty. This chapter provides us with a few possible answers, but even these are questionable. The impulse response model discussed in Section 9.2.2 makes no allowances for variations in the internal state of the particular process. The estimators that were described in Section 9.3 do not remove the noise in the measurement, they simply attenuate certain frequencies more than the others. The calculations shown in Section 9.4 used input data that was based on guesswork. The resulting answers are only as good as the initial guesses.

Even though computer models may not provide perfect answers, they can nevertheless be an effective tool when used correctly. We will often learn more about the object under study while creating the model than we will gain from the results that it produces. It takes true wisdom to decide how realistic a model must be, and what is enough to satisfy our needs.

The next chapter considers the use of computer models by a team that works under project management. They will be used when the product is being defined and continue to be used up to the point where the hardware is built and tested. It is interesting to see what risks are involved due to imperfect modeling and what happens when the moment of truth arrives.

Exercises

1   Create the random number generator programs described in Section 2.4.1 and view their outputs.

2   Create the column vectors U and V that are shown in Table 9.1 and normalize U by creating a column vector x that has zero mean value.
    Find the coefficients `C(k)` of the following polynomial that minimizes `sum((Y-V).^2)`:

$$Y(k) = C(1) + C(2)*x(k) + C(3)*x(k)^2 + C(4)*x(k)^3$$

3   Use the same vector U as in Exercise 1 and create a vector V = 30 + 0.1*U^2. Add random noise to V with a variance of 1 unit.
    Find the coefficients `C(k)` of the following polynomial that minimize `sum((Y-V).^2)`:

$$Y(k) = C(1) + C(3)*x(k)^2$$

   Find the coefficients `C(k)` of the following polynomial that minimize `sum((Y-V).^2)`:

$$Y(k) = C(1) + C(2)*x(k) + C(3)*x(k)^2$$

4   Create the state estimator program shown in Section 9.3.4. Generate an accelerometer signal Ai that varies as follows. From 0 to 75 seconds: `Ai=0`. From 75 to 175 seconds: `Ai=1` m/s². After 175 seconds: `Ai=0`.
    Integrate this to generate a speed that starts at an initial value of −60 m/s. Integrate again to generate a GPS position signal Xi.
    Run the state estimater and plot Xi, Xp, and Xe versus time.
    Repeat with random noise on Ai with different variances around 0.25 m s^{-2}.
    Repeat with random noise on Xi with different variances around 0.25 m.

5   Create the FIR differentiator filter program described in Section 9.3.5 and test its response to an input signal $u(k)$ that is shown in Figure 9.2. Plot the time response of output (y) to various inputs.

6 Check the numbers in the spreadsheet shown in Section 9.4.1.
How does the table look if we change the numbers in the demand function?

7 Section 9.4.2 defines the *Cobb–Douglas production function* as
$k = f(x,y) =$ the number of units produced by spending x on labor and y on capital.
Plot the contour lines in the XY plane for

$$k = 100 \, x^{\frac{3}{4}} \, y^{\frac{1}{4}}$$

where $k = 80\,000$, $100\,000$, $120\,000$, $14\,000$, $160\,000$,
while x varies over the range 600 to 2000.
Note that by *doubling both x and y* we double the production level.
The gradient vector at any point is normal to the contour line.
What is the direction of positive gradient?
Repeat the exercise for:

$$k = 100 \, x^{\frac{1}{2}} \, y^{\frac{1}{2}}$$

What shape do the contour lines now have?

8 Image processing using Python was briefly discussed in Section 9.5. Explore the cv2 library for further functions. For example, `cv2.equaliseHist` increases the contrast of an image. Search the internet for applications that have been created using Python to do various forms of image processing.

9 Models must be linearized before we can determine their frequency response. These approximations may be acceptable provided that the non-linearities have a secondary effect on plant behavior.
How do non-linearities affect the impulse response of a plant?
Model predictive control (MPC) was developed for the industrial process control industry, where plants have many inputs and outputs. MPC can allow for constraints in the operating conditions of the plant while determining what control action should be taken. This requires a considerable amount of computation, based on the impulse response of the plant.
Do an evaluation to determine the effectiveness of MPC.

10 The game of "noughts and crosses" is played on a board with three rows and three columns, where players take turns to place their noughts and crosses on unoccupied squares on the board.
Can you model the state of the game by a numerical matrix?
Can you do the same for the game of chess?

Bibliography

Cooper, J.R. and LeFevre, E.J. (1969). *Thermophysical Properties of Water Substance*. London: Hodder & Stoughton.

Hamming, R.W. (1962). *Numerical Methods for Scientists and Engineers*. New York: McGraw Hill.

Kuo, F.F. and Kaiser, J.F. (1966). *System Analysis by Digital Computer*. New York: Wiley.

Malcolm, M.A. and Moler, C.B. (1973). *URAND: A Universal Random Number Generator*, Stan-Cs-73-334, Computer Science Department, School of Humanities and Sciences, Stanford University, CA.

Martin M.A. (1962). *Digital Filters for Data Processing*, General Electric Co., Missile and Space Division, Tech. Info. Series Report No. 62-SD484.

Peterson (1961). *Error Correcting Codes*. New York: Wiley.

Tou, J.T. (1959). *Digital and Sampled Data Control Systems*. New York: McGraw Hill.

Trask, M. (1971). *Cybernetics*. London: Studio Vista.

10

Computer models in a development project

Rubin (2016, pp. 1–125) gives a narrative of possible events that can occur in the course of an engineering development project. This chapter shows how simulation studies play a large part in this particular project.

10.1 Introduction

Computer models can often be created in less time and cost less than hardware prototypes. Throughout every phase of industrial research, design, and development they can serve as a test-bed for the engineers. Such simulation models are often used to demonstrate the feasibility of new proposals before the start of an actual project. The simulator can be regarded as an electronic prototype or test bed that takes the place of hardware. They can also be used to study the design and help to avoid costly mistakes before expensive decisions are made.

Many companies engaged in engineering projects have found it necessary to employ professionals who have the specialized skills that are needed for the creation of simulation models. The first requisite for success is that the simulation engineers understand the behavior of the plant, the operating requirements, and the operating environment. It is even better if the designers understand the physical effects that determine the behavior of the plant, which will allow us to construct a simulation model that can to some extent duplicate its behavior. The simulation engineers will have to work closely with the development team in order to set up mathematical models that describe the behavior of the plant. The very creation of such simulation models forces everyone to delve deeper into the underlying physics of the plant, and can give valuable insight into plant operation that can aid both the plant designers and the simulation engineers. This can involve the study of design data, hardware test results, and operational data from similar plants.

Computer Models of Process Dynamics: From Newton to Energy Fields, First Edition.
Olis Rubin.
© 2023 The Institute of Electrical and Electronics Engineers, Inc.
Published 2023 by John Wiley & Sons, Inc.

The characteristics of the plant will have a major effect on the performance of the system, so it is necessary to develop a detailed understanding of its response to control inputs. Whereas the plant designers often concentrate on its steady state operation, the simulation models can be used to predict the dynamic behavior of the plant. In this way simulation engineers become valuable members of the project team that must make design decisions that involve trade-offs between product performance and constraints.

10.1.1 The scope of this chapter

The product considered in this chapter consists of an electric motor that rotates a camera so as to point it in a given direction. A computer model will be created to assist the design engineers who are responsible for developing a control system that stabilizes the camera on a particular object. This chapter strives to give readers the "virtual experience" of situations that can confront a simulation engineer in a real development project. Section 10.2 gives more details on the hardware and describes the creation of the computer model. The rest of the chapter shows how the simulation model can help the project team with making design decisions that ensure the success of the project. In Section 10.3 it is shown how the computer can be used by the project team to define a product that meets the specifications. Section 10.4 goes on to describe the design phase, where the simulation engineers provide the designers with data based on the "paper plant." The model will then be used to simulate the performance of the resulting design. Section 10.5 then illustrates events that may occur when the hardware is built and tested.

This case study will show us how important it is to identify pitfalls during the early phases of the project, and thereby help to avoid costly mistakes. The design team should use the computer model to do "what-if" studies where they try to anticipate everything bad that could happen. We may take great care to avoid careless errors in the process of creating the computer model, only to find when the plant is built that there was a mistake in the defining equations. Section 10.5 will show that even though the hardware appears to be relatively simple we can still encounter such complications at a late stage in the project.

Whereas the emphasis is on the creation of the model the reader needs to have some understanding of control system design. Appendix A.8 gives some applicable background material.

10.2 A motor drive model

There have been considerable advances in the design and construction of electric motors since they originally came into use. With the powerful magnetic materials and high-performance electronic switching devices that are available today many

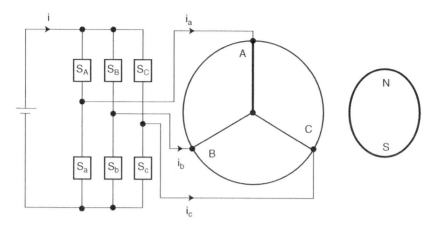

Figure 10.1 PWM inverter plus motor. *Source:* Reproduced with permission from Olis Rubin, *Control Engineering in Development Projects*, Norwood, MA: Artech House Inc., 2016 © 2016 by Artech House Inc.

motor drives now have the configuration shown in Figure 10.1. The rotor is made up of permanent magnets, where a two-pole rotor is represented by the circle marked (N S).

A typical arrangement of an inverter that drives the stator is also shown in the figure. This shows a three-phase switching bridge that controls the direction that the current (i) from the DC supply will flow through the three-phase windings of the stator. The system will include sensors that detect the position of the rotor and a controller that commands the electronic switches to operate in phase with its rotation. By this means it is possible to produce a motor that can be controlled to run at variable speed; see Rubin (2016, pp. 15–17).

The inverter blocks $[S_A]$, $[S_B]$, $[S_C]$, $[S_a]$, $[S_b]$, and $[S_c]$, contain solid-state switching devices. The three radial lines that join at the center of the circle marked A B C represent the three-phase windings of the stator connected together at a star point. This arrangement allows two of the three windings to be connected in series across the DC supply. For example, if $[S_A]$ and $[S_b]$ are switched on, the current (i_a) will then flow into the stator at the point A, through phase A and B, and out at point B. We thus have

$$i = i_a = -i_b$$

We can reduce the mean stator current by switching $[S_b]$ on for only a fraction of the time. If the frequency of the pulse-width modulation (PWM) is very high, the ripple in the current will be filtered out by the stator inductance and can be ignored in the computer model. We can also alternate between switches $[S_b]$ and $[S_c]$ so that the current flowing out of phase A is switched between phases B and C.

The current flowing through two stator windings produces the effect of a continuous coil. The magnetic field of the permanent magnet rotor, represented by the circle marked (N S) reacts with the stator current to produce a torque (m_m) as it rotates between the windings:

$$m_m = k\,i = \text{the torque on the motor shaft (Nm)} \qquad (10.1)$$

k = the motor constant (Nm A^{-1})

We can change the switching between the three phases as the motor rotates so that the equivalent stator current follows the rotor magnet. The motor torque (m_m) produced by a given current (i) is then nearly constant over all rotor angles.

10.2.1 A conceptual model

Figure 10.2 is a schematic description of the motor and its load. The relationships between these variables and parameters are considered in Rubin (2016, pp. 24–25). The voltage source (v) represents an electronic drive unit that supplies power to a brushless permanent magnet motor. The three-phase windings of the stator can be approximated by a single equivalent winding where

v = equivalent drive voltage (V)
i = equivalent stator current (A)
eb = equivalent stator back emf (V)
R = equivalent stator resistance (ohm)
L = equivalent stator inductance (henry)

These quantities are approximately related by the following differential equation:

$$v \approx eb + R\,i + L\,di/dt \qquad (10.2)$$

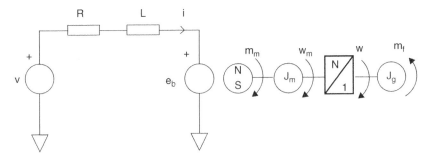

Figure 10.2 Physical variables and parameters. *Source:* Reproduced with permission from Olis Rubin, *Control Engineering in Development Projects*, Norwood, MA: Artech House Inc., 2016 © 2016 by Artech House Inc.

The current (i) flowing through the stator coils produces the torque (m_m) defined by Equation (10.1), which causes the permanent magnet rotor to rotate, where

w_m = the motor speed (rad s^{-1})

The mechanical drive between the motor and the load is also shown in Figure 10.2, where

w = the rotation rate of the load (rad s^{-1})
$N = w_m/w$ = the gear ratio between the motor and the load
m = the motor torque applied to the load through the gear ratio (Nm)
m_f = the load torque due to friction, that must be overcome by the motor (Nm)
J_m = the motor moment of inertia (kg m^2)
J_g = the load moment of inertia (kg m^2)

The motor torque (m_m) is defined at the rotor, but its effect on the load depends as follows on the gear ratio:

$m = N\, m_m$

This can be combined with Equation (10.1) to give the following:

$m = K\, i$

where $K = k\, N\, (\text{m A}^{-1})$.

The motion of the rotor magnet induces a back emf (eb) in the stator windings:

$eb = k\, w_m$

where k has the same numerical value as in Equation (10.1) but now has the dimensions $\text{V (rad s}^{-1})^{-1}$. We can also express this as a function of the rotation rate of the load:

$eb = K\, w$

where $K = k\, N$ now has the dimensions $\text{V (rad s}^{-1})^{-1}$.

We can then derive a differential equation that models the resulting angular rates of the rotor and the load:

$m - m_f = J_g(dw/dt) + N\, J_m(dw_m/dt)$

and since w and w_m are related by the gear ratio (N), this can be written as

$m - m_f = J_g(dw/dt) + N\, J_m\, N(dw/dt)$

We can also combine the two inertias as: $J = J_g + N^2 J_m$, which simplifies the above differential equation to

$$J\,(dw/dt) = m - m_f \tag{10.3}$$

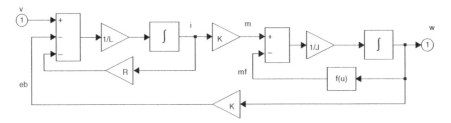

Figure 10.3 Block diagram representation of motor plus load. *Source:* Reproduced with permission from Olis Rubin, *Control Engineering in Development Projects*, Norwood, MA: Artech House Inc., 2016 © 2016 by Artech House Inc.

The differential equations (10.2) and (10.3) can be implemented as indicated in Figure 10.3, where the block $[f(u)]$ is used to simulate the load torque as a non-linear function $f(w)$ of angular rate. This model can be used to study the dynamic behavior of the plant as well as its steady-state operation, while the block diagram will be used to visualize interactions within the system.

10.2.2 The motor drive parameters

Before we can simulate these equations on the computer, we need to quantify the physical parameters of the plant. The simulation must also allow for the fact that hardware does not behave precisely like a textbook model. For example, the components that go into electric motors are machined within given tolerances, which implies that there will be tolerances on the physical parameters of the motor. When the manufacturer's data sheet contains a statement such as: "All parameters may vary by $\pm 10\%$," this could include the manufacturing tolerances as well as other effects.

Section 10.3.1 describes how the motor and the drive mechanics are designed to satisfy specified performance requirements. We will use the parameter values that are given in Rubin (2016, pp. 27–29):

$$R = 0.15 \text{ ohm} \pm 10\%$$

$$L = 0.5 \text{ mhenry} \pm 10\%$$

$$K_{max} = 20 \text{ V} \left(\text{rad s}^{-1}\right)^{-1}; \text{Nm A}^{-1}$$

$$K_{min} = 15 \text{ V} \left(\text{rad s}^{-1}\right)^{-1}; \text{Nm A}^{-1}$$

$$J_{min} = 300 \text{ kg m}^2$$

$$J_{max} = 400 \text{ kg m}^2$$

Note that K_{max} equals the product $N_{max} k_{max}$, while K_{min} equals $N_{min} k_{min}$.

Friction is often the most difficult plant parameter to determine because its behavior depends on so many different variables. For this reason, it is approximated by a linear model:

$$m_f = F\,w$$

where

$$F_{min} = 250\ \text{Nm}\ \left(\text{rad s}^{-1}\right)^{-1}$$
$$F_{max} = 450\ \text{Nm}\ \left(\text{rad s}^{-1}\right)^{-1}$$

This approximation may not be valid if the Coulomb friction has a significant effect.

10.2.3 Creating the simulation model

We can now create a computer model of the motor drive that is based on the block diagram shown in Figure 10.3 and nominal parameter values that lie within the above tolerance bands. Since we are working within a defined project plan that has little allowance for errors, we need to take special precautions to ensure that we produce valid results. We can try to ensure this by following a methodical procedure to create and verify the model. Although some readers may become impatient with the time and care that this involves, we cannot overemphasize the advantages of following such a process. Firstly, it gives us greater understanding of the plant itself. Secondly, if we try to do a rush job we will generally make mistakes, and the time to fix these errors will usually be far longer than the time taken to follow the recommended procedure. Rubin (2016, pp. 29–42) gives a detailed description of such a process, where extensive cross-checks are done at each stage by comparing simulation results and graphs with theoretical calculations. We will briefly show how this can be done.

It is often preferable to break up the model into recognizable subsystems that can be built up individually and tested separately before they are integrated into the simulation of the motor drive. For example, Figure 10.2 shows an electrical circuit that causes a current to flow through the stator together with the mechanics that produce the motion of the load. These two subsystems are linked by electromagnetic reactions within the motor, where the stator current causes a torque that acts on the load, while the motion of the load causes a back emf that reduces the stator current. The motor drive model can thus be built up using the subsystem blocks shown in Figure 10.4, where $Hs(s)$ represents the stator subsystem while $Hf(s)$ represents the mechanical subsystem. The interconnections between the subsystems are through the gains (K). The model includes an additional input (wv) that will be ignored for the moment. Readers can verify that this configuration

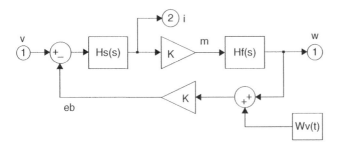

Figure 10.4 Simulation built up from subsystems. *Source:* Reproduced with permission from Olis Rubin, *Control Engineering in Development Projects*, Norwood, MA: Artech House Inc., 2016 © 2016 by Artech House Inc.

is equivalent to the model shown in Figure 10.3. The next sections will illustrate how subsystems are created and checked before they are integrated into the motor drive model, where further cross-checks are done. It could be argued that the intermediate step is not necessary since the motor drive model shown in Figure 10.3 is so simple, but we will see later that a methodical procedure can still offer certain advantages.

10.2.4 The electrical and mechanical subsystems

The stator subsystem is described by the following differential equation:

$$L \, di/dt = u - i R$$

where u equals the difference between the drive voltage (v) and the stator back emf (eb). This can be simulated as shown in Figure 10.5 by means of MATLAB-Simulink software where the triangular block is a gain, the circular block is a summer, and the square block [$1/s$] is an integrator.

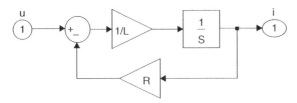

Figure 10.5 Stator subsystem. *Source:* Reproduced with permission from Olis Rubin, *Control Engineering in Development Projects*, Norwood, MA: Artech House Inc., 2016 © 2016 by Artech House Inc.

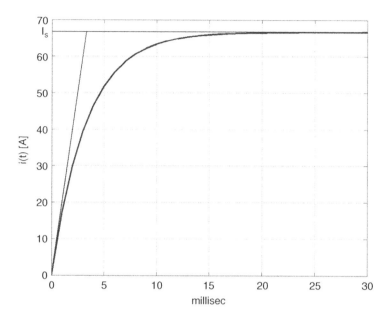

Figure 10.6 Step response of stator subsystem. *Source:* Reproduced with permission from Olis Rubin, *Control Engineering in Development Projects*, Norwood, MA: Artech House Inc., 2016 © 2016 by Artech House Inc.

We should verify that the parameters and variables are defined in consistent units. For example, since R is in ohms, we can define L to be in henrys so that the stator time constant:

$$T_s = L/R$$

will be in seconds.

We can test this subsystem before it is integrated into the motor drive model, by applying a step input (u) of 10 V. We will then obtain the transient shown in Figure 10.6. This can be cross-checked by the geometric construction shown in the figure. We can confirm that the point where the two tangents to the curve intersect corresponds to the time T_s. We will refer to the transfer function of this subsystem as $Hs(s) = I(s)/U(s)$.

The mechanical subsystem can be described by the following differential equation:

$$J \, dw/dt = m - w F$$

where the friction has been approximated by a linear coefficient.

We can again simulate it by means of a summer, an integrator, and two gains (1/ J and F), which can be verified by doing cross-checks. For example, since J is in kg m^2 and F is in Nm (rad s^{-1})$^{-1}$, the mechanical time constant:

$$T_f = J/F$$

will again be in seconds.

We will refer to the transfer function of the mechanical subsystem as

$$Hf(s) = W(s)/M(s) = (1/F)/(1 + sT_f)$$

We see from the parameter values given in Section 10.2.2 that T_f is in the vicinity of 1 second. On the other hand, Figure 10.6 shows that the stator responds within milliseconds. The two subsystems operate at very different time scales as well as representing different physical phenomena!

10.2.5 System integration

We can now integrate the two subsystems into the motor drive model shown in Figure 10.4 and test it by applying a step input (v) of 10 volts. This will produce the transient shown in Figure 10.7. The same result can be obtained by analysis.

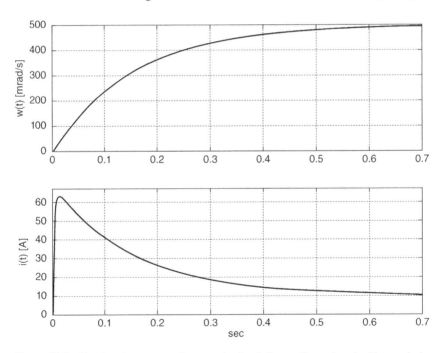

Figure 10.7 Simulated response of motor plus load. *Source:* Reproduced with permission from Olis Rubin, *Control Engineering in Development Projects*, Norwood, MA: Artech House Inc., 2016 © 2016 by Artech House Inc.

Section 6.3.2 described how we can derive the state equations and transfer function of a dynamic model. If the motor drive model shown in Figure 10.4 is saved in a Simulink file `motDrive.mdl`, the following MATLAB function will determine the matrices that define its state equations:

```
[A,B,C,D]=linmod('motDrive')
```

The system modes of motion are then determined by the statement

```
[T, D]  = eig(A)
```

where `D` is a diagonal matrix that contains the following eigenvalues:

```
D(1,1)   =  - 333          // rad s⁻¹
D(2,2)   =  - 5.3          // rad s⁻¹
```

This implies that the system has two modes that both settle exponentially. The transient response of the stator current $i(t)$ shown in Figure 10.7 is given by the following algebraic expression, where the coefficients `c0`, `c1`, and `c2` are chosen to match the figure:

```
i = c0 - c1*exp(-333*t) + c2*exp(-5.3*t)
```

We have seen that the stator current responds within milliseconds, while the rotor speed responds within seconds. Thus, the back emf will be negligible over the first few milliseconds, where the current transient looks nearly like Figure 10.6. This behavior corresponds to the term $-c_1 \exp(-333t)$, which rises with a time constant equal to 3 ms. The cross-checks that were done on the subsystems have given us valuable insight into understanding the transient behavior of the motor drive.

After this initial transient, the rotor speed (w) then starts rising almost exponentially and this generates a back emf (eb) that opposes the drive voltage. This causes the stator current to fall with a time constant equal to 189 ms to a final value where the motor torque just opposes the load friction. This behavior corresponds to the term $c_2 \exp(-5.3t)$.

The transfer function $\underline{H}(s)$ of the motor drive model can be derived from its state equation matrices `[A,B,C,D]`. Note that the model shown in Figure 10.4 has one input and two outputs, so $\underline{H}(s)$ is made up of two components, where one transfer function describes the response of the stator current $i(t)$ to the drive voltage while the other describes the response $w(t)$ of the load. These transfer functions have the same denominator $D(s)$. Since the roots of $D(s)$ are equal to the eigenvalues (`D`) of the matrix (`A`) we have:

$$D(s) = (s + 5.3)(s + 333)$$

The two transfer functions have different numerators, whose numerical values can be determined by the statement:

```
[num,den]=ss2tf(A,B,C,D,1)
```

The elements of the vector (den) define the coefficients of the polynomial $D(s)$ while num defines the two numerator polynomials.

Consider the transfer function $H_i(s)$ that defines the response of the stator current $i(t)$ to the drive voltage $v(t)$. The feedback loop shown in Figure 10.4 implies that the numerator of $H_i(s)$ must contain a single root that corresponds to the time constant (T_f) of the subsystem $Hf(s)$. We thus have:

$$H_i(s) = k_i \, (s + 1)/D(s)$$

where the value of the gain term (k_i) is chosen to match the steady state current shown in Figure 10.7.

10.2.6 Configuration management

During the design phase we will make increasing use of the simulation model as a test bed for evaluating system performance. Experiments will be done where control elements are added to the model and parameters are varied. We thus need a system to keep track of parameter changes and save them for comparison as the trade-offs between performance and operating constraints become clearer. The model block diagrams represent simulation files with parameters that are defined as variables in the operating workspace. Rubin (2016, p. 41) shows how numerical data can be defined in a MATLAB M file, while in Scilab it can be defined in an SCE file. For example, the value of the motor constant (K) can be defined by suitably commented instruction of the form:

```
K = 17.5;
```

We can execute such data files in order to create the variables prior to running the simulation. This allows us to use the same simulation model with different numbers as the need arises. We can use issue numbers in data file headers and comments that note reasons for design changes, etc. Having developed the simulation model, we can encapsulate it in a library that is kept under configuration management.

10.3 The definition phase

The first step is to agree on the *Design Requirements* that specify the performance of the product and its operating environment. The product is to be mounted on a moving vehicle. This motion will induce disturbances on the load. This chapter

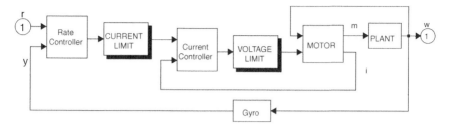

Figure 10.8 Motor drive schematic. *Source:* Reproduced with permission from Olis Rubin, *Control Engineering in Development Projects*, Norwood, MA: Artech House Inc., 2016 © 2016 by Artech House Inc.

will concentrate on the elevation of the camera, where the project team intends to use a control scheme such as that shown in Figure 10.8. The blocks marked MOTOR and PLANT correspond to the motor drive that is simulated in Figure 10.4. The operator manually commands the rotation rate of the camera by applying the input signal (r) to a rate controller that has feedback from an angular rate signal (w). There is also a current controller that follows commands from the rate controller and has feedback from the stator current (i).

The operator wishes to slew the camera to a designated direction within an acceptable time. This requirement will influence the choice of motor to be used in the drive, as will be shown in Section 10.3.1.

The controllers are required to stabilize the camera against disturbances that are caused by the motion of the vehicle. The source of these disturbances will be discussed in Section 10.3.2.

Since we have already created a generic simulation model of the motor drive, this can be used to play a supportive role in defining the design requirements for the plant. Our confidence in the simulation results will be highly dependent on how much experience we have gained on similar projects. This determines the margin of reserve that we should add to the specifications.

10.3.1 Selection of the motor

We can use the simulation model to calculate the capability of the motor drive to slew from one direction to another. Figure 10.8 shows a voltage limit between the current controller and the motor. This represents a physical limit that is imposed by the supply voltage (**V**) to the drive unit. This will determine the ultimate limit on the slew rate of the drive. For instance, consider the case where the friction torque (mf) in Figure 10.3 is zero. This block diagram then shows us that the motor torque (m) causes the load to accelerate until it reaches a steady-state speed where the back emf (*eb*) of the motor equals the input voltage (*v*). The maximum achievable no-load speed is thus given by

$$\mathbf{W}_o = \mathbf{V}/K \; \left(\text{rad s}^{-1}\right)$$

When the motor is at standstill the back emf is zero. Figure 10.3 then shows us that an input voltage (*v*) produces a steady-state current equal to v/R. The maximum achievable stall torque is thus given by

$$\mathbf{M}_s = K\,\mathbf{V}/R \; (\text{Nm})$$

It can be shown analytically that the torque–speed curve at full drive voltage is a straight line that satisfies the following equation:

$$(m/\mathbf{M}_s) = 1 - (w/\mathbf{W}_o)$$

This shows that increasing the motor speed reduces the torque. The motor power will also vary as a function of speed, where the maximum motor power is given by:

$$P_x = \mathbf{W}_o\,\mathbf{M}_s/4 = \tfrac{1}{4}\,\mathbf{V}^2/R$$

Using a power supply of 24 volts, a stator resistance of 0.15 ohms gives a P_x close to 1 kilowatt, which determines the power rating of this particular motor.

The top graph in Figure 10.7 shows the slew rate of the motor drive when 10 volts is applied to the stator. Thus 24 volts will take a third of a second to reach a steady-state slew rate of 69 degrees s^{-1}.

In addition to the torque that accelerates the load and the torque to overcome friction, the drive will generally have to overcome other load torques. The static friction often requires the motor to develop more torque when it starts from standstill than it needs when the load is moving. The motor may also have to provide a torque that overcomes any imbalance of the load.

We often have to limit the sustained current that flows through the stator coils to avoid overheating the motor. Figure 10.8 shows both a voltage limit and a current limit. Restricting the current through the stator coils limits the maximum achievable torque from the motor.

We will then have to design the linkages that drive the load. Increasing the gear ratio (*N*) will increase the achievable torque on the load but reduces the achievable speed. This changes the slope of the torque–speed curve, while the opposite occurs when *N* is reduced.

Readers who are interested can find more details in Rubin (2016, pp. 55–59) where motor torque–speed curves are shown.

10.3.2 Simulation of load disturbances

The design requirements should specify how well the motor drive should stabilize the camera against disturbances. The camera operator is concerned with angular

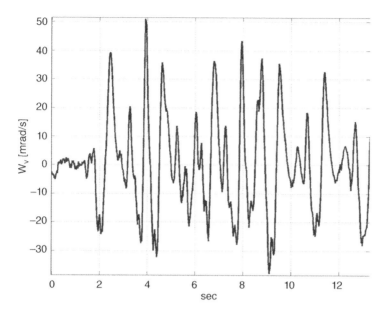

Figure 10.9 Recorded vehicle pitch rate. (*Source:* Reproduced with permission from Olis Rubin, *Control Engineering in Development Projects*, Norwood, MA: Artech House Inc., 2016 © 2016 by Artech House Inc.)

deviations of the boresight from the object of interest. The controllers shown in Figure 10.8 are meant to limit perturbations on the angular rate of the load. Rubin (2016, pp. 52–53) provides some discussion on ways to arrive at a suitable specification, and then assumes that the rms rate accuracy should be less than 0.5 mrad s^{-1}. We now need to determine the operating environment under which this specification should be met. If we have a prototype vehicle it should be tested to determine its pitching motion. A representative recording of the vehicle pitch rate $wv(t)$ is shown in Figure 10.9, while Appendix A.4 shows how we can determine the spectrum of this signal. There is a dominant oscillation at a frequency band around 1.3 Hz (8 rad s^{-1}).

Figure 10.4 shows how the vehicle pitch rate $wv(t)$ will induce an electromagnetic torque in the motor. The stator will rotate with the vehicle while the rotor is linked to the load through a gear ratio (N). This implies that the stator rotates at a rate $N(w - wv)$ relative to the rotor giving an induced emf in the stator:

$$eb = K (w - wv)$$

With a constant drive voltage this emf causes the stator current to change as follows:

$$i = eb/R$$

There is then a resulting change in motor torque that will drag the load behind the vehicle:

$$m = K i = (K^2/R)(w - wv)$$

Using the parameter values given in Section 10.2.2, the motor torque produced by this effect lies within the following limits:

$$K_{max}^2/R_{min} = 2900 \text{ Nm} \left(\text{rad s}^{-1}\right)^{-1}$$

$$K_{min}^2/\mathbf{R}_{max} = 1360 \text{ Nm} \left(\text{rad s}^{-1}\right)^{-1}$$

When the recorded vehicle pitch rate $wv(t)$ is added to the motor drive model, it induces a current $i(t)$ in the stator that is shown in Figure 10.10 together with the resulting perturbation $w(t)$ on the load. The simulation was done with K^2/R equal to 2000 Nm $(\text{rad s}^{-1})^{-1}$ while the drive voltage (v) was kept constant. This perturbation is 40 times larger than the operational specification. We will thus have to design controllers to improve the overall disturbance rejection.

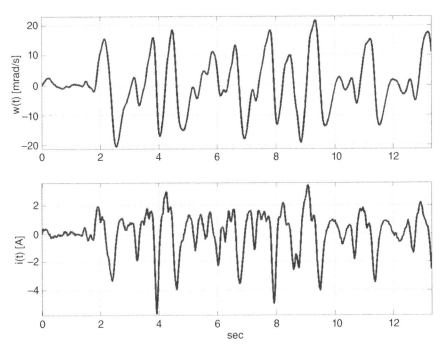

Figure 10.10 Perturbation in current and pitch rate. *Source:* Reproduced with permission from Olis Rubin, *Control Engineering in Development Projects*, Norwood, MA: Artech House Inc., 2016 © 2016 by Artech House Inc.

10.4   The design phase

We will now go on to the design of controllers that stabilizes the motor drive system against disturbances. The intended control scheme is shown in Figure 10.8. The simulation model will be used to provide design data, as well as to simulate the performance of the resulting design in the operating environment.

It is possible to reduce the load perturbations shown in Figure 10.10 by creating a drive voltage that opposes the induced emf $K(w - wv)$. The designers intend to use the scheme that is shown in Figure 10.11 to achieve this. In addition to the current feedback loop shown in Figure 10.8, this scheme makes use of a feedforward signal that is derived from a rate gyro that measures the pitch rate $wv(t)$ of the vehicle. Whereas the rate gyro is an accurate instrument, there are other factors that can degrade the efficacy of the feedforward compensation. The designers have reason to doubt whether they can accurately match the motor gain (K) to oppose the back emf that is produced by vehicle pitch motion, and will therefore make a conservative estimate that there is still a residual perturbation of around 3 mrad s^{-1} after feedforward compensation.

The current feedback loop can further oppose the effect of the induced emf. Appendix A.8 sketches the basic principles whereby the current controller can be designed in the frequency domain. The designers will thus ask us to determine the frequency response of the motor drive model.

10.4.1   Calculation of frequency response

We will use the procedure that is described in Rubin (2016, pp. 219–220) to compute the frequency response of the motor drive model from its state equation matrices (A, B, C, D), which were calculated in Section 10.2.5. The following MATLAB statement creates a state equation model of the motor drive:

```
SYS = ss(A,B,C,D);
```

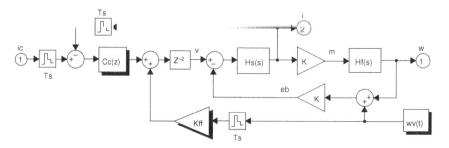

Figure 10.11   Simulated current control system. *Source:* Reproduced with permission from Olis Rubin, *Control Engineering in Development Projects*, Norwood, MA: Artech House Inc., 2016 © 2016 by Artech House Inc.

This can then be used to calculate the magnitude (mg) and phase (ps) of its frequency response:

```
[mg,ps]= bode(SYS,frequency);
```

where frequency defines a set of frequency points in rad s^{-1}.

For example, the following statement creates a vector of frN frequency points that are logarithmically spaced between the values fo and fn:

```
frequency = logspace(log10(fo), log10(fn), frN);
```

We can use the following instructions to access the results [mg,ps] for further use:

```
zz = size(mg);
mag = ones(zz(1,zz(3)));
phs = mag;
mag(:,1:frN) = mg(:,:,1:frN);
phs(:,1:frN)= ps(:,:,1:frN);
magdB = 20*log10(mag);
```

This will create vectors (magdB) and (phs) that describe the response of the plant over the frequency band. For example, the frequency response of the motor drive can be plotted by the instructions:

```
semilogx(frequency,magdB);
semilogx(frequency,phs);
```

The Bode plot shown in Figure 10.12 shows how the stator current responds to the drive voltage.

Before giving this Bode plot to the designers we can do a cross-check by drawing four tangents to the gain curve, which have slopes of 0 ; 20 ; 0, and −20 dB decade^{-1}. These tangents intersect at three frequencies that correspond to the values 1, 5.3, and 333 rad s^{-1} that were determined in Section 10.2.5. We also see that the low frequency gain of the Bode plot (approximately 0 dB) agrees with the steady state response in Figure 10.7 while the mid frequency gain (approximately 15 dB) agrees with the initial peak of the current transient.

10.4.2 The current control loop

The project team has decided to use digital controllers. This is simulated in Figure 10.11 where the sample and hold block represents the analog to digital converter (ADC) between the hardware and the controller, while a delay block [z^{-2}] is used to simulate latency in the data links together with the computation time within

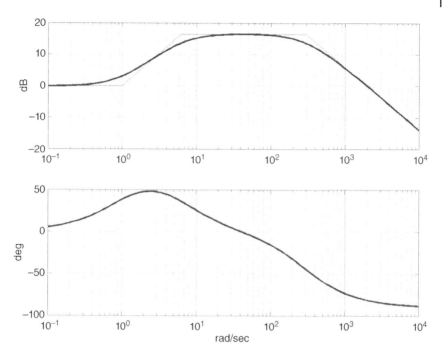

Figure 10.12 Frequency response of stator current. *Source:* Reproduced with permission from Olis Rubin, *Control Engineering in Development Projects*, Norwood, MA: Artech House Inc., 2016 © 2016 by Artech House Inc.

the computer. It will be assumed that this corresponds to a delay of 0.4 ms. Appendices A.8.1 and A.8.2 show how a digital PI controller can be programmed, while it is simulated in Figure 10.11 by the subsystem block that is labeled $Cc(z)$.

As described in Rubin (2016, pp. 70–73), the designers can simplify their calculations by modeling the digital controller as a continuous transfer function $Cc(s)$ in series with a time delay $\exp(-s\,Td)$, which models the delay of 0.4 ms plus the effect of a sample and hold. Appendix A.7.1 shows that this can be approximated by a delay of half the sample period, where Ts equals 0.0002 second, giving Td equal to 0.0005 second. Appendix A.7 shows that this will add a phase lag: Pd = frequency*Td to that of the controller. Appendix A.8 recommends that a control loop should be designed to have a phase margin of about 45 degrees. Figure 10.12 shows that the phase lag of the stator current is approaching 80 degrees at 1000 rad s^{-1}, where the phase lag (Pd) approaches 30 degrees. The designers could thus tolerate a loop gain of unity at this frequency and still have ample margin for the phase lag that is introduced by the controller. Section 10.3.2 showed dominant disturbances around 8 rad s^{-1}, while Figure 10.12 shows that the gain of the plant at this frequency is comparable with its gain at 1000 rad s^{-1}. The designers will thus wish to evaluate the effect of a PI controller to boost the low-frequency loop gain. They could perform rapid experiments by creating it as a transfer function model (SYSC):

```
Ti = 0.0033;                                  // second
Kp = 0.3;
numC = Kp*[Ti, 1];
denC = [Ti, 0];
SYSC = tf(num, den);
```

The above example corresponds to:

$$Cc(s) = 0.3 \left[1 + 300\, s^{-1}\right]$$

The following statement then calculates its gain (mgC) and phase (psC):

```
[mgC,psC] = bode(SYSC,frequency);
```

The frequency response of the current loop can then be found by adding mgC (in dB) to the gain (magdB) of the plant and the phase (psC + Pd) (in degrees) to phs. The designers can vary Kp and Ti in order to find controller parameters that meet the performance requirements. Readers who are interested in the design of the current control loop can find more details in Rubin (2016, pp. 69–81), where graphs and calculations are presented.

The designers can use the MATLAB command c2d() to convert the continuous controller to its discrete equivalent $Cc(z)$, which can then be implemented in the simulation model shown in Figure 10.11. We can then check the closed-loop behavior of the current control loop by testing its response to a step command (ic) of 1 amp. Figure 10.13 shows that the stator current closely follows the command without overshoot or resonance, further confirming that the design has an ample phase margin.

Having confirmed the design, we can proceed to verify how well the current control system counteracts the effect of vehicle motion. This is simulated in Figure 10.11 by the output of the block marked wv(t), which is added to the motion of the load so as to induce a stator emf. The same signal is used to simulate the rate gyro output, which generates the feedforward signal. It was stated in Section 10.4 that the designers are uncertain how well they can match the feedforward to the physical effect. We will model this by assuming that there is a 15% difference between the motor parameter (K) and the controller gain (Kff). The response of the system to the wv(t) will then be as shown in Figure 10.14. The resulting perturbation is now within the specified 0.5 mrad s^{-1}.

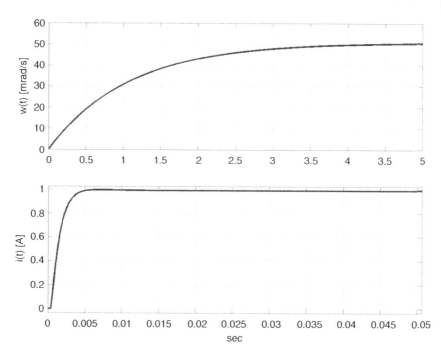

Figure 10.13 Closed-loop step response to commanded current. *Source:* Reproduced with permission from Olis Rubin, *Control Engineering in Development Projects*, Norwood, MA: Artech House Inc., 2016 © 2016 by Artech House Inc.

It is important to realize that a digital simulation is implemented by means of discrete operations, which are subject to an underlying sample rate. The Max step size of a Simulink model can be set by means of the Simulation function in its menu bar (see the MATLAB user documentation and help). Figure 10.13 was created by running the model with a step size that was less than 0.1 ms. We can run into difficulties if the step size is too long. This is illustrated in Figure 10.15, which shows a false instability when the step size is increased to 3 ms. This is because the sample rate is then insufficient for such a fast loop.

10.4.3 Design review and further actions

The computer model has been used to quantify the control requirements, to provide data for the designers, and to do a cross-check on their design. The design was based on the assumption that the control equipment introduced an effective delay of 0.5 ms.

The designers can program the digital controller in a language such as C# by using the difference equations that are given in Appendix A.8.1. It may then be

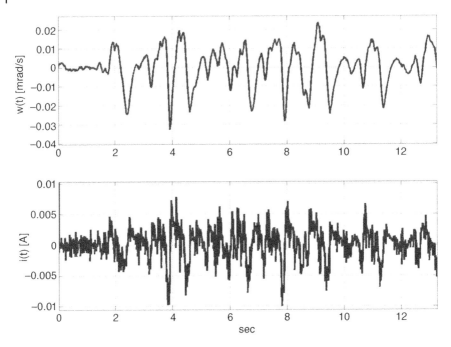

Figure 10.14 Perturbations reduced by current control scheme. *Source:* Reproduced with permission from Olis Rubin, *Control Engineering in Development Projects*, Norwood, MA: Artech House Inc., 2016 © 2016 by Artech House Inc.

compiled to run on a micro-controller that drives the switching bridge shown in Figure 10.1. The controller must also switch between stator windings as the motor rotates. The system could also be implemented with analog electronics.

The simulation model shown in Figure 10.11 can serve as a test bed to investigate system performance under worst-case operating conditions, where we can check the sensitivity of the design to variations in plant parameters. We can run the sample and hold blocks with a larger `Ts` in order to see whether the control loop can tolerate longer delays in the digital controller. It is found that the phase lag produced by increasing the sample period to 1.1 ms will drive the system to the verge of instability. This effect can be compared with the instability that was shown in Figure 10.15. It thus seems that `Ts = 0.2` ms was a good choice.

A good designer will do cross-checks by comparing different calculations against one another. One of the reasons for doing this is that the results are different faces of the same coin, and thus help the designer to look at the system from different angles. Rubin (2016, pp. 74–80) simulates the digital controller by a Padé approximation of the delay (`Td`) in series with a continuous controller, which gives a closed loop step response that is similar to Figure 10.13. It then goes on to find an analytic expression for the closed loop response: $Ha(s) = I(s)/Ic(s)$.

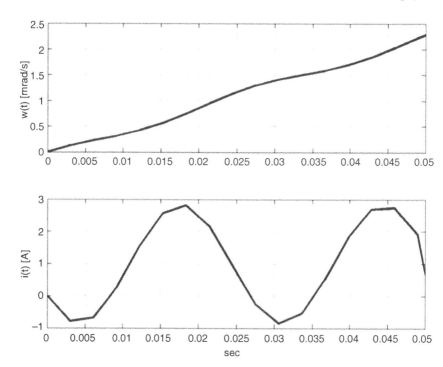

Figure 10.15 Step response with long simulation step size. *Source:* Reproduced with permission from Olis Rubin, *Control Engineering in Development Projects*, Norwood, MA: Artech House Inc., 2016 © 2016 by Artech House Inc.

However, we must realize that the simulation models, frequency responses, and transfer functions are all derived from the original differential equations, so any mistakes made at this level will show up in the different results.

We also need to review our computer model. For example, we should confirm that the bearing friction is adequately approximated by the viscous coefficient (F). The drive uses PWM that switches the stator between full positive and negative supply voltage. We should investigate to what extent the resulting ripple in the motor tor que allows us to linearize our model of the bearing friction.

10.4.4 Rate feedback

Whereas the current control loop suppresses perturbations to the motor current it does not counteract torques that act directly on the load. In fact, it actively reduces the ability of the motor to counteract perturbations due to such torques. This is illustrated in Figure 10.13, which shows how the steady-state current is virtually unaffected by a change in motor speed of 50 mrad s^{-1}. This implies that the current loop will inhibit the production of a motor torque to oppose any such perturbation.

The vehicle pitch motion $wv(t)$ shown in Figure 10.9 will act through the friction in the bearings to produce a torque that acts directly on the load. The equation of motion given in Section 10.2.4 can be augmented as follows to include this effect:

$$J\, dw/dt = m - F(w - wv)$$

Figure 10.16 shows how this can be simulated. Readers will notice that the output of the subsystem block $[Wv(t)]$ is added to the motion (w) of the load, whereas the friction torque in the bearings depends on the relative motion between the vehicle and the load. Vehicle motion was physically measured and recorded in a data file that can then be read into the computer model. The simulation engineers will have to ensure that the data is correctly scaled in rad s^{-1}. If the polarity of the signal is important, it is also necessary to ensure that it is correctly added to the model. The same observations apply to its use in Section 10.3.2.

Figure 10.9 shows that the vehicle pitch rate resembles zero mean random noise. If we believe that the hardware responds symmetrically to this motion, we would probably accept an error in polarity, as it should have little effect on the resulting rms perturbation. It is likely that the approximation of the friction in the various bearings by a single linear coefficient gives a more misleading result.

The vehicle pitch motion can be simulated as shown above within the mechanical subsystem block $[Hf(s)]$, which is shown in Figure 10.11. It will then produce the perturbation shown in Figure 10.17, which is once again out of specification! Since we do not expect the motor to react to this motion, we can do a cross-check by applying the signal $wv(t)$ as an input to the mechanical subsystem without connecting it to the motor drive model. Its response corresponds to a time constant T_f, which is close to 1 second.

The load disturbances can be counteracted by the rate feedback loop that is shown in Figure 10.8. The angular rate (w) of the load is measured by a gyro and used as a feedback signal that goes to a rate controller. The rate control loop operates around a current feedback loop whose closed-loop response is given by a transfer function $Ha(s)$. Figure 10.13 shows that this responds to commands within milliseconds, and its transfer function can be approximated by a gain of unity.

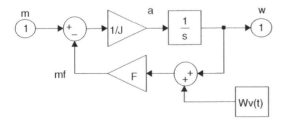

Figure 10.16 Mechanical subsystem. *Source:* Reproduced with permission from Olis Rubin, *Control Engineering in Development Projects*, Norwood, MA: Artech House Inc., 2016 © 2016 by Artech House Inc.

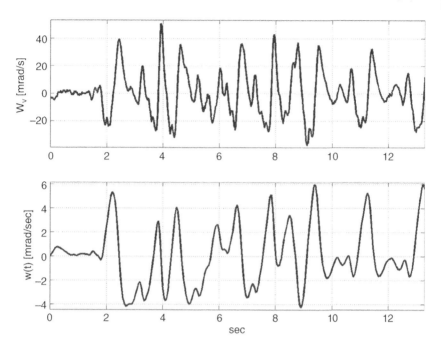

Figure 10.17 Vehicle pitch rate and load perturbation due to friction. *Source:* Reproduced with permission from Olis Rubin, *Control Engineering in Development Projects*, Norwood, MA: Artech House Inc., 2016 © 2016 by Artech House Inc.

The upper plot of Figure 10.13 shows that the response of the load $w(t)$ to a change in current can be approximated by a transfer function:

$$Hf(s) = W(s)/Ic(s) = 0.05/(1 + s)$$

The current feedback has thus significantly simplified the task of designing the rate loop. Rubin (2016, pp. 81–98) present graphs and calculations that show the design of a well-damped rate loop, which reduces the load perturbations to well within the specification. The bandwidth of this loop is about 20 rad s^{-1}, so it is adequate to use a continuous controller within the simulation model. This can then be used as a test bed to investigate system performance. We recall that the time constant of the mechanical subsystem depends on the load inertia and the bearing friction, where our knowledge is questionable. We should thus pay particular attention to the simulation of Coulomb friction, stiction, and mass imbalance. The model can also be used to determine whether the system can meet the slew requirements discussed in Section 10.3.1. We can then investigate whether we need anti-windup (see Appendix A.8.2) to allow for current and voltage saturation. The need for all these tests amply justifies the effort that we spent on creating our computer model.

10.5 A setback to the project

The project will arrive at a point where the team can integrate the control system with the hardware. Rubin (2016, pp. 101–105) describes this process and its consequences in more detail. When the engineers close the rate loop they will find to their dismay that they cannot increase the controller gain above 7% of the design value without provoking an unacceptable oscillation of the system! With this gain the disturbance rejection will be hopelessly inadequate!

> *Such unpleasant surprises can occur when we go from the computer to the hardware! It is from such experiences that we learn to take suitable precautions in future projects!*

The project team, which includes us, actually has two problems:

1) The rate loop gives insufficient disturbance rejection.
2) The rate loop simulation model differs significantly from the plant.

We reach a consensus that we must first resolve the *simulation* problem before we can solve the *control* problem, so we participate in sessions to determine why the simulation model differs from the plant. We firstly verify that the *known* effects within the plant are correctly simulated, structurally and numerically. After this we compile a short list of effects that were neglected in the simulation, such as dead times in the control hardware or software and backlash, dead-bands, static friction, and structural resonances in the drive train and the sensor mounting. It is now possible to quantify these effects by hardware tests. A test is done where the motor is abruptly stopped while it is running at speed. We find that this causes the load to oscillate, as shown in Figure 10.18. While the mechanical designers look for the causes of this vibration, we can use the simulation model to investigate the consequences of such a structural resonance on the control system.

10.5.1 Elastic coupling between motor and load

This structural resonance could be caused by elasticity in the drive train between the motor and the load. There can then be a torsional deformation in the linkages that produce an angular deflection (θ) between the motor and the load. The simulation model shown in Figure 10.19 includes this effect, where the torsion between the motor and the load is determined by

$$d\theta/dt = (wm/N) - w(t)$$

The input (wm/N) in Figure 10.19 represents the motion of the motor (wm) divided by the gear ratio (N) of the linkages. The output (w) is the angular rate

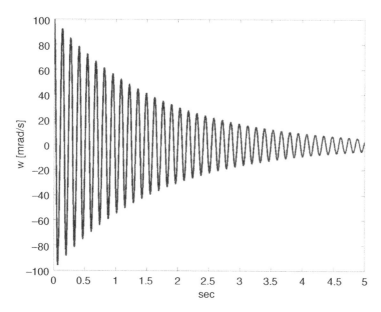

Figure 10.18 Induced oscillation of the load. *Source:* Reproduced with permission from Olis Rubin, *Control Engineering in Development Projects*, Norwood, MA: Artech House Inc., 2016 © 2016 by Artech House Inc.

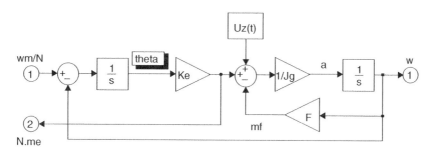

Figure 10.19 Load mechanics with elastic coupling. *Source:* Reproduced with permission from Olis Rubin, *Control Engineering in Development Projects*, Norwood, MA: Artech House Inc., 2016 © 2016 by Artech House Inc.

of the load. The mechanical time constant of the load on its own is given by a differential equation:

$$Jg \, dw/dt = Ke \, \theta - F \, w + Uz(t)$$

where Jg is the moment of inertia of the load while F is the associated bearing friction.

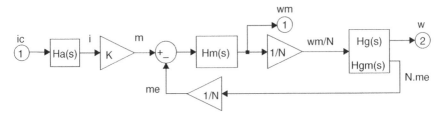

Figure 10.20 Simulation of motor and load. *Source:* Reproduced with permission from Olis Rubin, *Control Engineering in Development Projects*, Norwood, MA: Artech House Inc., 2016 © 2016 by Artech House Inc.

The input $Uz(t)$ simulates any external moments that act on the load, such as the moment due to pitching of the vehicle acting through the bearing friction.

The difference $(wm/N - w)$ between the angular rates is integrated to determine the torsion (θ) of the elastic linkage. This in turn produces a torque $(Ke\ \theta)$ that drives the load. The same torque acts through the linkages to produce a load (me) on the motor. Figure 10.19 has a second output $(N\ me)$ that must be reduced by the gear ratio (N) to determine the load on the motor.

The overall simulation of the motor and the load is shown in Figure 10.20, where the model defined by Figure 10.19 is included as the subsystem block $[H_g(s)\ H_{gm}(s)]$.

The subsystem block $[Hm(s)]$ simulates the mechanical time constant of the motor, as given by the differential equation:

$$Jm\ dwm/dt = (m\ me) - f\ wm$$

where Jm is the moment of inertia of the motor while f is the associated bearing friction.

The motor and the load are thus free to move independently. Some readers may ask why we have not included the effect of the back emf on the stator current. We can again refer to Figure 10.13, which shows that once the current has settled to a steady state it is virtually unaffected by the continuing change in motor speed. This implies that the current feedback almost totally suppresses the effect of the back emf.

The subsystem block $[Ha(s)]$ simulates the response of the current feedback loop, where the lower plot in Figure 10.13 shows that the current responds to commands (ic) within a few milliseconds. Figure 10.18 shows a resonance of the load in the vicinity of 50 rad s^{-1}. We can expect this to severely limit the bandwidth of the rate loop, so that the lag introduced by $Ha(s)$ will probably have little effect on the design of the controller. We can thus approximate $Ha(s)$ by a pure gain. A command (ic) from the rate controller then produces a motor torque that is approximately given by $m = K\ ic$.

Section 10.2.4 considered the combined effect, $J = Jg + N^2 Jm$, of the load inertia and that of the motor. We will assume that $Jg = 0.85\,J$. The friction parameters (f and F) can be determined by using the subsystem shown in Figure 10.19 to simulate the hardware test described in Section 10.5. This is done by observing the settling of the load from an initial angular rate (w) while the input signal (wm/N) is clamped to zero. The elasticity of the linkage will then interact with the load inertia to produce a torsional oscillation that is damped by the friction. Varying the stiffness (Ke) changes the frequency of the oscillation, while varying the friction (F) affects the damping. We can then modify the coefficients in the model so as to duplicate the hardware oscillation shown in Figure 10.18. This oscillation also corresponds to the poles of a transfer function $Hg(s)$. We can thus do a cross-check on these results by using the block diagrams shown in Figures 10.19 and 10.20 to derive an algebraic expression for this transfer function.

We can calculate the frequency response of the computer model by using the MATLAB functions as we did in Section 10.4.1. The response $H(j\omega)$ in rad s^{-1} per A, of $W(j\omega)$ to $Ic(j\omega)$ is shown in Figure 10.21. This shows a resonant peak

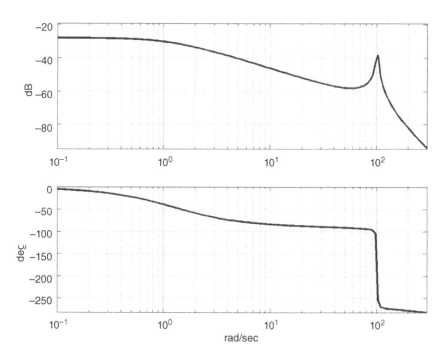

Figure 10.21 Resonant frequency response $H(j\omega)$ of load. *Source:* Reproduced with permission from Olis Rubin, *Control Engineering in Development Projects*, Norwood, MA: Artech House Inc., 2016 © 2016 by Artech House Inc.

in the drive train at 100 rad s^{-1} with a gain that is just above −40 dB. At this point we must give a word of warning! This Bode plot was made with 100 frequency points that cover a span of over three decades. The resulting frequency resolution is far too low to determine the maximum value of this peak. If we were to recalculate the gain over a frequency span of one octave, centered around 100 rad s^{-1}, we would find that the peak is about 10 dB higher!

We see that the phase lag shown in Figure 10.21 at frequencies below 10 rads^{-1} is close to that of the mechanical subsystem, which is modeled in Figure 10.16. This can be approximated by the transfer function $0.05/(1 + s)$. The elasticity of the linkages thus has very little effect over the low-frequency range, but adds a resonant peak, together with an abrupt phase lag, at 100 rad s^{-1}. It is the effect of this resonance that causes our present control problem.

If we now simulate a controller around the revised plant model and vary the proportional gain (K_p) we find that the closed-loop response to a step disturbance of 10 Nm varies as shown in Figure 10.22. The system is stable when K_p is equal

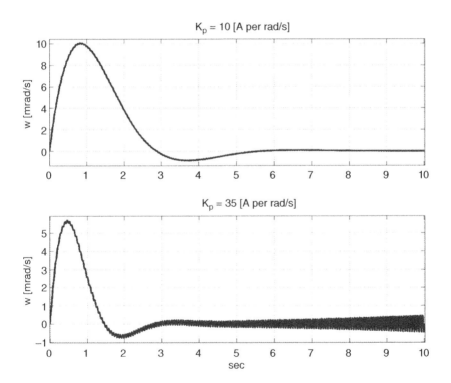

Figure 10.22 Closed-loop response to step disturbance. *Source:* Reproduced with permission from Olis Rubin, *Control Engineering in Development Projects*, Norwood, MA: Artech House Inc., 2016 © 2016 by Artech House Inc.

10 A per rad s^{-1}, but there is a growing oscillation at the resonant frequency when K_p is increased to 35 A per rad s^{-1}. This is a situation where an insufficient gain margin in the loop causes a resonance where the motor and the load oscillate in antiphase. We must avoid this instability by limiting the loop gain to -10 dB at 100 rad s^{-1}. The low frequency gain of the rate loop is thus drastically reduced, as we found when we tested the hardware!

The designers now have a significant challenge to solve this problem. The simulation model can be used as a prototype to assist them by doing "what-if" studies when they investigate modifications to the design. They may consider the use of a notch filter in the rate controller to suppress the resonant gain, or a highly tuned lead compensator that counteracts the abrupt phase lag in the mechanics. Perhaps they can use feedforward from an accelerometer to counteract the disturbance on the load. The mechanical designers can also investigate modifications to stiffen the linkages or increase their damping. There is no guarantee that there is a ready-made solution.to the problem!

There is always the unpleasant option of re-negotiating the contract to allow for reduced performance.

10.6   Discussion

> "Good engineering judgement is based on experience.
> Experience is based on bad engineering judgement"
>
> Anonymous
> (*Source:* Rights Managed)

Project engineers have to learn from experience how to minimize development costs by recognizing potential control problems during the concept and design phases, before resources are spent on building the plant. We have followed a case study that illustrates the adverse consequences that can occur if we overlook a critical aspect that causes such a problem. Simulation models can be of great assistance to the designers at the early stages of a project when they are used as prototypes to do "what-if" studies, but it is necessary to "get them right." Could we perhaps have foreseen that there would be a problem with structural resonance? Engineers who are working on such models could study operational data from similar plants and hardware test results. The very creation of such models forces everyone to delve deeper into the underlying physics of the plant. The more we understand the physical principles that determine the behavior of the plant, the more we can rely on a simulation model as a tool for prototyping and testing.

Readers will typically encounter problems that were not considered in the above example. Maybe next time it will not be a problem with structural resonance but the effect of imbalance in the load, or perhaps there will be too much backlash in the drive, or excessive Coulomb friction. We may also have to consider other factors such as the commutation of the current between stator windings as the motor rotates, or the effect of stator current on the flux density in the airgap, or the sensitivity of the system to variations in plant parameters.

> "The successful campaigner always studies the lay of the land"
>
> Napoleon

Simulation can continue to assist us over all phases of a project. The design can be evaluated by simulation before testing the hardware. Hardware tests can then be done while the plant is in the process of being built. The simulation may sometimes have to be modified to correct discrepancies between its behavior and that of a component in the plant, while in other cases there may have to be modifications to the hardware. We can also make use of simulation during operating trials on the plant where we verify that the product meets its specifications. Such test programs often look at system performance over a wide range of operating conditions. It is sometimes possible to convince the client that we can accept simulated results as a proxy for hardware tests that may be hazardous, or entail too much risk on the plant. Physical tests may also give inexplicable results. This could be because the data rate of the measurements is too low or because the results are influenced by unwanted external disturbances. Sometimes we cannot measure a critical plant variable. At other times we may simply wish to reduce the time and cost of commissioning and qualification by using simulator studies to reduce the scale of hardware testing.

There is also a thriving industry that produces simulators to train the operators how to run the plant. The flight simulators discussed in Chapter 6 are a striking example of such an application.

Section 10.2 illustrated the value of following a methodical procedure to create and verify a computer model. Even the most carefully implemented computer models should always be used with healthy skepticism until they can be verified by tests on the hardware. We must be prudent when commissioning the plant, since modeling errors can cause deviations in dynamic behavior that make the difference between the success or failure of a system.

Before venturing to interpret the results obtained from the computer it is necessary to acquire a feel for the dynamic behavior of the hardware. This can be obtained by watching the physical motion of an object, such as a servo as it settles to its final position or hunts around it. If this motion cannot be appreciated (because it is too fast or too slow) it can be recorded and played back at an adjusted time scale, similar to an action replay of a sporting event. A similar effect can be obtained by watching the output of a simulator on a suitable graphic display.

Readers can implement simulation models such as those that appear in this book and experiment with different parameters. Section 10.2 is there to help with such an effort. The plots produced by a simulation model resemble those produced by hardware whose motion is recorded and played back on a computer. Once readers have acquired a good feeling for dynamic behavior, they will also have a better understanding of the time plots that appear in this book.

Exercises

1   Creation of a computer model
    (a)   Consider the differential equations that model the rotation of a motor. Choose nominal numbers for the coefficients, within the ranges given in Section 10.2.2.

      If a drive of 10 V is applied to this motor, what steady state speed, current, and torque will then be produced?

      Calculate the deviation in speed when the coefficients are varied within the ranges given in Section 10.2.2.

      Find the extreme values of speed that result from the above tolerance bands.

    (b)   Implement a simulation model of the motor using the approach described in this chapter.

      Your simulation should have the form shown in Figures 10.4, 10.5, and 10.16. It is preferable to define the numerical values of the model parameters in a separate file. Choose nominal numbers within the ranges given in Section 10.2.2.

      Determine the response to a 10 V step input, and check the steady-state speed, current, and torque against the results found in part (a).

    (c)   Do a sensitivity study for parameter variations within the tolerance bands given in Section 10.2.2.

      Is there any way whereby we can reduce the scale of this work?

    (d)   Calculate the frequency response of the stator current to the voltage input.

2   Readers can emulate the role model that was presented in Chapter 3 and use their ingenuity to create a computer model of a four-cylinder internal combustion engine with fuel injection that drives a machine through a gearbox.

    The system description resembles Section 10.2.1, where the engine replaces the electric motor, while the machine operates at constant speed. Suppose that the engine delivers 60 kW of shaft power at an operating speed of 3000 rpm, with a gear reduction of 25 to 1. The load torque is dominated by friction, while the load inertia is in the vicinity of 3000 kg m^2.

You can simplify the problem by assuming that the fuel injection produces square pulses of pressure within the cylinders, and can "guess" at the values of any other system parameters that are deemed to be necessary for defining the model.

Bibliography

Rubin, O. (2016). *Control Engineering in Development Projects, Dedham*. MA: Artech House.

11

Postscript

11.1 Looking back

We have followed a series of case studies that began with ways of programming a computer to perform simple repetitive mathematical processes. This was extended to digital methods for solving differential equations. We also saw how scientists created theories to describe the behavior of the physical world around us. Newton then postulated mathematical laws to describe the motion of physical bodies. By combining our computer skills with our knowledge of science we could simulate the behavior of mechanical motion, to the extent of creating a flight simulator. These skills are of great value in the workplace.

We then saw how scientists used the concept of scalar and vector fields to develop equations that describe the propagation of energy through continuous media. There were case studies that showed how this mathematical framework could be exploited to create computer models that simulate the continuous flow of energy. By this means we progressed to complex applications that will challenge the most competent professional. By combining computer modeling with mathematical analysis we could gain a better understanding of the underlying physics.

Further challenges arise when we are dealing with imperfect knowledge or questionable data. It is reasonable to state that the limit on what can be achieved in the field of modeling does not lie with the computer, but with the knowledge of its creators.

The case studies presented in this book are intended to illustrate the general principles rather than to give particular recipes. We have studied computer models that can serve as basic prototypes for the simulation of many different dynamic processes. These consistently used a feedback structure to solve the applicable differential equations. Section 5.3.2 showed how truncation and roundoff could then produce errors in their results. We can probably reduce truncation errors by using a higher-order integration algorithm similar to those presented in Section 2.7.

Computer Models of Process Dynamics: From Newton to Energy Fields, First Edition.
Olis Rubin.
Published 2023 by John Wiley & Sons, Inc.

This then allows us to use a longer step length, and thereby reduce roundoff errors. We could also be confronted by other challenges.

For example, we could find that the mathematical description by means of differential equations also includes implicit algebraic equations similar to those discussed in Section 2.6. We saw there how we could use an iterative solver to search for a solution. We will illustrate the use of such a solver within the model of a dynamic process by considering the following differential equation:

$$dx/dt = y$$

together with the following implicit algebraic equation:

$$xy = 1$$

We can determine the value of y by using a solver that is based on the techniques discussed in Section 2.6. This can be programmed as follows:

```
function y = inv_solve(x, yo, A, G, kmax)
        y = abs(yo);
        e = 1 - abs(x)*y;
        k = 0;
        while abs(e)>A & k<kmax
                y = y + G*e;
                e = 1 - abs(x)*y;
                k = k+1;
        end
        y = y*sign(x);
endfunction
```

The `while` loop will generally operate until the absolute estimation error abs (e) is smaller than the specified accuracy (A), where the gain (G) is chosen to produce satisfactory convergence. Readers can experiment with different values of these parameters while deciding on an acceptable number of iterations. This is best done before the solver is encapsulated within the function `inv_solve()`. Note that the solver has not been designed to handle the situation where x approaches zero.

Since y corresponds to $1/x$ we can use the solver within a program that simulates the above differential equation:

```
for k = 1:K
        y = inv_solve(x(k), y, A, G, imax)
        x(k+1) = x(k) + dt*y
end
```

We leave it to the readers to evaluate its behavior with different initial conditions and step lengths.

Note that the above differential and algebraic equations can be combined to give:

$$dx/dt = 1/x$$

which can be simulated by the following program:

```
for k = 1:K
    x(k+1) = x(k) + dt/x(k)
end
```

Readers can compare the results that are produced by these two approaches.

The operation of the solver can be interpreted as a search for the value of *y* that minimizes the quadratic function $(1 - xy)^2$. It is thus a simple example of a least-squares estimator, many of which have been used in more general applications. The literature gives references to various other more sophisticated solvers that give better results in particular applications.

11.2   The operation of a simulation facility

Some of us will still remember the elaborate procedures that were developed to ensure the successful operation of an analog simulation facility. Apart from being confronted with a rat's nest of wires, we had to contend with voltages that had to be adjusted at the beginning of each session. Digital simulation platforms do not give these problems, but it is nonetheless recommended that the users follow a formal procedure when creating their models. It is not suggested that any single set of rules can hold for all situations, or that when two engineers follow a given procedure they will necessarily achieve the same result. However, a procedure that is logical and well reasoned must improve their chances of obtaining a satisfactory solution, and for that it is well worthwhile. It is also important to document each step of the process to ensure that all information is immediately at hand when results are questioned. The time spent in good preparation usually saves a far greater waste of time that is spent in debugging the computer program.

Chapter 10 showed how computer models can be of help in an engineering project. Before the work begins we should have a clear statement of what is required. This gives us a fair idea as to the accuracy that is needed and the operating frequency. The mathematical equations that describe the hardware should be written as exactly and completely as possible. Approximations can be made later, but omissions made at this stage can come back to haunt us. We have used a digital simulation platform that creates a block diagram as we program the computer. We would probably have drawn a rough block diagram to visualize the signal flow and the mathematical operations to be performed. The model was created by building it up from subsystems, where higher-order differential equations were broken up into first-order equations whose time responses could be cross-checked against simple exponential expressions. We then used mathematical analysis to perform cross-checks on the response of the complete model. By these means we had reasonable confidence that the model functioned correctly.

11.3 Looking forward

We have reached the end of our guided tour and it is now time to take our leave. There are many different areas where you, the reader, can exploit your talents, ranging from science and technology to business and the life sciences. For some applications the use of a computer model is well established and the defining equations are well known. In other areas it will be a daunting task to create a mathematical description of the physical process. There are great opportunities to do work in the study of life sciences. Theories that describe the workings of economics, which is greatly influenced by irrational human behavior, are still in their infancy (Ball, 2005). We saw in Chapter 3 how scientific progress generally depends on a series of inspired guesses. Edison is quoted to have said that creativity takes 90% perspiration and 10% inspiration. My experience is that deep thought and then sleeping on the problem often produces a solution. Lewis Carroll, who was a mathematician turned humorist, was a believer in parlour games (Carroll, 1885). It may well be that a spirit of light-heartedness helps to spur creativity.

There is also much work to be done in the creation of realistic models of various complex physical processes. One such application would be a meteorological model of the planet Earth.

Readers who enter the field of modeling will often work in *teams* that include experts who understand the physical phenomena and specialists who are experienced in implementing the model on the computer. Although a computer is just a giant number cruncher, a computer model can give us a new window to the world. It is often during the process of *creation* that we gain the most insight into the object of our attention. It would be ideal if all the team members were to approach the project with an open mind, since the model will often provide insights that were not anticipated before the work began. Seemingly unnecessary studies and experiments will sometimes produce dividends that by far exceed their expenditure. Chapter 10 serves as a warning of the problems that may occur if we overlook an important effect. Previous experience is a good defense against such occurrences, but there is always the unexpected. This is where a spirit of enquiry may help. Socrates spoke of himself as a midwife who knew how to ask the proper questions to draw the truth from a man. We can all ask a few well-chosen questions that help to clarify the nature of the choices to be made at all stages of the work.

We will also have to deal with customers who will base technical/management decisions on answers given by the model. It is understandable that there will be commercial pressure to meet deadlines that will discourage our spirit of enquiry, but the wise manager will also know that:

"Speed is no advantage if we are going in the wrong direction"
Anonymous

Bibliography

Ball, P. (2005). *Critical Mass*. London: Arrow Books.
Carroll, L. (1885). *A Tangled Tale*. London: Macmillan.

Appendix A

Frequency response methods

A.1 Complex exponential functions

Section 4.6 defined a phasor $\mathbf{z}(t)$ with unit magnitude that rotated anticlockwise in the complex plane at an angular rate ω rad s^{-1}. This was expressed as a complex function:

$$\mathbf{z}(t) = \cos(\omega t) + j \sin(\omega t)$$

where

$$j = \sqrt{-1}; \quad j^2 = -1; \quad j^3 = -j; \quad j^4 = 1; \text{ etc.}$$

Section 4.6.1 went on to define the sinusoidal components of $\mathbf{z}(t)$ to be:

$$\cos(\omega t) = 1 - (\omega t)^2/2! + (\omega t)^4/4! - \cdots$$

$$\sin(\omega t) = (\omega t)/1! - (\omega t)^3/3! + (\omega t)^5/5! \cdots$$

Section 4.5.1 defined an exponential function of t as

$$\exp(\omega t) = 1 + (\omega t)/1! + (\omega t)^2/2! + (\omega t)^3/3! \cdots$$

We can combine these concepts to define a *complex exponential function*:

$$\exp(j\omega t) = 1 + j\omega t/1! - \omega^2 t^2/2! - j\omega^3 t^3/3! \cdots$$

giving

$$\exp(j\omega t) = \cos(\omega t) + j \sin(\omega t)$$

We can thus define the phasor $\mathbf{z}(t)$ to be equivalent to $\exp(j\omega t)$. Section 4.6 showed how such a phasor could be used to represent the sinusoidal oscillation of a dynamic system.

Computer Models of Process Dynamics: From Newton to Energy Fields, First Edition.
Olis Rubin.
© 2023 The Institute of Electrical and Electronics Engineers, Inc.
Published 2023 by John Wiley & Sons, Inc.

We can use calculus to show that the derivative of $\mathbf{z}(t)$ is also a phasor:

$$d\mathbf{z}/dt = -\omega \sin(\omega t) + j\omega \cos(\omega t)$$

whence

$$d\mathbf{z}/dt = j\omega \exp(j\omega t)$$

The integral of $\mathbf{z}(t)$ will include a sinusoidal oscillation that is also a phasor: $(1/j\omega) \exp(j\omega t)$.

A.2 Frequency response

A linear, time-invariant plant responds to a sinusoidal input by settling to a sinusoidal oscillation with the same frequency. For example, consider a plant that is described by the following differential equation:

$$T \, dx/dt = p(t) - x(t) \tag{A.1}$$

We know from Section 4.5 that the transient response of such a plant would include an exponential function $\exp(-t/T)$ that will settle to zero at a rate that is determined by its time constant (T).

Now consider the following sinusoidal input to the plant:

$$p(t) = \cos(\omega t)$$

This will cause its output $x(t)$ to settle at the following oscillation:

$$x(t) = a \cos(\omega t) + a\omega T \sin(\omega t)$$

where

$$a = 1/\left(1 + \omega^2 T^2\right)$$

This satisfies Equation (A.1) since its derivative is given by

$$dx/dt = -a\omega \sin(\omega T) + a\omega^2 T \cos(\omega t)$$

Consider the case where the plant was initially at rest:

$$p(t) = 0 \text{ and } x(t) = 0 \text{ for } t < 0$$

and the application of the above sinusoidal input begins at $t = 0$.
The plant will then respond with the following output:

$$x(t) = a(\omega) \cos(\omega t) + b(\omega) \sin(\omega t) + c \exp(-t/T)$$

where
$$a(\omega) = 1/(1 + \omega^2 T^2)$$
$$b(\omega) = \omega T \, a(\omega)$$
$$c = -a(\omega)$$

The exponential transient will settle out and the sustained response of the plant will be determined by the values of $a(\omega)$ and $b(\omega)$. Rubin (2016, pp. 31–36) shows time plots that illustrate this behavior.

It is then possible to estimate $a(\omega)$ by determining the mean value of the product $2p(t)\,x(t)$.

We can also generate a signal $q(t)$ that is in quadrature with $p(t)$:

$$q(t) = \sin(\omega t)$$

and estimate $b(\omega)$ as the mean of $2q(t)x(t)$.

These operations are based on the trigonometric relations:

$$2\cos^2(\omega t) = 1 + \cos(2\omega t)$$

$$2\sin^2(\omega t) = 1 - \cos(2\omega t)$$

$$2\sin(\omega t)\cos(\omega t) = \sin(2\omega t)$$

The sustained response of the plant can also be described by an expression of the following form:

$$x(t) = H\cos(\omega t - \phi)$$

where we can calculate the gain of the plant as

$$H = \mathrm{sqrt}\left(a^2 + b^2\right)$$

Substituting the above analytic expressions for $a(\omega)$ and $b(\omega)$ we see that

$$H(\omega) = 1/\mathrm{sqrt}\left(1 + \omega^2 T^2\right)$$

We can also calculate the phase lag that is given by the plant as

$$\phi = \mathrm{arc}\ \tan(b/a)$$

which is given by the following analytic expression:

$$\phi(\omega) = \mathrm{arc}\ \tan(\omega T)$$

We can define the input $p(t)$ to the plant to be the real part of a phasor:

$$\mathbf{p}(t) = \exp(j\omega t)$$

Section A.1 showed how the derivative of the above phasor can be represented by the product $j\omega\mathbf{p}(t)$. The frequency response of a derivative operator can thus be given by the following analytic expression:

$$\mathbf{D}(\omega) = j\omega$$

Similarly, the frequency response of an integral operator is

$$\mathbf{I}(\omega) = 1/j\omega$$

The frequency response of the above plant to such a phasor input is then given by the following complex number:

$$\mathbf{H}(j\omega) = (1 - j\omega T)/\left(1 + \omega^2 T^2\right)$$

which corresponds to the following gain and phase lag:

$$\mathbf{H}(j\omega) = H \, \exp(j\phi)$$

where $H(\omega)$ and $\phi(\omega)$ are given by the above analytic expressions.

The output $x(t)$ of the plant is then given by the real part of the phasor:

$$\mathbf{x}(t) = \mathbf{H}(j\omega) \, \mathbf{p}(t) = H \, \exp(j\phi) \, \exp(j\omega t) = H \, \exp(j\omega t + j\phi)$$

which is the same sinusoidal oscillation as before.

There are commercial instruments that operate on this principle to measure the response of a plant over a frequency band. Rubin (2016, pp. 209–211) has plots that show how $p(t)$ and $x(t)$ can be used to determine the frequency response of a plant, as given by values $a(\omega)$ and $b(\omega)$. In more general cases, we may have to resolve phase ambiguities, such as deciding whether ϕ represents a lag of ϕ degrees or a lag of $\phi + 360$ degrees.

A.3 Fourier series

Figure A.1 shows a square wave signal $p(t)$ and a triangular wave $x(t)$. The following Scilab program was used to synthesize these periodic signals out of sinusoidal components.

```
function x = FourierSeries(T,S,W)
    N = max(size(W));
    if max(size(S))~=N then
        disp('Matrices S & W incorrectly defined')
        return
    end
    x = 0*T;
    for k = 1:N
        x = x + S(k)*exp(%i*W(k)*T);
    end
endfunction
```

```
w = 1;
W = w:2*w:300*w;
Sp = ones(1,150)./(%i*W);
T = [0:66]*%pi/30;
P = FourierSeries(T,Sp,W);
Sx = Sp./(%i*W);
X = FourierSeries(T,Sx,W);
```

The variable (w) defines the fundamental frequency (rad s^{-1}) that determines the period of $p(t)$ and $x(t)$. The elements of the vector (W) define the frequencies: w, 3*w, 5*w, ...

The function FourierSeries(T,Sp,W) synthesizes the signal $p(t)$ as a weighted sum of these sinusoidal components, where the weights are given by the vector (Sp). The amplitude of the harmonic components at the frequencies: 3*w, 5*w, ... vary inversely with their frequency. When these harmonics are added to the sinusoidal signal, they produce the square wave $p(t)$ shown in Figure A.1. The vector (T) defines the instants where $p(t)$ is computed.

Suppose that $p(t)$ is the input to a plant whose output $x(t)$ is the integral of $p(t)$. Then $x(t)$ will be the triangular wave shown in Figure A.1. Section A.2 shows that the frequency response of this plant has a gain that varies inversely with frequency,

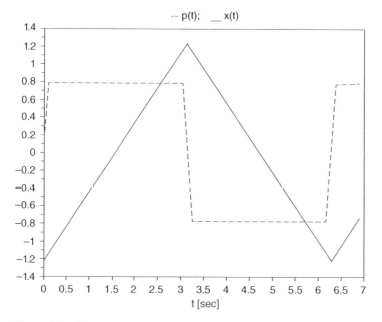

Figure A.1   Square wave and its integral.

while it adds a phase lag of 90 degrees to all the sinusoidal components in the input. The function FourierSeries(T,Sp,W) synthesizes this output $x(t)$ by using the vector (Sx) to define the amplitude and phase of the harmonics. For example, the magnitude of Sx./Sp varies inversely with frequency.

The above program demonstrates that the integral operation in time is equivalent to multiplication in the frequency domain. The function FourierSeries() has used complex exponential components in order to provide phase information as well as magnitude (see Section A.1). The vectors Sp and Sx can thus be complex numbers.

A.3.1 Fourier spectrum and laplace transform

Section A.3 illustrated how a periodic time signal $x(t)$ could be synthesized as the sum of sinusoidal components. It is also possible to perform the inverse operation to determine the amplitude of such sinusoidal components for a given signal $x(t)$. Suppose that we have sampled the signal and stored the data in a vector (U) where U(k) is the value at the kth instant. The discrete Fourier transform of the signal can be found by using the MATLAB or Scilab instruction:

```
Su = fft(U)
```

This produces a vector (Su) where Su(k) is a complex number that defines the amplitude and phase of the kth harmonic. The Help facilities or User Guide give further information regarding the fundamental frequency of the Fourier series and those of the harmonics.

The technique used to compute the Fourier transform is similar to that described in Section A.2. The complex number (Su) at the frequency ω is computed from the time average of the product $u(t) \exp(-j\omega t)$. We can show that the time average of $\exp(j\omega t) \exp(-j\omega t)$ is equal to that of $\cos^2(\omega t) + \sin^2(\omega t)$.

This operation can be further generalized to define the Laplace transform of $x(t)$ as the following integral over all positive time:

$$X(s) = \int x(t) \exp(-st)dt$$

where

$$s = \sigma + j\omega$$

Readers should consult textbooks on the subject to determine the necessary conditions on $x(t)$ for the above definition to be valid and when Laplace transforms satisfy the following important theorem:

If the Laplace transform of $x(t)$ is given by $X(s)$, then the Laplace transform of dx/dt is given by $s X(s)$.

We can use the Laplace transform mechanistically to find analytic solutions to differential equations.

A.4   Power spectra

Consider the random motion of a vehicle that is travelling over rough terrain, or that of a ship at sea, or an aircraft that is flying through turbulence. We can use a motion sensor, such as an accelerometer, to measure such a signal $u(t)$. Suppose that we have sampled this signal and stored it in a vector (U). Its Fourier spectrum, Su = fft(U), is a vector of complex numbers that define the amplitude and phase of the individual frequency components.

If T is a vector of sample instants that produced the original data, we can reconstruct the time series by the instruction:

```
U = FourierSeries(T,Su,W)
```

where the function FourierSeries() was defined in Section A.3.

We then define the power spectrum of U to be a function of frequency that is derived from the Fourier spectrum by the instruction:

```
Pu = Su.*conj(Su)
```

The quantities Pu(k) are real numbers, so the power spectrum does not contain phase information. This means that we can vary the phase angles of the individual frequency components that defined the original signal $u(t)$ at will, without altering its power spectrum. There are thus very many time signals that all have the same power spectrum. This implies that if we only know the power spectrum of a signal we cannot predict its variation with time, so we can properly regard it as being random.

The MATLAB functions, pwelch and pyulear, can also be used to do spectral analysis.

Suppose that the random motion $u(t)$ produces a physical force that acts on a mechanical structure. The force will cause motion $x(t)$ within the structure that will depend on its frequency response $H(j\omega)$, which can be represented as a complex number. Section A.3 gave an example where we calculated the response of a linear plant to a periodic input that has been broken up into its Fourier components. By the principle of superposition, the overall response of the plant is given by the sum of its individual responses to these components. In the present case we will create a vector (G) whose elements G(k) are equal to $H(j\omega)$ at the fundamental frequency of the Fourier series and those of the harmonics. The Fourier spectrum of the output $x(t)$ is then given by

```
Sx = G.*Su
```

so its power spectrum is given by

```
Px = Sx.*conj(Sx)
```

We can thus define a quantity $Q = G.*conj(G)$, where $Q(k)$ is the power gain of the kth harmonic.

Remark: The voltage gain |G| in dB is calculated as 20 log10(|G|) and corresponds to a power gain |G|^2 calculated as 10 log10(|G|^2).

Remark: Although we need phase information to design a control loop, after we have determined its closed-loop response we no longer need phase information to calculate its disturbance rejection.

A.4.1   Effect of sampling on a power spectrum

A sensor that measures a physical quantity often adds high-frequency noise to the measurement. When this noise is sampled at a relatively low frequency, the frequency of the resulting noise is reduced. The upper plot in Figure A.2 shows

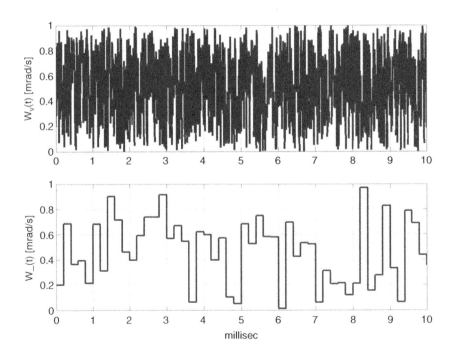

Figure A.2   Sampled gyro noise. (*Source:* Reproduced with permission from Olis Rubin, *Control Engineering in Development Projects*, Norwood, MA: Artech House Inc., 2016 © 2016 by Artech House Inc.)

high-frequency noise on the output $w_v(t)$ of a gyro that measures the vehicle pitch rate. If this is sampled, it produces low-frequency noise $w_-(t)$ that is shown in the lower plot. It is this signal that is seen by the digital controller. This phenomenon, known as frequency aliasing, can aggravate problems in the system, which can be avoided by inserting an analog anti-alias filter at the output of the sensor. We should generally specify a digital system that is much faster than the bandwidth of the control loop and ensure that the sample rate of the analog-to-digital converter (ADC) is greater than five times the filter bandwidth.

A.5   Pulse width modulation

High-performance electronic switching devices are typically used to drive electro-mechanical devices, such as electric motors. Suppose that we have a circuit where a motor winding can be connected to a DC voltage (V) by a solid-state switching device and shorted to earth by another. The mean current through the winding can then be controlled by pulse width modulation (PWM) of the switches, where the winding is connected to the voltage for part of the time and shorted to earth for the rest of the PWM cycle. Suppose that the winding has a resistance (R) and an inductance (L). The current $i(t)$ flowing through the winding will then obey the following differential equation:

$$L\,di/dt = e - iR$$

where $e(t)$ switches between V and zero.

   If the PWM cycle time is relatively short compared with the time constant (L/R), the current will have a relatively small ripple about a mean value. We can simulate this effect by means of the following program, which contains software that generates the PWM:

```
L = 0.5e-3;             //   [henry]
R = 0.15;               //   [ohm]
V = 24;                 //   [volt]
dt = 0.01e-3;           //   step length [s]
P = 100;                //   PWM cycle time [simulation
                        //   steps]
D = 0.5;                //   Duty cycle; fraction
                        //   of PWM cycle
t(1)  = 0;              //   initial time
E(1)  = V;              //   initial value of e(t)
I(1)  = (V/(2*R)) - 10; //   estimated initial i(t)
c = 0;                  //   counter that generates PWM
```

```
for k=1:20*P
    I(k+1) = I(k) + (dt/L)*(E(k)-I(k)*R);
    t(k+1) = t(k) + dt;
    c = c + 1;
    if c>P then
        c = 0;
    end
    if c<D*P then
        E(k+1) = V;
    else
        E(k+1) = 0;
    end
end
```

The program uses a counter to generate a sawtooth signal $c(t)$ that determines the pulse width where the voltage $e(t)$ is equal to 24 volts. If we wish to apply a mean of 12 volts to the motor, we would set the duty cycle to D = 0.5. The pulse width would then be D*P simulation steps, which correspond to the clock pulses in a digital controller, while the PWM period is equal to P steps. This generates a square wave $e(t)$ similar to that shown in Figure A.1, where $e(t)$ is saved in a vector E(k) that switches between 0 and 24 volts and has a period of 1 ms. The resistance and inductance of the winding then produce a current $i(t)$ that resembles the triangular wave shown in Figure A.1, where $i(t)$ is saved in a vector I(k) that has a mean value of 80 A and a triangular ripple current that has a peak-to-peak amplitude of 12 A. The mean value of $e(t)$ is equal to V/2 volts, while that of $i(t)$ equals V/(2*R). Section A.3 shows that the Fourier series of a triangular wave has a fundamental component whose amplitude is nine times greater than that of the third harmonic. The mechanical inertia of the motor and its load will further attenuate higher harmonics, so that we can approximate the ripple current by a sinusoidal signal. The power spectrum of $i(t)$ can thus be expressed by a constant term plus a single frequency component.

A.6 Circuit analysis

Consider a simple circuit that consists of an alternating voltage source $v(t) = V \cos(\omega t)$ that is connected across a resistance (R) in series with an inductance (L). Electrical engineers can determine the frequency response of this circuit by considering the impedance of the elements to the alternating current. This is given by

$$Z(j\omega) = R + j\omega L = |Z| \exp(j\phi)$$

where

$$Z^2 = R^2 + (\omega L)^2$$
$$\tan(\phi) = \omega L/R$$

The sinusoidal current through the circuit is given by

$$i(t) = I \cos(\omega t - \phi)$$

where

$$I = V/R$$

The voltage drop across the resistance will then be

$$V_R(t) = R\, i(t) = R\, I \cos(\omega t - \phi)$$

while the voltage drop across the inductance is given by

$$V_L(t) = L\, \mathrm{d}i/\mathrm{d}t = \omega L\, I \sin(j\omega t - \phi)$$

Appendix A.1 shows how the sinusoidal voltages and currents in this circuit can be represented by phasors in the complex plane. Therefore,

$$\mathbf{V}(t) = V \exp(j\omega t)$$
$$\mathbf{I}(t) = I \exp(j\omega t - \phi)$$
$$\mathbf{V}_R = R\, \mathbf{I}(t)$$
$$\mathbf{V}_L = j\omega L\, \mathbf{I}(t)$$

Appendix A.2 also shows that the phasor $\mathbf{V}_L$ will lead $\mathbf{V}_R$ by 90 degrees.

The drive voltage across the circuit must equal the sum of the volt drops across the resistance and inductance so that:

$$\mathbf{V} = \mathbf{V}_R + \mathbf{V}_L$$

We can visualize this by drawing the phasors $\mathbf{V}_R$ and $\mathbf{V}_L$ at right angles to one another and adding $\mathbf{V}$ as the hypotenuse of a right-angled triangle. The length of $\mathbf{V}$ is thus given by Pythagoras as

$$V^2 = V_R{}^2 + V_L{}^2 = I^2 \left[R^2 + (\omega L)^2 \right]$$

while its angle, ahead of $\mathbf{V}_R$, is given by

$$\tan \phi = V_L/V_R = \omega L/R$$

This geometric analysis allows us to find the frequency response of the circuit. For instance, the frequency response [amps/volts] between the voltage $V(j\omega)$ and the current $I(j\omega)$ will be given by

$$H(j\omega) = 1/Z(j\omega)$$

These concepts can be extended to networks with multiple loops by using theorems due to Kirchhoff, Thévenin, and others.

A.7 Transfer functions of time delays

Consider a signal $y(t)$ that represents a signal $u(t)$ which has been delayed by a time T_D:

$$y(t) = u(t - T_D)$$

The Laplace transform of $u(t)$ is defined as the following integral over all positive time:

$$U(s) = \int u(t) \, \exp(-st) \, dt$$

where it is implied that $u = 0$ over all negative time.

The Laplace transform of $y(t)$ is thus the following integral over all time greater than T_D:

$$Y(s) = \int u(t - T_D) \, \exp(-st) \, dt$$

Since this is an infinite integral, we can write it as

$$Y(s) = \int u(t) \, \exp(-sT_D) \, \exp(-st) \, dt$$

which is integrated over all positive time, whence we have

$$Y(s) = \exp(-sT_D) \, X(s)$$

The frequency response of the time delay is thus given by

$$Y(j\omega)/X(j\omega) = \exp(-j\omega T_D) = \exp(-j\phi)$$

This has a gain of unity and a phase lag (ϕ) that is proportional to frequency:

$$\phi = \omega T_D$$

If we wish to manipulate transfer functions that include time delays by simple algebra, we need to approximate them by polynomials. We can then write the frequency response of the delay element as

$$D(j\omega) = \exp(-j\omega T_D/2)/\exp(j\omega T_D/2)$$

A first-order Padé approximation of $D(j\omega)$ is obtained by using truncated series in place of the exponential functions:

$$D_P(j\omega) = [1 - (j\omega T_D/2)]/[1 + (j\omega T_D/2)]$$

Its gain is equal to unity, while its phase lag is given by

$$\tan(\phi/2) = \omega T_D/2$$

Readers can calculate the phase error given by this approximation and decide whether it is acceptable over a particular frequency band.

A.7.1 Time delays due to sampling

Suppose that the sinusoidal signal $x(t)$ shown in the top plot of Figure A.3 is sampled at intervals (Ts) by an ADC and stored in the memory of a digital

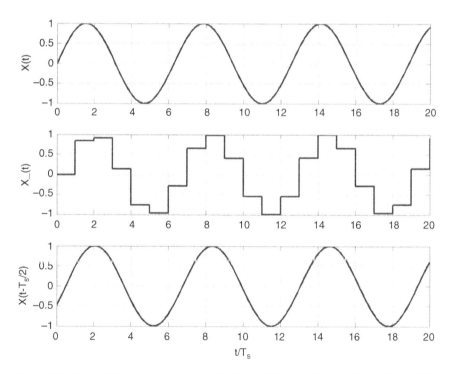

Figure A.3 Time delay due to sampling of a sinusoidal signal. (*Source:* Reproduced with permission from Olis Rubin, *Control Engineering in Development Projects*, Norwood, MA: Artech House Inc., 2016 © 2016 by Artech House Inc.)

computer. The sampled values can be described by a discrete series x(k) where k =0,1,2,3,..., which represents the values of $x(t)$ at the instants (k*Ts).

Now suppose that the computer sends this signal to a digital-to-analog converter (DAC) that periodically updates its output at the same instants (k*Ts). The output will then be a continuous stepped signal x_(t), shown by the middle plot in Figure A.3. The overall effect is simulated in the MATLAB and Scilab platforms by a sample-and-hold block. This can be compared with the bottom plot in the figure, which shows a signal that has been delayed by a time equal to Ts/2. If we can ignore the ripple in the stepped signal we can approximate the effect of a sample-and-hold by the addition of a delay equal to Ts/2 seconds.

Rubin (2016, pp. 235–238) compared the settling of a feedback loop that contains a sample-and-hold block with that of a loop that contains a transport delay block (*Ts/2*). It was shown in this case that the approximation by a time delay gave adequate results. If the sampling frequency in a control loop is too low it can cause an unacceptable time lag.

A.7.2 Integration of sampled signal

The previous section considered the effect of a sample-and-hold operation on a proportional controller. We will now consider the effect of adding an integral term to the controller. We could use the rectangular integration algorithm described in Section 2.7.1 to generate a signal w(k) that approximates the time integral of $x(t)$. This leads to the following difference equation:

w(k+1) = w(k) + Ts*x(k)

Then w(k) can be sent to a DAC at the instants (k*Ts) in order to generate a continuous stepped signal w_(t). The size of the steps are equal to the integral of x_ (t) over the intervals from k*Ts to (k+1)*Ts.

We can determine the frequency response of this discrete integrator where we firstly represent it by a Z-transfer function. The Z-transform variable (z) is defined to be the opposite of a time delay operator:

$$z = \exp(sTs)$$

We will not go into the mathematics behind the Z-transform analysis of digital systems, but will simply use the variable (z) to describe discrete signals as the following series:

$$X(z) = x(0) + z^{-1}x(1) + z^{-2}x(2)...$$
$$W(z) = w(0) + z^{-1}w(1) + z^{-2}w(2)...$$

If we assume that $w(0) = 0$, we then have

$$zW(z) = w(1) + z^{-1}w(2) + z^{-2}w(3)...$$

Substituting these series for $W(z)$, $zW(z)$, and $X(z)$ into the above difference equation, we obtain

$$z\,W(z) - \mathbf{W}(z) = Ts\,X(z)$$

The Z-transfer function of rectangular integration is then defined as

$$R(z) = W(z)/X(z) = Ts/(z - 1)$$

Readers can expand $R(z)$ as a binomial series and compare the product $R(z)X(z)$ with the finite impulse response model discussed in Section 9.2.2.

The transfer function (SYS) of a continuous integrator ($1/s$) can be defined in the MATLAB workspace:

```
SYS = tf(1,[1, 0]);
```

We can then use the following MATLAB instructions to find its Z-transform:

```
Ts = 0.0002;            % [seconds] sample period
SYSd = c2d(SYS,Ts);
[Nd,Dd] = tfdata(SYSd);
```

These operations give the following result for the Z-transfer function of a digital integrator:

$$N_d(z)/D_d(z) = 0.0002/[z - 1]$$

We could use the following MATLAB instruction to calculate its frequency response:

```
[magd, phsd] = dbode(Nd, Dd, Ts, frequency);
```

At 1000 rad s^{-1} (where there are 31 samples per cycle), its phase lag will be 96 degrees whereas that of a continuous integrator is 90 degrees. The operating bandwidth of the controller should not go far beyond this frequency in order to limit the adverse effects of sampling.

A.7.3   Alternative analysis of discrete integration

We can find a simple approximation that models the effect of sampling for a discrete integrator. We start with the following analytical expression for the frequency response of the Z-transfer function that is given in Section A.7.2:

$$Ts/[\exp(j\omega Ts) - 1] = Ts\,\exp(-j\omega Ts/2)/D(j\omega)$$

where

$$D(j\omega) = \exp(j\omega Ts/2) - \exp(-j\omega Ts/2)$$

The denominator $D(j\omega)$ can be expanded as

$$D(j\omega) = 1 + j\omega Ts/2 - \omega^2 Ts^2/8 - j\omega^3 Ts^3/48\cdots - 1 +$$
$$j\omega Ts/2 + \omega^2 Ts^2/8 - j\omega^3 Ts^3/48\cdots$$
$$D(j\omega) = j\omega Ts - j\omega^3 Ts^3/24\cdots = j\omega Ts\left[1 - \omega^2 Ts^2/24\cdots\right]$$

We will approximate $D(j\omega)$ by $j\omega Ts$. At the frequency $(0.5/Ts)$ rad s^{-1} this has an accuracy of 1%.

We can thus approximate the frequency response of the discrete integrator by adding a delay $(Ts/2)$ to that of the continuous integrator:

$$Ts/[\exp(j\omega Ts) - 1] \approx \exp(-j\omega Ts/2)/j\omega$$

The phase lag of this approximation in the operating frequency band is virtually the same as that found by using the Z-transfer function and the MATLAB function dbode().

A.8 Feedback loops

Feedback occurs naturally in a physical system such as a pendulum, where the force of gravity pulls the pendulum back towards the vertical. The Watt governor is an early example of feedback in an engineering product. This alters the steam being fed into an engine when its speed deviates from the setpoint. It is advisable that simulation engineers who work on projects that involve feedback controllers understand some basic principles of feedback such as those presented in Rubin (2016, pp. 243–250).

Figure A.4 shows a generic feedback loop where the open loop transfer function $L(s)$ represents the combined effect of a controller in series with an actuator, a plant, and a sensor. Note that we have assumed that all the components in the loop can be modeled by transfer functions. The purpose of the feedback is to drive the measured output of the plant (y) to follow the command (c), but in practice there can be a control error: $e = c - y$. Taking Laplace transforms of these signals we have

$$E(s) = C(s) - Y(s)$$
$$Y(s) = L(s)E(s)$$

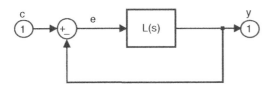

Figure A.4 Generic feedback loop.

giving

$$E(s) = C(s) - L(s) E(s)$$

This allows us to derive the following closed-loop frequency response:

$$E(j\omega) = S(j\omega) C(j\omega)$$

where

$$S(j\omega) = 1/[1 + L(j\omega)]$$

The function $S(j\omega)$ is often called the sensitivity of the loop. It can also be used to describe the ability of the control loop to counteract disturbances that act on the plant. For example, we could simulate a sinusoidal disturbance at a frequency (ω_d) as a force that acts on a computer model of the plant and find that it produces sinusoidal perturbations $\sim y(t)$ on its output. If we now add a control loop around the plant we should find that the amplitude of the perturbations are reduced by a factor $|S(j\omega_d)|$. We see that the perturbations can be further reduced by increasing the loop gain $|L(j\omega_d)|$. For example, a loop gain of 20 dB will reduce perturbations to about 10% of their uncontrolled amplitude. We have to take care that increasing the loop gain does not cause the feedback loop to resonate. We can test for this by applying a sinusoidal input $c(t)$ and doing a frequency sweep. This will propagate around the loop, giving sinusoidal signals $e(t)$ and $y(t)$ that are related as follows:

$$E(j\omega) = C(j\omega) - Y(j\omega)$$
$$Y(j\omega) = L(j\omega) E(j\omega)$$

If we represent these signals as phasors (see Section 4.6 and Figure 4.5), we can arrange them in a triangle, as shown in Figure A.5. This represents a plot in the complex plane, where the real and imaginary axes are not shown and the angular positions of the phasors correspond to $t = 0$.

The plant will generally have an inertia that absorbs energy. This reduces its response to high-frequency inputs. If the control loop is designed so that $|L(j\omega_d)|$ is larger than unity, the loop gain will generally fall to unity at a frequency (ω_x) somewhere above ω_d. If we apply a sinusoidal input $c(t)$ at a frequency (ω_x), the phasor $\mathbf{y}(t)$ will lag behind $\mathbf{e}(t)$ by an angle $\phi(\omega_x)$ while their amplitudes will be equal. The phasor $\mathbf{c}(t)$ will be the base of the isosceles triangle that is shown in Figure A.5. The angle (p) that is shown in the figure is known as the phase margin of the feedback loop. It tends to zero when the phase lag $\phi(\omega_x)$ approaches 180 degrees.

We see that the magnitude of the signals $y(t)$ and $e(t)$ become larger if we reduce the phase margin. The feedback loop then amplifies the sinusoidal motion of the load. This phenomenon is known as resonance. As a rule of thumb, control loops

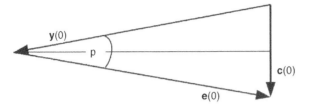

Figure A.5 Phasor triangle for the feedback loop.

can be designed to have an open-loop phase lag that is less than 135 degrees at gain crossover, giving a phase margin (p) of 45 degrees. We often have to make a design tradeoff between increasing the gain of the controller in order to achieve adequate disturbance rejection and limiting the gain to avoid excessive closed loop resonance. Rubin (2016, pp. 243–250) gives design details with frequency response plots that show how we can design controllers that add gain at the disturbance frequency or add phase lead to avoid resonance.

A.8.1 Digital PI controllers

Digital controllers are generally implemented on microcontrollers or larger process automation systems. These are generally programmed through integrated development environments that support their proprietary programming languages. The plant output sensor is sampled by an ADC while the control command is sent via a DAC to the plant actuator. When the computer receives a new sample $y(k)$ from the sensor it computes a new control error $e(k) = S(k) - y(k)$, that is used by the controller to generate a new control command $u(k)$. We will assume that the actuator drive then generates a continuous stepped signal $u\_(t)$ such as that shown in Figure A.3. This operation is known as a sample-and-hold, and it is shown in Section A.7.1 that it has the effect of adding a time delay $T/2$ to the loop, where T is the time interval between samples. Even if $u(k)$ is computed and transmitted through the DAC at virtually the same instant (kT) that the sample $y(k)$ was taken, we still have the delays due to the latency of the data links and the effect of sample-and-hold. The designer must thus ensure that the speed of the digital control platform is commensurate with the bandwidth of the control loops. This can be analyzed using the techniques given in Section A.7, as well as Section A.4.1, and can then be verified by means of simulation. We should also be aware that the visible frequency response of the plant can be modified by the effects of sampling. For example, consider a plant that has a transfer function $H(s)$ that is driven by a sampled input while its output goes through a synchronous sampler. The theory of sampled data systems shows that the frequency response from input to output is given by the vector addition of the following complex quantities:

$$H^*(j\omega) = (1/T)\{H(j\omega) + H[j(\omega + \Omega)] + H[j(\omega - \Omega)]$$

$$+ H[j(\omega + 2\Omega)] + H[j(\omega - 2\Omega)] + \cdots\}$$

where $\Omega = 2\pi/T$ is the sampling frequency (see Tou, 1959).

We will generally make the sample period (T) as small as possible, so that the controller can react quickly to plant disturbances. This usually implies that $H[j(\omega + \Omega)]$ has relatively little effect on $H^*(j\omega)$ at the operating frequencies of the control loop, so that we can then approximate $H^*(j\omega)$ by the frequency response $H(j\omega)$ of the continuous plant. We can then begin the design of the digital controller by analyzing the frequency response of a continuous time control loop.

Section A.8 described a feedback control system that acts to reduce the control error $e(t)$. This would include a controller that generates a command $u(t)$ to an actuator. A continuous PI controller would use the following control law:

$$u(t) = K_p e(t) + (K_p/T_i) \int e(t)\, dt$$

A digital control computer uses samples that it receives from an ADC to determine the discrete sequence e(k) that approximates the continuous evolution $e(t)$ of the control error. It is then possible to create an algorithm that will generate a sequence of control commands u(k) that represents the sampled output $u(t)$ of the above continuous controller. Section 2.7 presented several algorithms that approximate the integration of a continuous signal, such as $e(t)$. These involved difference equations that operated on discrete sequences, such as e(k). Suppose that such an algorithm produces a discrete sequence f(k) that approximates the integral of $e(t)$. The control commands u(k) that go to the DAC can then be formed as a weighted sum of e(k) and f(k).

The following simple difference equation corresponds to rectangular integration of $e(t)$:

```
f_R(k)  =  f_R(k-1)  +  T*e(k)
```

where T is the sample period.

We will also consider trapezoidal integration:

```
f_T(k)  =  f_T(k-1)  +  (T/2)*(e(k)+e(k-1))
```

and Simpson's formula for integration:

```
f_S(k)  =  f_S(k-2)  +  (T/3)*(e(k)+4*e(k-1)+e(k-2))
```

We can write a program to test the time response of these digital integrators to a change in control error. Their responses to a unit impulse in e(k) are shown below. The impulse is applied at k=3, while

```
T = 0.05 sec.
```

k	e(k)	f_R(k)	f_T(k)	f_S(k)
1	0.	0.	0.	0.
2	0.	0.	0.	0.
3	1.	0.05	0.025	0.0166667
4	0.	0.05	0.05	0.0666667
5	0.	0.05	0.05	0.0333333
6	0.	0.05	0.05	0.0666667
7	0.	0.05	0.05	0.0333333

The rectangular integrator responds immediately, the trapezoidal integrator responds more slowly, while the Simpson integrator has an oscillatory response. These sequences define the impulse responses of the above digital integrators and will be referred to as h_R(k), h_T(k), and h_S(k).

Section 9.2.2 considered what would happen if a signal e(k) that is built up as a string of such impulses at the instants k*T is used as the input to a system that has an impulse response h(k). It is shown that such a system will produce an output:

```
f(k) = e(k)h(0) + e(k-1)h(1) + e(k-2)h(2) + ...
```

where we have neglected the free settling of the system from its initial conditions.

For example, a step in the control error e(k) at k = 3 will cause the rectangular integrator to immediately ramp up at a rate of 0.05 per sample. The trapezoidal integrator will ramp up at the same rate with a small lag, while the Simpson integrator will have an oscillation about this mean ramp rate.

Section A.7.2 uses Z-transform theory to describe the sequence e(k) as the following series:

$$E(z) = e(0) + z^{-1}e(1) + z^{-2}e(2) + \cdots$$

The sequence f(k) will be a similar function F(z). If we neglect the free settling, we can describe the impulse response of the system by the following Z-transfer function:

$$H(z) = F(z)/E(z)$$

We can similarly use Z-transform theory to describe a difference equation by a Z-transfer function.

For example, the rectangular integration formula:

```
fR(k)  =  fR(k-1)  +  T*e(k)
```

can be described by the following *Z*-transfer function:

$$H_R(z) = T z/(z-1) = T z^{1/2}/(z^{1/2} - z^{-1/2})$$

We can then find its frequency response by making the following substitution:

$$z = \exp(j\omega T) = \cos(\omega T) + j\sin(\omega T)$$

which gives

$$H_R(j\omega) = T[\cos(\omega T/2) + j\sin(\omega T/2)]/$$
$$[\cos(\omega T/2) + j\sin(\omega T/2) - \cos(\omega T/2) + j\sin(\omega T/2)]$$

This can be simplified to the following:

$$H_R(j\omega) = (-jT/2)[\cos(\omega T/2) + j\sin(\omega T/2)]/\sin(\omega T/2)$$

from which we can calculate the gain and phase shift:

$$H_R(j\omega) = |H_R| \exp(j\phi_R)$$

where
$$|H_R| = (T/2)/\sin(\omega T/2)$$
$$\tan(\phi_R) = (\omega T/2) - (\pi/2)$$

$H_R(j\omega)$ is a good approximation to a continuous integrator:

$$1/j\omega = (1/\omega) \exp(-j\pi/2)$$

The phase error is less than 1.5 degrees at frequencies below $1/(20T)$ rad s^{-1}, while the gain error is less than 0.1 dB at frequencies below $1/(2T)$ rad s^{-1}.

The frequency response of the PI controller is given by the vector sum of the proportional and integral terms. The integrator dominates at frequencies below $1/(T_i)$ rad s^{-1}, which should be well below the sample frequency.

The trapezoidal integration formula:

```
fT(k)  =  fT(k-1)  +  (T/2) * (e(k)+e(k-1))
```

corresponds to the following *Z*-transfer function and frequency response:

$$H_T(z) = (T/2)(z^{1/2} + z^{-1/2})/(z^{1/2} - z^{-1/2})$$
$$H_T(j\omega) = -j(T/2)\cos(\omega T/2)/\sin(\omega T/2)$$

It has a phase lag of exactly 90 degrees, while its gain is a reasonable approximation to $1/\omega$:

$$| HT | = (T/2)/\tan(\omega T/2)$$

The final choice for a particular application will probably lie between a rectangular or trapezoidal integrator. They can be compared by simulating their closed-loop performance. Chapter 10, Section 10.4.2, simulates a digital PI controller with rectangular integration, where it is found to give an acceptable closed-loop step response.

Simpson's formula for integration also gives a frequency response that has a phase lag of exactly 90 degrees:

```
f_S(k)  =  f_S(k-2)  +  (T/3)*(e(k)+4*e(k-1)+e(k-2))
```

$$H_S(j\omega) = -j(T/3)[2 + \cos(\omega T)]/\sin(\omega T)$$

A.8.2   Programming a PI controller

A PI controller that incorporates the rectangular integrator described in Section 2.7.1 can be programmed as follows:

```
e(k+1)   = yc(k+1)  -  y(k+1);
Int(k+1) = Int(k)   +  T*e(k+1);
c(k+1)   = Kp  *  (e(k+1)  +  Int(k+1)/Ti);
```

Here y is the controlled variable, yc is the setpoint, T is the sample period, Int is the output of the integrator, and c is the control command, while Kp and Ti are the controller gains.

Having designed the controller, it can be programmed in a language such as C# and compiled to run on a microcontroller that drives the hardware. Before we do so, we still have a few practical points to consider.

We often have to deal with actuator saturation. Chapter 10 describes the design of a motor control system where the drive voltage is limited by the power supply. If the motor must quickly slew the load to a new position, it will be limited by the maximum voltage. This will cause a control error, and the integrator will ramp up its output (Int) in a vain attempt to drive the motor beyond its limits. This phenomenon is known as *integrator windup*. When the load reaches the new position the error will reverse, but the PI controller will be delayed while the integrator is "unwound." The following program can be used to prevent this by limiting the control command to a prescribed value (max):

```
e(k+1) = yc(k+1) - y(k+1);
Int(k+1) = Int(k) + T*e(k+1);
c(k+1) = Kp * (e(k+1) + Int(k+1)/Ti);
if abs(c(k+1)) > max  then            //  anti-windup
    Int(k+1) = Int(k);
    c(k+1) = max * sign(c(k+1));
end
```

The following program first computes the derivative (d) of the error and the derivative (b) of the control command. The control command c(k+1) is then computed as the integral of b. This configuration is used in process control systems, where it has the advantage that a human operator can override the integrator and directly move its output to a suitable value. It is then possible to revert to automatic control, where the PI controller will start from this value. This is known as *bumpless transfer*. The program also prevents windup:

```
e(k+1) = yc(k+1) - y(k+1);
d = (e(k+1) - e(k)) / T;
b = Kp * (d + e(k+1)/Ti);
c(k+1) = c(k) + T*b;
if abs(c(k+1)) > max  then            //  anti-windup
    c(k+1) = max * sign(c(k+1));
end
```

We can program a generic PI controller as an object that can be called by the main program whenever the controlled variable (y) arrives on the data bus. It then computes the control command that the main program sends to the applicable actuator driver. The code will be written in a language that depends on the particular compiler.

Bibliography

Cheng, D.K. (1966). *Analysis of Linear Systems*. Reading. MA: Addison-Wesley.

Kuo, F.F. (1966). *Network Analysis and Synthesis*. New York: Wiley.

Rubin, O. (2016). *Control Engineering in Development Projects*. Dedham, MA: Artech House.

Starkey, B.J. (1958). *Laplace Transforms for Electrical Engineers*. London: Iliffe & Sons.

Tou, J.T. (1959). *Digital and Sampled Data Control Systems*. New York: McGraw-Hill.

Appendix B

Vector analysis

B.1 The use of vector analysis

Many of the quantities of physics are conveniently represented by vectors. As examples we mention force, displacement, velocity, acceleration, fluid flow, the flow of heat, and electric currents. Such quantities are represented graphically by arrows of length proportional to their *magnitude*, and pointing in the appropriate *direction*.

The position of a body in space can be described by a vector:

$$\mathbf{R} = x\,\mathbf{i} + y\,\mathbf{j} + z\,\mathbf{k}$$

x, y, z = Cartesian coordinates of the body relative to the origin of the system
$\mathbf{i}, \mathbf{j}, \mathbf{k}$ = unit vectors along the positive directions of the Cartesian axes X, Y, Z

In Section B.2 we show how physical motion can be described by means of vectors.

B.2 Vector analysis of motion

The physical motion of rigid bodies can be analyzed by means of vector analysis. If we neglect its rotation, the motion of a body can be described by the position of its center of gravity as a function of time. This can then be described by a vector:

$$\mathbf{R}(t) = x(t)\,\mathbf{i} + y(t)\,\mathbf{j} + z(t)\,\mathbf{k}$$

The rate of change in position can then be described by a velocity vector:

$$\mathbf{V}(t) = d\mathbf{R}/dt = (dx/dt)\,\mathbf{i} + (dy/dt)\,\mathbf{j} + (dz/dt)\,\mathbf{k}$$

Computer Models of Process Dynamics: From Newton to Energy Fields, First Edition.
Olis Rubin.
© 2023 The Institute of Electrical and Electronics Engineers, Inc.
Published 2023 by John Wiley & Sons, Inc.

$\mathbf{V}(t)$ is always tangential to the trajectory, so the rate of travel along the trajectory is given by

$$(ds/dt)^2 = |V|^2 = V \cdot V = (dx/dt)^2 + (dy/dt)^2 + (dz/dt)^2$$

We can form a unit vector in the direction of $\mathbf{V}$:

$$\mathbf{T}(t) = \mathbf{V}(t)/ \mid \mathbf{V} \mid \ = (d\mathbf{R}/dt)\,(dt/ds) = d\mathbf{R}/ds$$

whence

$$\mathbf{V}(t) = \mathbf{T}\,(ds/dt)$$

The acceleration of the body is then given by a vector:

$$\mathbf{A}(t) = d\mathbf{V}/dt = \mathbf{T}\,(d^2s/dt^2) + (d\mathbf{T}/dt)\,(ds/dt)$$
$$= \mathbf{T}\,(d^2s/dt^2) + [(d\mathbf{T}/ds)\,(ds/dt)]\,(ds/dt)$$

$\mathbf{T}\,(d^2s/dt^2)$ = the acceleration along $\mathbf{V}$

$\mathbf{T}$ is defined to be a unit vector so $d\mathbf{T}$ is normal to $\mathbf{T}$

The acceleration of the body normal to the velocity vector causes a change in heading. This is equivalent to a rotation $(d\theta/dt)$ of the unit vector $(\mathbf{T})$, where

$$d\mathbf{T} = \mathbf{T}(s + ds) - \mathbf{T}(s) = d\theta$$

For motion in the horizontal plane $\mathbf{T}$ points to left or right while its magnitude defines the rate of turn.

If there is no tangential acceleration, the trajectory $\mathbf{R}(t)$ will trace the arc of a circle:

$$ds = r\,d\theta$$

where

r = a turning radius

If we now define a unit vector $(\mathbf{N})$ that is normal to the velocity vector $(\mathbf{V})$:

$$\mathbf{N} = (d\mathbf{T}/dt)/ \mid d\mathbf{T}/dt \mid \ = (d\mathbf{T}/ds)/ \mid d\mathbf{T}/ds \mid$$

We can combine these relationships with that for $d\mathbf{T}/d\theta$ to obtain

$$(d\mathbf{T}/ds)\,(ds/dt)^2 = \mathbf{N}|V|^2/r = \text{the centripetal acceleration, normal to } \mathbf{V}$$

The acceleration vector of the body thus has a tangential and a normal component:

$$\mathbf{A}(t) = \mathbf{T}\,(d^2s/dt^2) + \mathbf{N}\,|V|^2/r$$

The equations of motion for the rigid body are thus given by

$$dV/dt = \mathbf{T}\left(d^2s/dt^2\right) + \mathbf{N}\,|V|^2/r = \mathbf{T}\,F_T/m + \mathbf{N}\,F_N/m$$

where

F_T and F_N = the tangential and normal forces on the body
m = the mass of the body

B.2.1 Rotation of a rigid body

Before we analyze rotational motion, we must define the relative directions of the Cartesian axes. We will use a right-handed coordinate system where the X axis points forward, the Y axis points sideways to the right, and the Z axis points downwards. We must also define an operation between two vectors known as their vector product. We will begin by defining the vector products of the unit vectors $(\mathbf{i}, \mathbf{j}, \mathbf{k})$ in the X, Y, Z directions to satisfy the following relationships:

$$\mathbf{i} \times \mathbf{j} = -\mathbf{j} \times \mathbf{i} = \mathbf{k}$$
$$\mathbf{j} \times \mathbf{k} = -\mathbf{k} \times \mathbf{j} = \mathbf{i}$$
$$\mathbf{k} \times \mathbf{i} = -\mathbf{i} \times \mathbf{k} = \mathbf{j}$$
$$\mathbf{i} \times \mathbf{i} = \mathbf{j} \times \mathbf{j} = \mathbf{k} \times \mathbf{k} = 0$$

(We can rotate the coordinate system about any axis and these relationships will still be true. For example, we can rotate it 180 degrees about the X axis, so that $\mathbf{j}$ points to the left and $\mathbf{k}$ points upwards.)

If $\mathbf{m}$ and $\mathbf{n}$ are orthogonal vectors we can define a coordinate system $(\mathbf{i}, \mathbf{j}, \mathbf{k})$ where

$$\mathbf{m} = a\,\underline{\mathbf{i}}$$
$$\mathbf{n} = b\,\underline{\mathbf{j}} + c\,\underline{\mathbf{k}}$$

The vector product is then given by

$$\mathbf{v} = \mathbf{m} \times \mathbf{n} = ab\underline{\mathbf{k}} - ac\underline{\mathbf{j}}$$

The length of the vector $\mathbf{v}$ will be

$$|\mathbf{v}| = \sqrt{(\mathbf{v} \cdot \mathbf{v})} = \sqrt{\left(a^2 b^2 + a^2 c^2\right)} = |\mathbf{m}|\,|\mathbf{n}|$$

If $\mathbf{m}$ and $\mathbf{n}$ are co-linear vectors we can find a scalar constant (a) where:

$$\mathbf{n} = a\,\mathbf{m}$$

The scalar product is then given by:

$$\mathbf{m} \cdot \mathbf{n} = \mathbf{m} \cdot (a\,\mathbf{m}) = a\,|\mathbf{m}|^2 = |\mathbf{m}||\mathbf{n}|$$

Consider a rigid body that rotates about an axis which passes through the origin of the coordinate system. Its angular velocity is represented by a vector:

$$\Omega = \omega_x\,\mathbf{i} + \omega_y\,\mathbf{j} + \omega_z\,\mathbf{k}$$

while its angular speed is given by

$$\omega = \sqrt{(\Omega \cdot \Omega)} = \sqrt{\left(\omega_x^2 + \omega_y^2 + \omega_z^2\right)}$$

The vector (Ω) is defined to point along the axis of rotation in the direction given by the thumb of the right hand whose fingers are wrapped about the axis in the direction of rotation.

Now consider a particle within the body whose position is defined by the vector **P** that can be decomposed into an axial component (**A**) where

$$|\mathbf{A}| = |\mathbf{P}|\,\cos\theta$$

and a radial component (**R**), where

$$|\mathbf{R}| = |\mathbf{P}|\,\sin\theta$$

R is at right angles to the axis, and will have components of the form

$$\mathbf{R} = x\,\mathbf{i} + y\,\mathbf{j} + z\,\mathbf{k}$$

The length of the vector **R** will be

$$r = \sqrt{(\mathbf{R} \cdot \mathbf{R})} = \sqrt{\left(x^2 + y^2 + z^2\right)}$$

The particle moves around the rotation axis in a circle with a radius r; thus its tangential speed will be

$$v = \omega\,r$$

Now consider the vector product:

$$\mathbf{V} = \Omega \times \mathbf{R} = \left(\omega_x\mathbf{i} + \omega_y\mathbf{j} + \omega_z\mathbf{k}\right) \times (x\mathbf{i} + y\mathbf{j} + z\mathbf{k})$$

Using the above relationships for $\mathbf{i} \times \mathbf{j}$, etc., we have

$$\mathbf{V} = \left(\omega_y z - \omega_z y\right)\mathbf{i} + \left(\omega_z x - \omega_x z\right)\mathbf{j} + \left(\omega_x y - \omega_y x\right)\mathbf{k}$$

Because Ω and **R** are mutually orthogonal vectors:

$$|\mathbf{V}| = |\Omega||\mathbf{R}| = \omega\,r$$

Thus **V** corresponds to the tangential velocity, which is at right angles to both vectors Ω and **R**.

The axial component (**A**) of **P** is parallel to the angular velocity vector, so

$$\Omega \times P = \Omega \times (A + R) = k(\Omega \times \Omega) + (\Omega \times R) = \Omega \times R$$

B.2.2 Center of gravity

The mass of a particle in a rigid body is given by

$$dm = \rho(x, y, z)\, dv$$

where ρ is the density of the particle and dv is its volume.

The mass of the body is given by the integral of dm over its volume:

$$m = \iiint \rho(x, y, z)\, dv = \iiint \rho(x, y, z)\, dx\, dy\, dz$$

If the origin of the coordinate system is at the center of mass the following integrals will be zero:

$$N_{yz} = \iiint x\,\rho(x, y, z)\, dv = \iiint x\,\rho(x, y, z)\, dx\, dy\, dz$$

$$N_{xz} = \iiint y\,\rho(x, y, z)\, dv = \iiint y\,\rho(x, y, z)\, dx\, dy\, dz$$

$$N_{xy} = \iiint z\,\rho(x, y, z)\, dv = \iiint z\,\rho(x, y, z)\, dx\, dy\, dz$$

Gravity will act on a particle in a rigid body to produce a force:

$$dF_g = k\, g\, \rho(x, y, z)\, dv$$

where its position relative to the center of mass is defined by a vector:

$$P = x\, i + y\, j + z\, k$$

This vector has a vertical component ($z\, k$) and a horizontal component:

$$II - \lambda\, i + y\, j$$

The vector moment of the force about the center of mass is defined to be

$$dM_g = P \times dF_g = H \times dF_g = (y i - x j)\, g\, \rho(x, y, z)\, dv$$

The integral of dM_g over the volume of the body is thus equal to zero:

$$M_g = g\left(N_{xz}\, i - N_{yz}\, j\right)$$

If the body is now rotated 90 degrees about the Y axis, the moment ($g\, N_{xy}$) is again equal to zero.

B.2.3 Moment of inertia

Now consider the following integrals:

$$I_{yz} = \int\int\int x^2 \rho(x,y,z)\, dv = \int\int\int x^2 \rho(x,y,z)\, dx\, dy\, dz$$

$$I_{xz} = \int\int\int y^2 \rho(x,y,z)\, dv = \int\int\int y^2 \rho(x,y,z)\, dx\, dy\, dz$$

$$I_{xy} = \int\int\int z^2 \rho(x,y,z)\, dv = \int\int\int z^2 \rho(x,y,z)\, dx\, dy\, dz$$

The moments of inertia of the body are defined to be

$$I_x = I_{xz} + I_{xy} = \int\int\int \left(y^2 + z^2\right) \rho(x,y,z)\, dv$$

$$I_y = I_{yz} + I_{xy} = \int\int\int \left(x^2 + z^2\right) \rho(x,y,z)\, dv$$

$$I_z = I_{yz} + I_{xz} = \int\int\int \left(x^2 + y^2\right) \rho(x,y,z)\, dv$$

Consider a rigid body that rotates with an angular velocity (Ω) about an axis that passes through its center of mass. The tangential speed of a particle within the body is given by

$$|V| = |\Omega||R| = \omega r$$

where its radial position is defined by the vector R having a length r. The kinetic energy of the particle is then given by

$$dE = \tfrac{1}{2}\rho(x,y,z)\, dv\, |V|^2 = \tfrac{1}{2}\rho(x,y,z)\, dv\, (\omega r)^2$$

If the body rotates with an angular velocity $(\omega\, i)$ about the X axis, its kinetic energy is given by

$$E = \tfrac{1}{2}\omega^2 \int\int\int \left(y^2 + z^2\right) \rho(x,y,z)\, dv = \tfrac{1}{2}I_x \omega^2$$

Rotation about the Y and Z axes give similar relationships.

The products of inertia of the body are defined to be

$$J_{xy} = \int\int\int xy\, \rho(x,y,z)\, dv = \int\int\int xy\, \rho(x,y,z)\, dx\, dy\, dz$$

$$J_{yz} = \int\int\int yz\, \rho(x,y,z)\, dv = \int\int\int yz\, \rho(x,y,z)\, dx\, dy\, dz$$

$$J_{xz} = \int\int\int xz\, \rho(x,y,z)\, dv = \int\int\int xz\, \rho(x,y,z)\, dx\, dy\, dz$$

The tangential velocity of the particle is given by

$$\mathbf{V} = \boldsymbol{\Omega} \times \mathbf{P} = \left(\omega_y z - \omega_z y\right)\mathbf{i} + \left(\omega_z x - \omega_x z\right)\mathbf{j} + \left(\omega_x y - \omega_y x\right)\mathbf{k}$$

where its position relative to the center of mass is

$$\mathbf{P} = x\,\mathbf{i} + y\,\mathbf{j} + z\,\mathbf{k}$$

The momentum of the particle is given by the following vector:

$$d\mathbf{M} = \boldsymbol{\Omega} \times \mathbf{P}\,\rho(x,y,z)\,dv$$

The moment of momentum is the momentum times the lever arm, and is given by the following vector:

$$d\mathbf{H} = \mathbf{P} \times (\boldsymbol{\Omega} \times \mathbf{P})\,\rho(x,y,z)\,dv$$

The angular momentum of the body is given by the integral of $d\mathbf{H}$ over its volume:

$$\mathbf{H} = \iiint \mathbf{P} \times (\boldsymbol{\Omega} \times \mathbf{P})\,\rho(x,y,z)\,dv$$

Substituting the above expressions for $\mathbf{P}$ and $(\boldsymbol{\Omega} \times \mathbf{P})$ we obtain:

$$\mathbf{H} = H_x\,\mathbf{i} + H_y\,\mathbf{j} + H_z\,\mathbf{k}$$

where

$$H_x = \omega_x I_x - \omega_y J_{xy} - \omega_z J_{xz}$$
$$H_y = \omega_y I_y - \omega_z J_{yz} - \omega_y J_{xy}$$
$$H_z = \omega_z I_z - \omega_x J_{xz} - \omega_y J_{yz}$$

These can be written as a matrix equation:

$$\mathbf{H} = \underline{\mathbf{I}}\,\boldsymbol{\Omega}$$

where the moments and products of inertia are components of the matrix ($\underline{\mathbf{I}}$).

If the body is rotating about a shaft that is parallel to the X axis, where its center of mass is at a radial distance d from the shaft, then its moment of inertia about the shaft is given by

$$I_s = m\,d^2 + I_x$$

B.2.4 Equations of motion for a rigid body

The velocity of the center of mass in inertial coordinates is defined as a vector ($\mathbf{V}$). We can form a unit vector in the direction of $\mathbf{V}$:

$$\mathbf{T}(t) = \mathbf{V}(t)/V$$

$$V = |\mathbf{V}|$$

The derivative of this in body coordinates is given by

$$d\mathbf{V}/dt = d(\mathbf{T}V)/dt = \mathbf{T}\,dV/dt + V\,d\mathbf{T}/dt$$

The body has an angular velocity ($\mathbf{\Omega}$) with respect to the inertial coordinates. The tip of the vector ($\mathbf{T}$) thus moves in a circle, which gives

$$d\mathbf{T}/dt = \mathbf{\Omega} \times \mathbf{T}$$

Thus we have

$$d\mathbf{V}/dt = \mathbf{T}\,dV/dt + \mathbf{V}(\mathbf{\Omega} \times \mathbf{T}) = \mathbf{T}\,dV/dt + \mathbf{\Omega} \times \mathbf{V}$$

Note that $d\mathbf{V}/dt$ is the acceleration of the body with respect to inertial space, but it is expressed here in body coordinates.

All the forces ($\mathbf{f}_i$) acting on the body will combine to produce a resultant force, expressed in body coordinates:

$$\mathbf{F} = \Sigma\,\mathbf{f}_i$$

If we assume that the mass (m) of the body is constant, the acceleration of its center of mass (in body coordinates) is then given by

$$\mathbf{F} = m\,d\mathbf{V}/dt = m\,[\mathbf{T}\,dV/dt + \mathbf{\Omega} \times \mathbf{V}]$$

Each force acts on the body at a point that is defined by a position vector ($\mathbf{p}_i$) relative to the center of mass. The forces thus produce moments about the center of mass that combine to give a resultant moment:

$$\mathbf{M} = \Sigma\,\mathbf{p}_i \times \mathbf{f}_i$$

where $\mathbf{M}$ is in body coordinates.

This causes a rate of change of angular momentum:

$$\mathbf{M} = d\mathbf{H}/dt = \underline{\mathbf{I}}\,d\mathbf{\Omega}/dt + \mathbf{\Omega} \times \mathbf{H} = \underline{\mathbf{I}}\,d\mathbf{\Omega}/dt + \mathbf{\Omega} \times (\underline{\mathbf{I}}\,\mathbf{\Omega})$$

Appendix C

Scalar and vector fields

C.1   One-dimensional thermal systems

Chapters 7 and 8 consider the simulation of scalar and vector fields, where most of the models are one-dimensional. We will begin by analyzing the heat transfer processes that are described in Chapter 7. A prototype model of a one-dimensional heat transfer process would be a long thin cylindrical body with flat ends that are at right angles to its axis. If the one end is hot and the other end is cold while the sides are insulated, the heat will flow from the hot end to the cold in straight lines parallel to the axis. The temperature distribution within such a solid body will be a function $T(x)$, where x is the distance from one end. Scientists argue that this temperature profile is a physical state of the body, which is referred to as a temperature field.

Chapter 7 creates a finite element computer model by dividing the solid body into a number of sections. To simplify the computation, it is preferable that these elements are identical. The cylinder would thus be divided into equal lengths, whose ends are at right angles to the axis. We can represent the temperature profile in a computer as a vector (T) where the element T(n) represents the temperature at the center of the nth section. Suppose that we have stored such a vector (T) that consists of N elements. We can then create a Scilab function that is akin to differentiation:

```
function Tx = grad(T,dx,N)
    for n=1:N-1
        Tx(n) = (T(n+1)-T(n))/dx;
    end
endfunction
```

Computer Models of Process Dynamics: From Newton to Energy Fields, First Edition.
Olis Rubin.
© 2023 The Institute of Electrical and Electronics Engineers, Inc.
Published 2023 by John Wiley & Sons, Inc.

This program can be regarded as an operator that converts an input (T) into an output (Tx), which is the discrete equivalent of a derivative. As dx tends to zero, the above function tends to the differentiation operator that converts an input $T(x)$ into an output $T_x = dT/dx$.

There is a mature mathematical methodology that has been developed for analyzing the properties of scalar and vector fields. In general, the temperature distribution within a solid body can be described by a three-dimensional scalar field, where $T(x, y, z)$ is the temperature at a point (x, y, z). Under certain circumstances the description of the scalar field can be reduced to $T(x, y)$ or to $T(x)$. In the parlance of field theory, the above derivative can be regarded as a one-dimensional vector pointing in the positive X direction, which is aligned with the unit vector **i**, as defined in Appendix B. It will then be written as

$$T_x(x) = \mathbf{grad}(T) = \mathbf{i}\, dT/dx$$

The **grad**( ) operator thus converts a scalar field $T(x)$ into a vector field $T_x(x)$. We see that if dT/dx is negative, $T_x(x)$ points backwards down the X axis.

Since heat flows from a hot body to a cold body, the heat flow (W m^{-2}) from one section of the finite element computer model to the next is given by

```
Q = - (K/dx) * grad(T,dx,N) // in the opposite direction to the
                            // temperature gradient
K/dx = the thermal conductivity (W K⁻¹) of a section
```

Whereas K/dx reduces inversely with the length (dx) of the finite element, it increases proportionally with the cross-sectional area of the cylinder.

The heat flow through a point (x) can also be represented by a vector field:

$$\mathbf{Q} = k\,\mathbf{grad}(T)$$

k = the thermal conductivity of the material
The heat flow vector can also be written as

$$\mathbf{Q}(x) = \mathbf{i}\,Q(x)$$

We see that if the scalar $Q(x)$ is negative, $\mathbf{Q}(x)$ points backwards down the X axis.

This is a good time to review the use of a *derivative* as an *operator*. Suppose that the temperature profile can be described as an analytic function, such as $T(x) = \sin(x)$. We can then use the rules of calculus to determine dT/dx as an algebraic function of x. However, we should remember that the rules of calculus were derived from the premise that d/dx is an operator that converts an input $T(x)$ into an output dT/dx.

We also need to review the above grad() operator. The finite element computer model of a one-dimensional thermal field represents the vector quantities $T_x(x)$ and $\mathbf{Q}(x)$ by their magnitudes Tx(n) and Q(n). Their profiles along the length of the cylinder are represented by one-dimensional arrays (T and Q), which are somewhat ambiguously referred to as "vectors." The meaning of this term thus depends on the context in which it appears. If the vector (T) has N scalar elements, then we see that the grad(T,dx,N) operator will produce a vector (T) that has N-1 scalar elements, so the vector (Q) also has N-1 scalar elements. For example, the vector component Q(2) represents the heat flow from the second section of the cylinder to the third. Thus, if Q(2) is negative, the heat will flow from the third section to the second. We are thus able to model a one-dimensional vector field by a finite element scalar field.

C.1.1 The diffusion equation

Heat can flow into or out of a finite element. We can create a Scilab function that will calculate the heat flow out of each section:

```
function Dx = div(Q,dx,N)
    for n=1:N-1
        Dx(n) = (Q(n+1)-Q(n))/dx;
    end
endfunction
```

This program executes the same computation as grad(Q,dx,N) but performs an entirely different function. The inputs Q(n) are heat flow vectors while the outputs Dx(n) are scalar quantities. For example, Dx(3) represents the net heat outflow from the third section to sections 2 and 4. Thus heat will flow into the third section if Dx(3) is negative.

Since heat flow into a body causes its temperature to rise, the evolution of a one-dimensional temperature field is given by the following equation:

$$\mathrm{d}T/\mathrm{d}t = Dx/C$$

where C is the heat capacity (J K^{-1}) of each section.

The discrete evolution of T at time steps k*dt can be simulated by the following computer program:

```
for k = 1:K
    Z = [T0; T(:,k); T10];
    Tx = grad(Z,dx,N+2)
    Q = -(K/dx)*Tx
    Dx = div(Q,dx,N+1)
    T(k+1) = T(:,k) + dt*Dx/C
end
```

Suppose that the initial temperature profile is a positive half-sine wave while the ends of the body are connected to temperatures T0 and T10, which are held at zero.

Heat will then flow out of the body, so the divergence will also be a positive half-sine wave.

As dx tends to zero the `div()` function tends to the divergence operator that is used in the calculus of vector fields. The divergence of a one-dimensional flow field $Q(x)$ is defined as follows:

$$\mathbf{div}(\mathbf{Q}) = \mathbf{div}(\mathbf{i}\,Q) = dQ/dx$$

This is a scalar field that represents the net heat outflow (W m^{-3}) from the point x.

The above computer program combined the operations `div()` and `grad()` to calculate the evolution of a one-dimensional temperature field. The equivalent operation in vector field calculus will then be

$$\mathbf{div}(\mathbf{grad}(T)) = d^2T/dx^2$$

The net heat outflow from a point x in the temperature field is thus given by the following expression:

$$Dx(x) = -k\,\mathbf{div}(\mathbf{grad}(T))$$

In a one-dimensional field the second derivative (d^2T/dx^2) gives the same result as the $\mathbf{div}(\mathbf{grad}())$ operation, but it must be borne in mind that we have gone from a scalar temperature field to a vector heat flow field to a scalar heat field that defines the outflow of heat from the point x.

The evolution of the temperature field $T(x, t)$ is then determined by the following partial differential equation, known as a *diffusion equation*:

$$k\,\mathbf{div}(\mathbf{grad}(T)) = c\,\partial T/\partial t$$

$c =$ the heat capacity (J K^{-1}) per unit volume of the material

The $\mathbf{div}(\mathbf{grad}(T))$ operator now corresponds to a partial derivative $(\partial^2 T/\partial x^2)$.

C.2 Harmonic analysis of a one-dimensional diffusion equation

This technique can be used to determine the evolution of a one-dimensional field from a given initial shape. It has limited application for modeling physical systems, but is nevertheless useful as a simple cross-check to verify the behavior of a computer model. It can be applied to both diffusion and wave motion, and to solve the Laplace equation.

We will illustrate the use of the technique by considering the following diffusion equation that could describe the evolution of a one-dimensional temperature field:

$$\mathbf{div}(\mathbf{grad}(T)) = h^2 \left(\partial T/\partial t\right)$$

To do harmonic analysis we assume that the solution to the equation is composed of various modes of motion, as given by the following Fourier series:

$$T(x,t) = \Sigma\, Ai(t)\, Si(x)$$

The function $Si(x)$ defines the shape of a temperature profile while $Ai(t)$ describes its evolution with time.

We can describe an arbitrary temperature profile by the above Fourier expansion. For example, we could synthesize a triangular wave by using the following infinite Fourier series:

$$S(x) = \sin(wx) - \sin(3wx)/9 + \sin(5wx)/25...$$

The higher harmonics will generally settle much faster than the first harmonic, so it is probably adequate in most situations to restrict the analysis to a single harmonic.

Consider a temperature profile that is represented by a single mode, which we will define as $A(t)\, S(x)$. The diffusion equation then reduces to

$$A(t)\, d^2S/dx^2 = h^2\, S(x)\, dA/dt$$

These are ordinary derivatives since $S(x)$ and $A(t)$ are functions of single variables. We can then rearrange this equation to move the variables x and t into the two different sides:

$$\left(d^2S/dx^2\right)/S(x) = h^2\, (dA/dt)/A(t)$$

This equation can only be satisfied if the two sides are constant. We will suppose that this constant has a value $-w^2$. We then have two ordinary differential equations that define $A(t)$ and $S(x)$:

$$d^2S/dx^2 = -w^2\, S(x)$$
$$dA/dt = -\left(w^2/h^2\right) A(t)$$

The first differential equation gives the shape of the temperature profile as a sinusoidal function. Suppose that we wish to model a temperature field whose value is always zero at its boundaries, which are given by $x = -L/2$ and $x = L/2$. We could then assume that the temperature profile is given by

$$S(x) = \cos(x\,\pi/L)$$

which implies that $w = \pi/L$.

The second differential equation then shows that the amplitude of the temperature profile will settle exponentially with a time constant $u = (h/w)^2 = (hL/\pi)^2$:

$$T(x,t) = A(0) \exp(-t/u) \cos(x\pi/L)$$

The heat flow vector is given by:

$$\mathbf{Q}(x,t) = -k\,\mathbf{grad}T(x,t) = -\mathbf{i}\,k\,A(t)\,dS/dx = -\mathbf{i}\,(k\pi/L)\,A(t)\,\sin(x\pi/L)$$

$\mathbf{Q}(x,t)$ changes direction at $x=0$; thus heat flows outwards from the center of the region and so the heat energy stored in the body reduces with time. $\mathbf{Q}(x, t)$ increases in magnitude as we move out from the center of the region, so there is divergent flow at all points in the thermal field. We have

$$\mathbf{div}(\mathbf{i}\,Q) = k\,(\pi/L)^2\,A(t)\,\cos(x\pi/L)$$

which is positive over the whole region, so there is a net heat loss from all points.

This means that heat diffuses out of the region. $A(t)$ determines the rate at which the temperature profile drops with time. It is understandable that the thermal time constant (u) increases with the square of the length (L), since heat capacity is proportional to L, while conductivity is inversely proportional to L.

C.2.1 Vibration of a stretched string

Chapter 8 considers the phenomenon of wave propagation. Section 8.2.1 derives a wave equation that has the following form:

$$\mathbf{div}(\mathbf{grad}(y)) = (1/c^2)\,\partial^2 y/\partial t^2$$

The wave equation can be used in vibration analysis. Section 8.4 considers the simulation of a standing wave in a vibrating string that is stretched between the points $x = -L/2$ and $x = L/2$.

As we did in Appendix C.2, we will assume that the solution consists of a single mode shape $S(x)$, which evolves with time as a function $A(t)$. The functions $A(t)$ and $S(x)$ are again given by separate ordinary differential equations:

$$d^2S/dx^2 = -(w/c)^2\,S(x)$$

$$d^2A/dt^2 = -w^2\,A(t)$$

The vibration profile is a sinusoidal function:

$$S(x) = \cos(x\pi/L)$$

while the string oscillates at a frequency that is inversely proportional to its length:

$$A(t) = A(0)\, \cos\left(t\,\pi/Lc\right)$$

C.3 Transfer function analysis of one-dimensional wave propagation

Figure 8.4 in Chapter 8 shows what happens when a finite element model is used to simulate the propagation of an energy wave through a continuous medium. The wavefront is progressively distorted as it travels down the model, making it necessary to introduce attenuation within the elements. The simulation was also terminated before the reflected wave could interfere with the time plots.

It is possible to determine an analytic expression that gives a better description of the wave motion down a lossless, infinite transmission line. We will begin with the one-dimensional wave equation that is given in Section 8.2.1:

$$\mathbf{div}(\mathbf{grad}(V)) = \left(1/c^2\right)\partial^2 V/\partial t^2$$

If we take the Laplace transform of the voltage field $V(x, t)$ to obtain a function $\mathbf{V}(x, s)$, this will transform the above equation to an ordinary differential equation, where the Laplace variable (s) can be regarded as an algebraic quantity:

$$d^2\mathbf{V}/dx^2 = \left(1/c^2\right)s^2\mathbf{V} - A(s, x, 0)$$

If all the voltages and currents down the line are initially zero, we have $A(s, x, 0) = 0$. If the sending end is at $x = 0$, the response of the voltage at a distance x is given by

$$\mathbf{V}(x, s) = \mathbf{V}(0, s)\left[\exp\left(-sT\right) + \exp\left(sT\right)\right]$$
$$T = x/c$$

The term $\exp(-sT)$ implies that the voltage at the sending end is delayed by a time T seconds before it reaches the point (x). This means that there is a voltage wave that travels down the line at a finite speed (c) without distortion or attenuation. The second term $\exp(sT)$ can be interpreted to mean that there is also a voltage wave that travels up the line from the point (x) towards the sending end. If we neglect reverse motion the above response becomes

$$\mathbf{V}(x, s) = H(s)\,\mathbf{V}(0, s)$$
$$H(s) = \exp\left(-sT\right)$$

This equation will be valid for an infinite transmission line that starts at $x = 0$. We suppose that there are initially no voltages across the capacitors or currents flowing through the inductors. If a voltage step $E(t)$ is applied at $x = 0$, it will take a time x/c to travel a distance x along the line.

C.3.1 A finite transmission line

Consider a lossless transmission line that stretches between $x = 0$ and $x = d$. Suppose that there are voltage waves that travel along the line at a finite speed (c). The time to travel from one end to the other is defined as $T = d/c$. The voltage profile along the line is given by the following general solution:

$$\mathbf{V}(x, s) = \mathbf{A} \exp\left(-[x/c]s\right) + \mathbf{B} \exp\left([x/c]s\right)$$

In order to simplify the algebraic expressions, we will assume that a voltage $E(t)$ is applied at $t = 0$ from the sending end, which is at $x = d$. If the line is initially at rest, the voltage at $x = 0$ is given by

$$\mathbf{A} \exp\left(-sT\right) + \mathbf{B} \exp\left(sT\right) = \mathbf{E}(s)$$

Now suppose that the line is shorted at $x = 0$, so that $V(0, t)$ is equal to zero. We then have

$$\mathbf{A} + \mathbf{B} = 0$$

These two equations can be solved to give the following:

$$\exp\left(-sT\right) - \exp\left(sT\right) = \mathbf{E}(s)/\mathbf{A} = -\mathbf{E}(s)/\mathbf{B}$$
$$\mathbf{A} = -\mathbf{B} = \mathbf{E}(s)/[\exp\left(-sd/c\right) - \exp\left(sd/c\right)]$$

Substituting these expressions in the general solution for $\mathbf{V}(x, s)$ we obtain:

$$\mathbf{V}(x, s) = \mathbf{E}(s)\left[\exp\left(-sx/c\right) - \exp\left(sx/c\right)\right]/\left[\exp\left(-sd/c\right) - \exp\left(sd/c\right)\right]$$

The transfer function $\mathbf{V}(x, s)/\mathbf{E}(s)$ can be split into the following factors:

$$\mathbf{P}(x, s) = \exp\left[-s(d - x)/c\right] - \exp\left[-s(d + x)/c\right]$$
$$\mathbf{R}(x, s) = \left[1 - \exp\left(-s2T\right)\right]^{-1} = 1 + \exp\left(-s2T\right) + \exp\left(-s4T\right) + \cdots$$

$\mathbf{P}(x, s)$ responds to a step input by giving a square pulse with a period equal to $2x/c$ seconds.

The transfer function $\mathbf{R}(x, s)$ corresponds to a series of time delays: $2T$, $4T$, ... $V(x, t)$ thus responds to a step input by giving a series of square pulses.

There are thus waves that travel in both directions, where the energy waves are reflected at the ends. These waves interfere with one another. This effect complicates the transfer function and frequency response analysis of physical systems. Diffusion is also bidirectional and therefore suffers from the same problem. If the analysis is used with caution, it can nevertheless provide some insight into system behavior.

C.3.2 Transfer function analysis of heat flow

Chapter 7 described a practical application where we used a thermocouple to measure the temperature on the outside surface of a wall that enclosed a high-temperature reactor. If we wish to detect relatively rapid changes in the operating conditions, we need to account for the time taken by the heat to diffuse through the wall. Figure 7.13 showed the frequency response of a finite element model that simulated this configuration. Because we are uncertain about the accuracy of this result, we would like to compare it with an analytic expression that describes the diffusion of energy through a continuous medium. We will begin with the one-dimensional diffusion equation that is given in Section C.1.1:

$$k\left(\partial^2 T/\partial x^2\right) = c\left(\partial T/\partial t\right)$$

We can scale the distance (x) so that the thermal conductivity of the material (k) is equal to its heat capacity (c) per unit volume. This reduces the diffusion equation to

$$\partial^2 T/\partial x^2 = \partial T/\partial t$$

If we take the Laplace transform of the temperature field $T(x, t)$ to obtain a function $\mathbf{T}(x, s)$, this will transform the above equation to an ordinary differential equation, where the Laplace variable (s) can be regarded as an algebraic quantity:

$$d^2\mathbf{T}/dx^2 = s\,\mathbf{T}$$

If we then take a second Laplace transform of $\mathbf{T}(x, s)$ to obtain $\mathbf{T}(r, s)$, we can factorize the resulting algebraic equation in r and s to obtain

$$r^2\mathbf{T} - s\mathbf{T} = \left(r + \sqrt{s}\right)\left(r - \sqrt{s}\right)\mathbf{T}(r,s) = 0$$

The positive root corresponds to the diffusion of heat in the reverse direction. Suppose that we consider the negative root only and neglect reverse flow. Replacing the term ($r\mathbf{T}$) by $d\mathbf{T}/dx$, we obtain

$$d\mathbf{T}/dx = -\sqrt{s}\,\mathbf{T}$$

This has a solution of the form:

$$\mathbf{T}(x,s) = \mathbf{T}(0,s)\,\exp\left(-x\sqrt{s}\right)$$

This equation will be valid for diffusion through an infinite wall that transmits heat in the positive X direction from its inner surface at $x = 0$.

The frequency response of the transfer function $H(s) = \exp(-x\sqrt{s})$ is given by

$$H(j\omega) = \exp\left(-x\sqrt{j\omega}\right) = \exp\left(-x\sqrt{\omega}(1+j)/\sqrt{2}\right)$$

giving

$$H(j\omega) = \exp[-P(\omega)] \exp[-jP(\omega)]$$

where $P(\omega)$ is a phase lag in radians:

$$P(\omega) = \left(x/\sqrt{2}\right)\sqrt{\omega}$$

C.3.3 The transfer function of a transmission line

Section 8.2 derives the following equations that describe the propagation of voltage and current fields $V(x, t)$ and $I(x, t)$ down a transmission line:

$$RI + L\,\partial I/\partial t = -\partial V/\partial x$$
$$GV + C\,\partial V/\partial t = -\partial I/\partial x$$

We will have *distortionless wave motion* when $R/L = G/C = A$, which gives the following equations:

$$AI + \partial I/\partial t = -(1/L)\,\partial V/\partial x$$
$$AV + \partial V/\partial t = -(1/C)\,\partial I/\partial x$$

As in Appendix C.3.2, we can transform the above partial differential equations into algebraic equations:

$$(A + s)\,\mathbf{I}(r,s) = -(r/L)\,\mathbf{V}(r,s)$$
$$(A + s)\,\mathbf{V}(r,s) = -(r/C)\,\mathbf{I}(r,s)$$

$\mathbf{V}(r,s)$ and $\mathbf{I}(r,s)$ are the Laplace transforms of $\mathbf{V}(x, s)$ and $\mathbf{I}(x, s)$

where

$\mathbf{V}(x,s)$ and $\mathbf{I}(x,s)$ are the Laplace transforms of $V(x, t)$ and $I(x, t)$

By eliminating $\mathbf{I}(r, s)$ from these equations, we obtain

$$(A + s)\,\mathbf{V} = \left(r^2/LC\right)\mathbf{V}/(A + s)$$

Now define the following:

$$c^2 = 1/LC$$
$$Q = (A + s)/c$$

whence we have

$$(Q + r)(Q - r)\,\mathbf{V} = \left(Q^2 - r^2\right)\mathbf{V} = 0$$

The positive root corresponds to wave propagation in the reverse direction. Suppose that we consider the negative root only, which gives forward motion. Replacing the term $(r\mathbf{V})$ by $d\mathbf{V}/dx$, we obtain

$$d\mathbf{V}/dx = -Q\mathbf{V}$$

This has a solution of the form:

$$\mathbf{V}(x, s) = \mathbf{V}(0, s)\ \exp(-Qx) = H(s)\ \mathbf{V}(0, s)$$

where

$$H(s) = \exp(-Ax/c)\ \exp(-[x/c]\,s)$$

This equation will be valid for an infinite transmission line that starts at $x = 0$, where there are initially no voltages across the capacitors or currents flowing through the inductors. If a voltage step $E(t)$ is applied at $x = 0$, it will take a time x/c to travel a distance x along the line. It will be attenuated by a factor $\exp(-Ax/c)$ as a result of line losses. The attenuation is independent of frequency, so there is no distortion in the shape of $V(x, t)$.

If R/L does not equal G/C the attenuation will vary with frequency and $V(x, t)$ will be distorted.

C.4   Two-dimensional thermal systems

A prototype model of a two-dimensional heat transfer process would be a flat rectangular plate with insulated faces. We will suppose that one side of the rectangle lies on the X axis while another lies on the Y axis. The temperature distribution within such a body will be a function $T(x, y)$, where x and y are the cartesian coordinates relative to the origin of the system. If we draw isothermal lines on the plate, they will resemble a contour map. At any given point we can draw a line at right angles to the isothermal curve. This will indicate the direction along which the temperature gradient is a maximum. We can model the temperature gradient as a two-dimensional vector $(\mathbf{G})$ whose magnitude equals this maximum value, while it points in the direction along which the value is a maximum. It turns out that the component of $\mathbf{G}$ in the X direction equals the partial derivative $T_x = \partial T/\partial x$, while that in the Y direction equals $T_y = \partial T/\partial y$. We can thus define a two-dimensional vector field $\mathbf{G}(x, y)$ that models the temperature gradient.

We can create a finite element computer model by dividing the solid body into a number of sections. To simplify the computation, it is preferable that these elements are identical. The plate would thus be divided into equal rectangles whose sides are parallel to the X and Y axes (like elements of a large chessboard). We can represent the temperature profile in a computer as a matrix (T) where the element T(n,k) represents the temperature at the center of the *n* by *k*th section. Suppose that we have stored such a matrix (T) that consists of X by Y points. We can then create a Scilab function that is akin to partial differentiation:

```
function [Tx, Ty] = grad(T,dx,X,dy,Y)
    for k=1:Y-1
        for n=1:X-1
            Tx(n,k) = (T(n+1,k)-T(n,k))/dx;
            Ty(n,k) = (T(n,k+1)-T(n,k))/dy;
        end
    end
```

The program converts a scalar input matrix (T) into two matrices (Tx and Ty) that approximate the components (T_x and T_y) of the gradient vector. The equivalent operation in the calculus of two-dimensional vector fields is given by

$$\mathbf{G}(x,y) = \mathbf{grad}(T) = \mathbf{i}\,\partial T/\partial x + \mathbf{j}\,\partial T/\partial y$$

As dx and dy tend to zero, the above function tends to the gradient operator, and this converts a scalar field $T(x, y)$ into a vector field $\mathbf{G}(x, y)$.

The magnitude of the heat flow (W m^{-2}) at any given point and the direction along which its value is a maximum can similarly be defined as a vector:

$$\mathbf{Q} = -k\,\mathbf{grad}(T) = \mathbf{i}\,Qx + \mathbf{j}\,Qy \tag{C.1}$$

Suppose that we have stored the two-dimensional flow field in two matrices (Qx and Qy). We can then create a function:

```
function D = div(Qx,dx,X,Qy,dy,Y)
    for k=1:Y-1
        for n=1:X-1
            Dx(n,k) = (Qx(n+1,k)-Qx(n,k))/dx;
            Dy(n,k) = (Qy(n,k+1)-Qy(n,k))/dy;
            D(n,k) = Dx(n,k) + Dy(n,k);
        end
    end
endfunction
```

The program converts the two matrices (Qx and Qy) into a scalar matrix (D). When the inputs approximate the components (Qx and Qy) of the heat flow vector, the element D(2,3) will represent the net heat outflow from a finite element that forms part of the body. This is made up of upward and downward heat flows, as well as to the left and right. The rectangle in question lies in the second row and third column of the chessboard.

As dx and dy tend to zero, the above function tends to a **div**() operation on a two-dimensional vector field $Q(x, y)$, which converts it into a scalar field that defines the outflow of heat from the point x, y:

$$D(x,y) = \mathbf{div}(\mathbf{Q}) = \partial Qx/\partial x + \partial Qy/\partial y$$

Equation (C.1) then gives

$$D(x,y) = \mathbf{div}(-k\,\mathbf{grad}(T)) = -k\left(\partial^2 T/\partial x^2\right) - k\left(\partial^2 T/\partial y^2\right)$$

Thus:

$$D(x,y) = -k\,\mathbf{div}(\mathbf{grad}(T))$$

where

$$\mathbf{div}(\mathbf{grad}(T)) = \partial^2 T/\partial x^2 + \partial^2 T/\partial y^2$$

The negative sign in the expression for $D(x, y)$ implies that heat flow is divergent when $\mathbf{div}(\mathbf{grad}(T))$ is negative. The evolution of a two-dimensional temperature field $T(x, y, t)$ is thus determined by the following diffusion equation:

$$k\,\mathbf{div}(\mathbf{grad}(T)) = c\,\partial T/\partial t$$

C.4.1   Harmonic analysis of the laplace equation

Consider a two-dimensional diffusion equation:

$$\mathbf{div}(\mathbf{grad}(T)) = (c/k)\,\partial T/\partial t$$

Suppose that the temperature field $T(x, y)$ has settled to a steady state condition where $\partial T/\partial t$ is equal to zero. The diffusion equation then reduces to the *Laplace equation*:

$$\partial^2 T/\partial y^2 = -\partial^2 T/\partial x^2$$

As in Appendix C.2, we will assume a solution that consists of a single mode shape, which varies as $A(x)$ in the X direction and as $S(y)$ in the Y direction. The functions $A(x)$ and $S(y)$ are again given by separate ordinary differential equations:

$$d^2 A/dx^2 = W^2\,A(x)$$
$$d^2 S/dy^2 = -W^2\,S(y)$$

The solution to the second equation is a sinusoidal function of y. We can use this to model a temperature field within a rectangular plate where the side lying on the X axis is kept at temperature zero. This is also true on the opposite side, where $y = B$. The temperature profile is then described by

$$T(x,y) = A(x) \sin (y\pi/B)$$

whence we see that

$$W = \pi/B$$

Suppose that the side that lies on the Y axis is in contact with a heat source. The above solution implies that the temperature profile is restricted as follows:

$$T(0,y) = A(0) \sin (y\pi/B)$$

We will nevertheless carry on to investigate the shape of $A(x)$.

We can take the Laplace transform of the first differential equation to obtain:

$$\left(s^2 - W^2\right) \mathbf{A}(s) = (s + W) (s - W) \mathbf{A}(s) = 0$$

This characteristic equation has the following general solution:

$$A(x) = a_1 \exp (- x\pi/B) + a_2 \exp (x\pi/B)$$

We will now assume that the fourth side is in contact with a heat sink, so the heat flow at all points has a component in the positive x direction. This leads us to ignore the divergent exponential function in A(x), from which we finally obtain

$$T(x,y) = \exp (- x\pi/B) \sin (y\pi/B)$$

Note that the temperature profile at the fourth side is also a sinusoidal function of y. We must acknowledge that the mathematical solution is somewhat synthetic and that the system was tailored to approximate the solution. We could possibly approximate real applications by increasing the number of modes, but would then have to verify the answer by other means.

We see that when the field produced by a two-dimensional wave equation settles to a steady state, it will also be given by the Laplace equation.

C.4.2   The rotation of a vector field

Many physical energy fields exhibit the characteristics of rotational motion. We saw in Section 3.4 that the electric current flowing through a straight wire produces a magnetic field that follows a circle around the wire, while a magnetic field that passes through a wire loop can cause an electric current to flow around the loop. We can also investigate the rotational properties of a fluid flow field, described in Section 3.5.1 by a velocity vector ($\mathbf{V}$) that follows curves called streamlines. The flow on the perfectly flat surface of a river can be described by a two-dimensional flow field in the XY plane, where we assume that the speed of flow in a thin slice just below the surface is not affected by depth. The velocity vector can then be described by

$$\mathbf{V}(x, y) = \mathbf{i}\, Vx + \mathbf{j}\, Vy$$

Now suppose that the river has perfectly straight banks that are aligned with the X axis, while we will also assume that the streamlines are perfectly straight, so that $\mathbf{V}(x, y) = \mathbf{i}\, Vx$.

If we now assume that the flow rate does not change as we move downstream, the velocity vector at any point (x, y) is independent of the x coordinate and is thus given by

$$\mathbf{V}(y) = \mathbf{i}\, Vx(y)$$

It is still possible to have shear flow between the streamlines, causing Vx to vary in the Y direction. Thus:

$$Vx(y + dy) = Vx(y) + dy\, dVx/dy$$

Consider two fluid elements where the initial position of element 1 is the point (x, y) while that of element 2 is the point $(x, y + dy)$. Their initial position of element 2 relative to element 1 can be expressed by a two-dimensional vector:

$$\mathbf{r} = \mathbf{j}\, dy$$

while its relative motion can be expressed by a velocity vector:

$$\mathbf{u} = \mathbf{i}\, dy\, dVx/dy$$

Now consider a light twig that floats on the surface of the water and moves with the streamlines. At the instant that it is at right angles to the flow its rate of rotation is equal to

$$|\,\mathbf{u}\,| / |\,\mathbf{r}\,| = dVx/dy$$

Vector field calculus represents this situation by a quantity that corresponds to the magnitude and direction of an angular velocity vector that points at right angles to the XY plane:

$$\mathbf{curl}(\mathbf{V}) = -\mathbf{k}\, dVx/dy$$

The minus sign results from the convention that is used in Appendix B.2.1 to define the cartesian axis system ($\mathbf{i}\,\mathbf{j}\,\mathbf{k}$).

If the river had flowed along the Y axis, the above situation would have corresponded to

$$\mathbf{curl}(\mathbf{V}) = \mathbf{k}\, dVy/dx$$

while a more general two-dimensional flow field would give

$$\mathbf{curl}(\mathbf{V}) = \mathbf{k}\,(\partial Vy/\partial x - \partial Vx/\partial y)$$

We can store a two-dimensional flow field in arrays `Vx(x,y)` and `Vy(x,y)` and then create a function:

```
function Cz = curl(Vx,dx,X,Vy,dy,Y)
    for k=1:Y-1
        for n=1:X-1
            cx(n,k) = (Vy(n+1,k)-Vy(n,k))/dx;
            cy(n,k) = (Vx(n,k+1)-Vx(n,k))/dy;
            Cz(n,k) = cx(n,k) - cy(n,k);
        end
    end
endfunction
```

As `dx` and `dy` tend to zero, the scalar variable `Cz(n,k)` tends to the magnitude of the vector function **curl(V)**, where **V** is a two-dimensional vector in the *XY* plane while the vector **curl(V)** is at right angles to the *XY* plane.

Aerodynamicists will often approximate fluid flow by defining the vector field **V** (*x*, *y*) to be the gradient of a scalar potential function *P*(*x*, *y*) that is akin to a pressure field. The flow field then becomes

$$\mathbf{V} = \mathbf{i}\,\partial P/\partial x + \mathbf{j}\,\partial P/\partial y$$

The curl of the flow field is then

$$\mathbf{curl}(\mathbf{V})) = \mathbf{k}\left(\partial^2 P/\partial x\partial y - \partial^2 P/\partial y\partial x\right)$$

Since we can reverse the order of differentiation, we have that **curl(V)** is zero. Such a potential flow field is thus irrotational.

Section 8.6 analyses the flow around a cylindrical obstacle by means of a potential function that is defined as follows in polar coordinates (*r*, *θ*):

$$P(r,\theta) = \cos(\theta)\left(r + a^2/r\right)$$

The cross-section of the cylinder and the flow around it is shown in Figure 8.8.

We can approximate this function in a discrete space that is composed of a matrix of finite elements. Consider a matrix of such elements that cover a rectangular area. Their *x* and *y* coordinates are defined by the vectors `X=0:8` and `Y=10:14`. In Figure 8.8 this is a rectangle that touches the top of the cylinder and covers part of the downstream flow field. The potential function, the flow field, and **curl(V)** can then be created as follows:

```
for k=1:5
    for n=1:9
        R(n,k)  = sqrt(X(n)^2 + Y(k).^2);
        Cs(n,k) = X(n)/R(n,k);
        A(n,k)  = R(n,k) + a^2/R(n,k);
        P(n,k)  = Cs(n,k)*A(n,k);
    end
end
[Vx, Vy] = grad(P,1,8,1,5);
Cz = curl(Vx,1,7,Vy,1,4);
```

This produces a 3 by 6 matrix (`Cz`) of zeros.

If **V** is a three-dimensional flow field, **curl(V)** will also have a component in the direction of **i** that corresponds to the rotation in the *YZ* plane and a further component in the direction of **j** that corresponds to the rotation in the *ZX* plane.

We can now return to Equation (3.4) in Section 3.4.2 that is derived from *Faraday's induction law*. This implies that any change $(\partial\mathbf{B}/\partial t)$ within a field (**B**) of magnetic flux density will induce an electric field (**E**) where **curl(E)** is given by $-\partial\mathbf{B}/\partial t$. The voltage induced in a wire loop that lies within this field will be equal to the integral of **E** around the loop. *Stokes's theorem* states that this is equal to the integral of **curl(E)** over the area that is circumscribed by the loop. We can visualize this by dividing the area into infinitesimal rectangular elements with sides dx and dy. Consider two elements that lie side-by-side, where **curl(E)** causes the field to circulate in the same sense around each element. Now consider the total flow along the side that is common to the elements. The direction of flow produced by one element will be opposite to that produced by the other element. The sum of **curl(E)** around the first element and that around the second element now flows around the rectangle that circumscribes their joint area. The summation of such infinitesimal elements corresponds to the integral of **curl(E)** over the whole area. All the rotational flows thus combine to produce the integral of **E** around the wire loop. This represents the potential to drive electric charges around the wire against its resistance.

C.4.3   Vector operations in polar coordinates

Consider the potential function $P(r, \theta)$ of a flow field where (r, θ) defines the position of a point in the *XY* plane in polar coordinates. By analogy with a gradient in cartesian coordinates, the gradient of $P(r, \theta)$ going outward from the origin equals the partial derivative $\partial P/\partial r$. If θ is kept constant, a displacement dr causes radial motion $\mathbf{r}$ dr, where $\mathbf{r}$ is a unit vector:

$$\mathbf{r} = \mathbf{i} \cos \theta + \mathbf{j} \sin \theta$$

On the other hand, if r is kept constant, a change, dθ, causes a displacement, d$s = r$ dθ, along the arc of a circle that has its center at the origin. This causes tangential motion $\boldsymbol{\theta}$ r dθ, where $\boldsymbol{\theta}$ is a unit vector:

$$\boldsymbol{\theta} = -\mathbf{i} \sin \theta + \mathbf{j} \cos \theta$$

The gradient of $P(r, \theta)$ going along the tangent to this circle will be $\partial P/\partial s = (1/r) \partial P/\partial \theta$. We can thus define a gradient operator that produces the following vector:

$$\mathbf{gradp}(P) = \mathbf{r} \, \partial P/\partial r + \boldsymbol{\theta}(1/r) \, \partial P/\partial \theta$$

By definition the velocity vector of the flow field is thus given by

$$\mathbf{V}(r, \theta) = \mathbf{r} \, Vr + \boldsymbol{\theta} Vq = \mathbf{gradp}(P)$$

The divergence of the vector $\mathbf{gradp}(P)$ is then

$$\mathbf{divp}(\mathbf{gradp}(P)) = Vr/r + \partial(Vr)/\partial r + (1/r)\partial(Vq)/\partial \theta$$

Substituting the partial derivatives for Vr and Vq, we obtain

$$\mathbf{divp}(\mathbf{gradp}(V)) = (1/r)\partial P/\partial r + \partial^2 P/\partial r^2 + \left(1/r^2\right)\partial^2 P/\partial \theta^2$$

Appendix D

Probability and statistical models

Statistical data is gathered so that we can make informed decisions on actions to be taken. Statistical analysis is only as good as the suppositions on which it is based and the uncertainties that are taken into account.

> "The words figure and fictitious both derive from the same Latin root, fingere. Beware!
>
> M.J. Moroney (1951)
> *Source:* Rights Managed, Penguin Random House

This appendix looks at a few statistical models that can be used to draw conclusions from the raw data. It is important to know whether the data is taken from a physical process that matches the characteristics of the chosen model.

D.1 The laws of chance

Rather than trying to define the notion of probability in words, we will do so by means of numbers. Just as a temperature scale (e.g. °C) was defined by physicists, so we can define a probability scale (p). We will start by defining $p = 1$ to mean *absolute certainty*, and p = 0 to mean *absolute impossibility*. We can fix our ideas by imagining a simple experiment where we place 100 marbles in a leather bag, mix them up well, and then draw out one marble. If we placed 100 white marbles in the bag, the probability that we draw out a white marble will be $p = 1$. On the other hand, if we placed 100 red marbles in the bag, p will be 0. If we put in 50 white marbles and 50 red marbles, the chance of drawing out a white marble will be equal to that of drawing out a red marble. The probability ($p = 1$) that the marble will *either* be white *or* red can be shared between the two possible results, giving

$p = 0.5$ for a white marble and $p = 0.5$ for a red marble. In general, the probability (p) that a randomly chosen marble will be white is given by

$$p = K/N$$

K = the number of white marbles in the bag
N = the number of marbles in the bag

We will now extend these ideas to a quality control plan where units that come off a production line are inspected, tested, and classified as "OK" or "defective." In some cases, such as with the testing of ammunition, the quality control involves a destructive test. All that we can do in such a situation is to draw a sample for testing in order to ensure that the percentage of defective items is small.

If we were to do a 100% inspection of a batch that contains N units and found K defectives, we could calculate $p = K/N$ as we did with the bag of marbles. If we were to take a reasonably large sample of n units and found k defectives, we could possibly use the same calculation to estimate the above probability (p) as

$$p_e = k/n$$

Suppose that we divide the whole batch into m samples of equal size, $n = N/m$. The number of defectives (k_1, k_2, ..., k_m) in these samples are not necessarily the same, but their sum will be equal to the total number of defectives (K) in the batch. Thus, the mean probability that a randomly chosen unit will be defective is given by K/N.

We can try to simulate what happens if we take a batch consisting of 1000 units and divide it into 10 samples, each containing 100 units. We can use the Scilab random number generator `grand()` to produce 10 numbers that simulate the number of defectives (k_i) in a sample containing 100 units. One run produced the following numbers:

```
ki = 8, 10, 9, 11, 10, 10, 16, 10, 7, 9
```

This was done by means of the following program:

```
m=10; n=100;   p=.1;
K = grand(m,1,"bin",n,p)';
meanK = sum(K)/m
x = K - meanK;
varK = sum(x^2)/m
sigma = sqrt(varK)
Pi = K/n
meanPi = meanK/m
```

The program calculated the mean value of K to be

```
meanK = 10
```

while its variance is calculated as

```
varK = 5.2
```

The *standard deviation* (`sigma`) represents the dispersion of the data about its mean value:

```
sigma = 2.3
```

We see that K is not spread symmetrically about its mean = 10 defectives. We could then calculate estimates of the probability (p):

```
Pi = 0.08, 0.1, 0.09, 0.11, 0.1, 0.1, 0.16, 0.1, 0.07, 0.09
meanPi = 0.1
```

D.2 The binomial distribution

Suppose that a large production batch contains 10% defectives. The probability that a single randomly chosen item will be defective is $p = 0.1$. We will have a probability (q) that a randomly chosen item will be OK. The item will certainly be classified as either defective or OK, so by the *Addition Law of Probabilities* we have $p + q = 1$.

Suppose that we now draw out a sample consisting of two units. The same probability (p) applies to both units. The probability that both items are defective is given by the *Multiplication Law of Probabilities*:

$$P(2) = p\,p = p^2 = 0.01$$

The probability that both items are OK (i.e. none are defective) is given by

$$P(0) = q^2 = (1 - p)^2 = 0.81$$

The probability that one item is defective can arise in the following two ways. The first item chosen can be OK while the second is defective. By the *Multiplication Law*, the probability of this happening is $q\,p$. Alternatively, where the first item chosen is defective and the second is OK, the probability is $p\,q$. If we are only concerned with the final result, irrespective of the order in which it comes about, the probability of one item being defective is given by the *Addition Law of Probabilities* as

$$P(1) = qp + pq = 2pq = 0.18$$

The *Addition Law* can also be used to combine the above three results in a binomial expression:

$$P(2) + P(1) + P(0) = (p + q)^2 = 1$$

This confirms the obvious, that we are certain to obtain one of these three results.

The following Scilab program computes the binomial probability distribution Pb where Pb(k) describes the number (k) of defectives in a sample that contains n units, where p is the probability that an item is defective:

```
Pb = binomial(p,n);
```

The answer (Pb) is a vector whose terms Pb(1), Pb(2), Pb(3), ... correspond to the probabilities $P(0)$, $P(1)$, $P(2)$, ... that were previously defined. For example:

```
Pb=binomial(0.1,1) produces the answer: Pb=[0.9 0.1]
Pb=binomial(0.1,2) produces the answer: Pb=[0.81 0.18 0.01]
Pb=binomial(0.1,3) produces the answer: Pb=[0.729 0.243
0.027 0.001]
```

The above analysis arrived at the first two answers, while we can compute the third answer by evaluating the expression $(p + q)^n$ for $n = 3$. Each time that we add one more item to the sample we introduce the possibility that we could now have $n + 1$ defectives, while we were previously limited to n defectives. The probability that all the items in the sample are OK therefore becomes smaller. This trend continues as we increase the sample size. The first six elements of the vector Pb=binomial(0.1,15) are shown in the top plot of Figure D.1. The remaining terms continue reducing. The probability that we have one defective is now larger than $P(0)$. The bottom plot of Figure D.1 shows the first 31 elements of the vector Pb=binomial(0.1,200). The probability that we have 20 defectives exceeds all other outcomes, while the probability distribution tends to be symmetrical about this number, which is equal to p*n. The spread of the distribution divided by p*n also becomes smaller as we increase the sample size.

If samples are drawn from a batch that contains 50% defectives (p=0.5), the resulting probability distribution is symmetrical about the value n/2, as shown by the following examples:

```
Pb=binomial(0.5,2) produces the answer: Pb=[0.25 0.5 0.25]
Pb=binomial(0.5,3) produces the answer: Pb=[0.125 0.375
0.375 0.125]
```

The binomial distribution for a sample size n=50 is shown in Figure D.2. It is clustered closely around its peak, at the value n/2.

Whereas Appendix D.1 simulated what happens when we take samples from a batch that contains defectives, we have now calculated what would probably

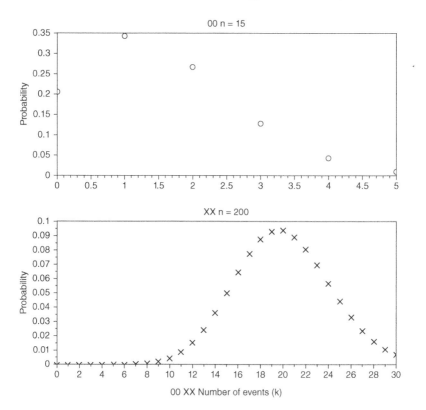

Figure D.1 Binomial distributions for increasing sample size.

happen. Whereas the two approaches may arrive at the same mean values, their variances could very well be different.

D.3 The Poisson distribution

Near my home, high on a hill, is a meteorological observatory. This is an area where there is a high incidence of powerline trips in the late summer due to lightning, so the electricity authority is interested in knowing the probability distribution that can be used to predict the occurrence of lightning strikes. The observatory counts the number (k) of lightning flashes that occur in a given time, but *it cannot count how many lightning flashes did not occur*, and so one cannot define a probability scale, $p = k/n$, as was done before. The great mathematicians of centuries ago encountered similar instances, where objects or events could be counted in a

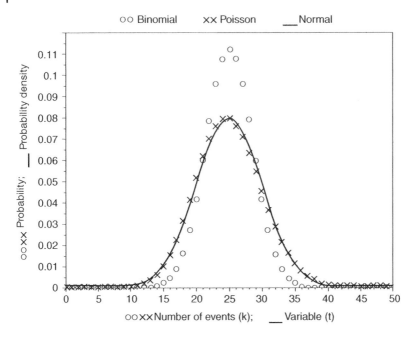

Figure D.2 Binomial, Poisson, and Normal distributions.

continuum of time, or space. It is remarkable that they found, empirically, a simple mathematical function (de Moivre, 1711, 1718; Poisson, 1857) that describes the probability $P(k)$ of observing a given number (k) of events in a continuous interval. This function, known as a Poisson distribution, is an appropriate model if the following conditions are true:

The number of times that an event occurs in a given interval can take on the values $k = 0, 1, 2, ...$
Events occur independently, and two events cannot occur at exactly the same instant.
No event can provoke further events.

Moroney (1951) describes an application of this distribution that was made by von Bortkiewicz (1898) when he investigated the number of soldiers in the Prussian army that were accidentally killed by horse kicks. Data from 10 army corps over a period of 20 years could be arranged in a table with 200 entries that corresponded to the number of deaths that occurred in a particular corps within a given year. It was then possible to count the number of times $n(k)$ that

k deaths occurred in any corps within any year. This could be arranged in the following table:

k	=	0	1	2	3	4
$n(k)$	=	109	65	22	3	1

There were no cases where there were more than four annual deaths per corps.

We see that there were 122 deaths in a table with 200 entries The average number of deaths per entry is thus z=0.61. We will now assume that z represents the average number of events that occur in a given interval. The following program can then be used to generate a vector (Po) that represents a Poisson distribution:

```
Px(1)  =  1;
for  k=1:K
     Px(k+1)  =  Px(k)*z/k;
end
P  =  exp(-z)*Px;
Po  =  200*P
```

We recognize the element Px(k+1) to be a term in the Taylor expansion of the exponential function exp(z), where sum(Px) tends to exp(z) as k increases without limit. The element P(k+1) gives the probability that an entry in the table is equal to k, where sum(P) tends to unity as k increases. This implies that the sum of all eventualities defines all possible outcomes.

When the above program is run with z=0.61 and K=4, it generates the following numbers:

```
k          P(k)               Po(k)
0.         0.5433509          108.67017
1.         0.3314440          66.288806
2.         0.1010904          20.218086
3.         0.0205551          4.1110108
4.         0.0031346          0.6269291
```

The Poisson distribution will be an appropriate model of the random process if the element Po(k+1) matches the number $n(k)$ that was derived from the original data. The fit between Po(k) and $n(k)$ is remarkably good, considering that we are dealing with events that are random by nature.

The probability function P(k) reaches a maximum value at the condition k=floor(z). In the above case this occurs at k=0. If the average number of events (z) is large, the peak of the probability function is at a correspondingly larger value of k. For example, if we run the above program with z=25 and K=50, it generates the plot of the Poisson distribution that is shown in Figure D.2. The mean and variance of the Poisson distribution are both equal to the parameter (z).

D.4   The normal distribution of errors (Gaussian Law)

We showed how the binomial distribution could be used to model how often an object with a given property could be found in a sample of a given size, while the Poisson distribution describes the number of times a given event could occur in a given period. These statistical models introduced the use of "frequency distributions" to describe the probability that a discrete event would occur. The need for a different type of statistical model arose when astronomers used relatively primitive telescopes to take bearings on the planets in order to calculate their orbits. The resulting readings contained significant errors, which impaired the accuracy of their calculations. An angular error in an astronomical measurement can be regarded as a random variable that is centered on the true direction of the celestial object. When astronomers take reasonable care, it is more likely that the errors will be small rather than large. If we plot a number of measurements as points on a graph, we should find that they are clustered around the true value, in a cloud that is denser near the center than at the edges.

This distribution of readings can be described by a function $f(x)$, where x is the distance from the true value, while $f(x)$ is the corresponding density of the cloud of points. Such a representation is commonly known as a probability density function. It is a form of "frequency distribution" that describes the number of times a given reading could occur around a given numerical value. Whereas we started with a finite number of measurements that were plotted as points on a graph, we can now take the limit as the number of measurements becomes infinite. The density function $f(x)$ now describes a continuous "cloud" around the true value. This process can be compared with the transition from numerical analysis to differential calculus. We can compute the probability that a measurement will lie between the values x_1 and x_2 by taking the integral of $f(x)\,dx$ between these values. The most commonly used density function is the so-called *Normal Law*, or *Error Law*. In its simplest form it can be written as

$$f(x) = X \exp\left(-x^2\right)$$

Since $f(x) = f(-x)$, the mean error is zero. The variable x lies between $-\infty$ and $+\infty$ with *absolute certainty* (probability $= 1$) so we define X accordingly. The error now has a variance given by the integral of $x^2 \exp(-x^2)\,dx$ from $-\infty$ to $+\infty$ that is equal to $\frac{1}{2}$.

This function first appeared in the work of de Moivre (1718). Then in 1801 Piazzi discovered the dwarf planet Ceres, and tracked its motion over three degrees across the sky before it disappeared behind the glare of the Sun. Some months later when it should have reappeared Piazzi could not locate it. Gauss heard about the problem and estimated its orbit by statistical analysis. This allowed von Zach to find it one year later. Gauss's predicted position was correct to within half a degree. The resulting fame that this brought him led to his appointment as Professor of Astronomy and Director of the Observatory in Göttingen. The Normal Law is often referred to as the Gaussian distribution. The method of *least squares* is probably the most widely used approach to approximate "noisy" data. We give an example of this approach in Section 9.3.2. The Normal distribution is intimately associated with the method of least squares.

We can modify the mean value and variance of the density function by a change of variable. The modified Normal distribution can be computed in Scilab as follows:

```
Mean = 25;
Std = 5;
x = 22:.5:28;
Nx = exp(-(x-Mean)^2/(2*Std^2));
Ix = Std*sqrt(2*%pi);
N = Nx/Ix;
```

where the quantity `Ix` equals the integral of $Nx(x)$ from $-\infty$ to $+\infty$.

Figure D.2 shows the Normal distribution that corresponds to a mean value of 25 and a standard deviation equal to 5.

In many cases the measurement error is due to several factors. For example, suppose that we use a thermocouple to measure the temperature of gas that is flowing through a duct. We could have errors (e1) due to unsteady flow through the duct, e2 due to temperature changes in the reference junction, and an error (e3) in the voltage measurement. If we can assume that these errors are additive, the overall error would be given by e1 + e2 + e3. The central limit theorem of statistics states that when a large number of independent random components are added together the resulting random signal tends to have a Normal distribution. This is often used to justify the validity of the Normal distribution. Figure D.2 shows comparative plots of Binomial and Poisson distributions. As n is increased, these distributions are even closer to a continuous Normal distribution.

D.5 Inspection by sampling

Moroney (1951) shows how we test a sample from a production line, where the defectives follow a statistical distribution. As the sample size is increased, the number of defectives become closely packed around the mean value. We reduce the amount of effort by taking a sample rather than inspecting all units, but the sample must be large enough to give us confidence that we are not accepting too many bad batches or rejecting too many good batches. Just how far we can increase the sample size will be limited by the number of units in the batch. We can use statistical tables such as those found in Selby (1967) to determine the necessary sample size.

Bibliography

Brownlee, K.A. (1953). *Industrial Experimentation*. New York: Chemical Publishing Company.

de Moivre A., *De Mensura Sortis seu; de Probabilitate Eventuum in Ludis a Casu Fortuito Pendentibus*, 1711

de Moivre, A. (1718). *The Doctrine of Chances*, 2e. London: W. Pearson.

Moroney, M.J. (1951). *Facts from Figures*. Middlesex: Penguin Books.

Poisson S.D., *Recherches sur la probabilité des jugements en matière criminelle et en matière civile*, 1837

Selby S.M. (1967). *Standard Mathematical Tables*, Cleveland, OH: The Chemical Rubber Co.

von Bortkiewicz, L. (1898). *Das Gesetz der kleinen Zahlen*. Leipzig: B.G: Teubner.

Index

Computer Models of Process Dynamics: From Newton to Energy Fields, First Edition.
Olis Rubin.
© 2023 The Institute of Electrical and Electronics Engineers, Inc.
Published 2023 by John Wiley & Sons, Inc.

Printed and bound by CPI Group (UK) Ltd, Croydon, CR0 4YY
05/09/2022
03145679-0001